SMALL SCALE INDUSTRIES AND ENTREPRENEURSHIP

SMALL SCALE INDUSTRIES AND ENTREPRENEURSHIP

G.P. PRASAIN
E. NIXON SINGH

Akansha Publishing House
NEW DELHI

AKANSHA PUBLISHING HOUSE
4649-B/21, Ansari Road
Darya Ganj, New Delhi - 110 002
Email: ektabooks@yahoo.com
Ph. : 23263193 / 9811582579

Small Scale Industries and Entrepreneurship

First Published 2007
ISBN 81-8370-096-9

[The responsibility for the facts stated, conclusions reached etc. is entirely that of the Authors. The publisher is not responsible for them, whatsoever.]

PRINTED IN INDIA

Published by M.P. Misra for Akansha Publishing House, New Delhi and Printed at Aryan Enterprises, Delhi.

Manipur University
CHANCHIPUR
IMPHAL - 795 003
MANIPUR, INDIA

Vice-Chancellor

Foreword

Industrial development of a country is considered to be an engine of growth to accelerate its over all economic development. Industrial development can not, however, progress without development of entrepreneurship. In fact promotion and development of small industries considered vital for ameliorating the scourge of unemployment with less capital investment is ultimately linked with development of entrepreneurship. Small business is a starting point for the first generation entrepreneurs and regarded as nursery for them. It has given a conceptual and applied platform for the entrepreneurship.

One of the disturbing signs of weakness of Indian economy is unemployment amongst the educated young men and women. It is all the more distressing to see young qualified professionals not gainfully employed. Since the economic growth and unemployment are mutually incompatible, this imbalance must be stalled by stimulation of a spectacular growth of small industry based on local resources and skill. In this context, it would be better if during the course of education and training in colleges and universities, emphasis is given for proper motivation for self employment along with the minimum procedural know-how necessary for starting a venture for self employment. If our students are given such entrepreneurship education they would be motivated to go for self employing ventures which would enable them to become **job givers** rather than **job seekers**. Therefore, I feel that the education must be given a new orientation so that our young generation, after completing their education, will have the skills, incentives and facilities to go for self employed enterprises. In this context, I hope that the present book which is an outcome of research work conducted by Dr. G.P. Prasain and Dr. B. Nixan Singh in the Department of Commerce, Manipur University will be useful for planners, policy makers and scholars who are interested in entrepreneurship research.

Prof. C. Amuba Singh
Vice-Chancellor

November 6, 2006

Preface

Entrepreneurship, of late, has attracted much public interest since it is the focus of bringing industrial growth and has been receiving the attention of the planners, policy makers, social scientists, economists, industrialists, financial institutions, administrators and academicians. Entrepreneurship is regarded as the most crucial factor in the economic development of the country. If some states like Manipur have remained underdeveloped today, it is because of the dearth of entrepreneurship. In underdeveloped regions, only a few men with growth perspective would come forward for changing the stationery inertia and creating pre-conditions for industrialisation, since they are motivated for higher achievements rather than financial gains.

More recently, enhancing small scale industries has been viewed as an effective way of fostering the private sector's contribution to both the growth and the equity objectives of development. Small scale industries are found in existence in every country. They play a key role in the industrialisation of developing countries. This is because they provide immediate large-scale employment and have a comparatively higher labour-capital ratio, they have a shorter gestation period and relatively smaller markets to be economic, they need lower investments, offer a method of ensuring a more equitable distribution of national income and facilitate an effective mobilization of resources of capital and skill which might otherwise remained unutilized, and they stimulate the growth of industrial entrepreneurship and promote a more diffused pattern of ownership and location

This book is a revised version of research work done in the Department of Commerce, Manipur University. The book focuses on the different aspects of entrepreneurship in small scale industries. It contains seven chapters. The first chapter deals with the concept of entrepreneurship and its relationship with economic development, the emerging trends of small scale industry with objectives and research design. Chapter II provides the socio-economic origins of entrepreneurs. Chapter III analyzes the entrepreneurial motivations and ambitions. The promotion of enterprises by the entrepreneurs is discussed in Chapter IV which is followed by Chapter V, evaluating the performance and growth of enterprises. Problems encountered by enterprises are analyzed in Chapter VI. The last chapter is devoted for findings and suggestions which pave way for certain discussion on policy implications.

Now it is our privilege to express sincere thanks to those who have helped us at various levels of work. At the outset, the authors wish to express sincere thanks to Prof. C. Amuba Singh, Hon'ble Vice-Chancellor, Manipur University for his encouragement and personal affection. We owe a deep sense of gratitude to Prof. N. Joykumar Singh, Dean, School of Social Science, Manipur University, without his guidance and inducement, this work would not have come to its successful completion.

We are thankful to Prof. Elangbam Bijoykumar Singh, Head, Department of Economics, Manipur University, H. Kulla Singh, Former Head, Department of Accounting and Finance, D.M. College of Commerce, Imphal for their valuable suggestions and persistent encouragement. We extend our sincere thanks to I. Pramodini Devi, Principal, D.M. College of Commerce, Imphal for her valuable guidance and advice extended to us throughout the process of publication of this book. We are deeply indebted to Prof. S.S. Khanka, Dean, School of Management Science and Head, Department of Business Administration, Tezpur University, Tezpur, who is also a great scholar in the field of entrepreneurship in the country, for the encouragement he has provided to us for completion of the work. We are thankful to Dr. R.K. Ranjan Singh, Registrar, Manipur University, Prof. N. Lokendra Singh, Director, College Development Council, Manipur University, Dr. N. Tejmani Singh, Dr. Rajmani Singha, Dr. Robita

Sorokhaibam and Dr. Kh. Dhiren Meetei from the Department of Commerce, Manipur University for their help and co-operation provided for the completion of the work.

Valuable suggestions and immense help were provided by Prof. A.R.M.Rehman, Dibrugarh University, Prof. H.C. Gautam, Guwahati University, Prof. Sudipti Benerjea, Kolkata University, Prof. P.K. Bhattacharjee, Kalyani University, Prof. N.C.Das, Guwahati University, Prof. P.K. Haldar, Tripura University, and Prof. N.C. Dey, Assam University, Silchar. In fact, words are inadequate to express our profound gratitude to them.

We are thankful to all the entrepreneurs who co-operated with us in the data collection and provided information about their industries. We will also like to express our gratitude to Shri M.P. Misra, Proprietor, Akansha Publishing House, New Delhi for taking keen interest in publishing the book in record time.

G.P. PRASAIN

E. NIXON SINGH

Contents

CHAPTER I

ENTREPRENEURSHIP AND SMALL SCALE INDUSTRIES

1.1 Introduction

Entrepreneurship of late, has attracted much public interest since it is the focus of bringing industrial growth and had been receiving the attention of the planners, policy-makers, social scientists, economists, industrialists, financial institutions, administrators and academicians. Entrepreneur-ship is regarded as the most crucial factor in the economic development of a country.

The spirit of enterprise makes a man entrepreneur. Such a spirit transformed him from a nomad to cattle rearer to a settled agriculturist, to a trader and to an industrialist. Thus entrepreneurs are persons who initiate, organize, manage and control the affairs of a business unit that combine the factors of production to supply goods and services, whether the business pertains to agriculture, industry, trade or profession. The economic development of a country is the hard work of entrepreneur. The development or underdevelopment is the result of the development or underdevelopment of entrepreneurship in the society. If today, some countries like India have remained underdeveloped, it is largely due to the dearth of an important input, viz, entrepreneurship. In recent years also, economists have shifted the emphasis from the growth rate of capital formation to that of entrepreneurship as the major factor of economic development.

Different writers defined the entrepreneurial functions in different ways. But the term 'entrepreneur' appeared in the French language much before the emergence of the concept of entrepreneurial function. In French language, it originally meant to designate "an organizer of musical or other entertainments". In the early 16th century, men engaged in military expeditions were referred to as entrepreneurs. From this usage it was easy to move to apply the word 'entrepreneur' to other type of adventure.[1]

After 1700, 'entrepreneur' was a word, which was frequently applied by the French government to bridge, harbour and fortification contractors. The same term was later applied to architects. Richard Cantillon, an Irishman living in France was the first to use the term 'entrepreneur' to refer to economic activities. He portrayed an entrepreneur as one discharging the function of direction and speculation. He defined an entrepreneur as a person who buys factor services at certain prices with a view to sell its product at uncertain prices in the future.[2] The 'classic' definition of entrepreneur which was to survive for almost two centuries, was given by J.B. Say. According to him, an entrepreneur is the most important agent of production who provides continuing management and brings together the factors of production.[3]

F.H. Knight propounded the theory that the entrepreneurs are a specialised groups of persons who bear risk and deal with uncertainty. Accordingly to him, entrepreneur is the economic functionary who undertakes such responsibility, which, by its very nature, cannot be insured or salaried. He also guarantees specified sums to others in return for assignments made to them. The supply of entrepreneurship involves three factors: namely, ability, willingness and power to extend such guarantees. Knight has gone a step ahead and has also located the psychological, social and economic factors which govern the supply of entrepreneurship. Adam Smith, the father of political economy, considered entrepreneur as a proprietary capitalist, a supplier of capital and at the same time working as manager intervening between the labour and the consumer. He argues that the fundamental economic determinant of growth is the rate of capital formation. David

Ricardo, a contemporary of J.B. Say, also attributed a significant role to the rate of capital accumulation in the process of economic development. According to him, the prime motive of the entrepreneur is to accumulate and without motive there should be no accumulation to facilitate capital formation and economic development. In his words, "the farmer and the manufacturer can no more live without profit than the labourer without wages".[4] He stressed that the motive for accumulation will diminish with every diminution of profit and will cease altogether when profits are so low as not to afford an adequate compensation for the risk and trouble which the entrepreneur encounters in employing his capital productivity. Alfred Marshall too, not only followed Smith-Ricardian path but reaffirmed the function of direction in production process and he repeatedly stressed that the function requires "no ordinary skill".

Modern interest in the entrepreneur as a key figure in economic progress stems in large part, as is well known, from the work of Joseph A. Schumpeter, In Schumpeter's system, entrepreneurship is essentially a creative activity. The entrepreneur is the innovator who introduces something new into the economy. The innovation may be a method of production not yet tested by experience in the branch of manufacture concerned, or a product with which consumers are not yet familiar, or a new source of raw-material or of new market hitherto unexploited, or other innovations in the strict sense of the term.[5] According to him, entrepreneurs are business leaders and not simple owners of capital. They are men of vision, drive and talent, who spot out opportunities and promptly seize them for exploitation. By virtue of their initiative, earnestness and activity, they accomplish significant advances in national production and incidentally obtained a good slice of the increasing national income as reward for their untiring efforts in the forms of profits, which they consider as the barometer of their success. Personal gain constitutes the spur of economic activity under private enterprise. In furtherance of their interest, entrepreneurs undertake business ventures and economic activity involving new combination of factors of production, which raise the level of productivity resulting in better utilization of resources. Hence, entrepreneurs constitute the generating force of motive of economic development.

According to Harvey Leibenstein,[6] the entrepreneurs fills market deficiencies through input-completing activities. Entrepreneurship involves activities necessary to create or carry on an enterprise where not all markets are well established or clearly defined and/or in which relevant parts of the production function are not completely known.

The Entrepreneurship Centre at Miami University of Ohio[7] has an interesting definition of entrepreneurship: "Entrepreneurship is the process of identifying, developing and bringing a vision to life. The vision may be an innovative idea, an opportunity, or simply a better way to do something. The end result of this process is the creation of a new venture, formed under conditions of risk and considerable uncertainty."

In summary, entrepreneurship is often viewed as a function, which involves the exploitation of opportunities, which exist within a market. Such exploitation is most commonly associated with the direction and/or combination of productive inputs. Entrepreneurs usually are considered to bear risk while pursuing opportunities, and often are associated with creative and innovative actions. In addition, entrepreneurs undertake a managerial role in their activities, but routine management of an ongoing operation is not considered to be entrepreneurship. In this sense entrepreneurial activity is fleeting. An individual may perform an entrepreneurial function in creating an organization, but later is relegated to the role of managing it without performing an entrepreneurial role. In this sense, many small-business owners would not be considered to be entrepreneurs. Finally, individuals within organizations (i.e. non-founders) can be classified as entrepreneurs since they pursue the exploitation of opportunities. Thus entrepreneurship is appropriately considered to be a form of entrepreneurship.

1.2 Entrepreneurship and Economic Development

Entrepreneurship is an important input influencing the economic development of the economy. If some states like Manipur have remained underdeveloped today, it is obviously because of the dearth of entrepreneurship. In underdeveloped regions only a few men with growth prospective would come forward for changing the stationary inertia and creating pre-conditions for industrialisations, since they are motivated for higher achievements rather than financial gains.

According to neo-classical economists, there is no room for enterprise and initiative. Both the micro and macro theories have assigned only a limited role to entrepreneurship. In the firm's behavioural analysis, the entrepreneur or the management group is viewed as a passive agent of the production process.

According to Adam Smith, the rate of capital formation is the fundamental determinant of economic development. The rate of capital formation in turn depends upon the relationship between minimum expected rate of profit and actual profit. The minimum profit required for a firm to stay in the industry and the actual profits would ultimately govern the economic development. Ricardo's theory explains the impact of change in wages on profit and capital accumulation. He suggested two policy variables namely socio-cultural environment and technological improvements, which increase the marginal productivity of capital and labour. In both analyses, the entrepreneurial role is totally ignored and the economic development takes place automatically.

The Schumpeterian model of economic development postulates that given rate of population growth, the dynamic evolution of capitalist economy is determined by its rate of innovations. This model implies that labour supply; resources, existing capital and the state of the arts only create potentiality for capital productivity, while it is the enterprise, which performs the miracle of transforming the potential into effective productivity. J.A. Schumpeter considered entrepreneurial function as a distinctive function, which yields distinct returns and entrepreneurial gains as monopoly gains, since, it occurs due to the fact that competitions only follow at a distance.[8]

The Schumpeterian concept of "innovations' is more fundamental than that of "entrepreneurship". The latter is simply the agent for affecting the former.[9] However, the role of entrepreneurs in the process of economic development cannot be overlooked. Technological innovations may not be fruitful resulting in development, unless they are put to economic use. In fact, the transformation of laboratory results to commercial production itself is an "innovation". It is the entrepreneur who materialises this vital transformation. As a matter of fact, Schumpeter has visualised innovative type of entrepreneurship in the process of economic development. However, if one analyzes the history of economic development of developed countries, he may not come across Schumpeterian entrepreneurs. In the words of the ancient proverb chosen by Marshall as the motto of the Principles, **Nature non facit saltum**. A country with little or no industrial tradition can hardly produce the innovators capable of substantial transformations without first producing, and in large numbers, the humble type of entrepreneurs. Economy shaking innovators, like great scholars, are the exceptional few who emerge at the summit of a broadly based pyramid. Such men do not appear and could not function until a certain level of educational, social and technical progress has been achieved. They are at once a product of development and an agent of further development.[10] But the need for Schumpeterian innovators in countries, which are beginning to industrialise, must not be over stressed. The technologies and products needed by these countries have already been developed in more advanced countries. Men are needed who can adapt these technologies and products to the particular conditions of less advanced countries.

It is McClelland's concept of personality aspects of entrepreneurship, which is more comprehensive and relevant for the study of this phenomenon in a backward region. He emphasises that people with high achievement motivation are likely to behave in an entrepreneurial way as they would not be satisfied with their present status in the society, they would prefer entrepreneurial function. Hence, it is clear that the quality of entrepreneurship need not be identified from attributed but from the functions performed by it.

Underdevelopment cannot be identified only with the under-utilization of material resources, as it is only a symptom. Under-utilization of human resources including the entrepreneurial skills is the surest diagnosis of underdevelopment. There are a few instances where development process has been initiated just by an accident. It may be pointed out that the quality and quantity of human resources, which include among others, entrepreneurial ability, skilled manpower, the state of administration and national character are the pre-requisites in order to change the initial conditions of the economy.[11] While entrepreneurship cannot be considered as a sufficient condition for growth activity, it is surely a necessary condition.

Entrepreneurship in underdeveloped regions has a different connotation. It does not emerge out of industrial background with well developed institutions to support and encourage it but it is characterised by the conditions associated with under-development. There, the entrepreneur in such region may not be an "innovator", but only an "imitator", who would copy the organisation, technology, and products of the innovators from the developed regions. His role as a constraints and conditions peculiar to his area of operation and the factors under which he conducts his minimal modest industrial activity.

In undeveloped regions, only a few men with growth perspective would come forward for changing the stationary inertia and creating preconditions for economic development, since they are motivated for higher achievements rather than financial gains. [12] The economic development in backward regions can be achieved through two forms of entrepreneurial activities. One is entrepreneurship emerging from individual efforts and another is that emerging from collective efforts. The first one may be called as "individualistic entrepreneurship" which is a peculiar form of leadership where all the functions of management are concentrated in a single hand.[13] Consequently, the entrepreneurs take all decisions in diverse fields of promotional and managerial activities. The second form of entrepreneurship is based on 'techno-structure'.[14] It emerges from mechanisation, division of labour, large scale production and production in anticipation of demand. This form of entrepreneurship is performed by a group of experts, who are not generally owners of the enterprise. The development of such a techno-structure would definitely accelerate the process of economic development. However, in an underdeveloped region, private techno-structure may not come forward to risk its capital in the absence of necessary infrastructure. Even the public sector techno-structure may also hesitate to penetrate into these regions despite the government's commitment to the dispersal of industries to the backwards areas. The characteristics of under development are in themselves the constraints for the development of a techno-structure private or public in a region devoid of any infrastructural facilities. Hence, only the first type of entrepreneurship can contribute for industrialisation of such regions. In India, since the public and co-operative techno-structure has its own limitations, it is the local entrepreneurship that must get itself involved in the process of economic development. It should be realised that economic development would not get momentum if much reliance is placed on the factors beyond local control. Therefore, it is absolutely necessary to break the vicious circle and initiate the process of economic development and industrialisation which may include, to start with small scale entrepreneurship as the most desirable factors.

Furthermore, entrepreneurship should be viewed in a wider perspective involving the Government, entrepreneur and financial institutions. Development cannot take place without active co-operation among these three factors. Very often, it is seen that Government stops at policy level and financial institutions take the responsibility only for financing but the entrepreneur is left to look after himself once a project is cleared.

1.3 Small Scale Industry: Concept and Significance

More recently, enhancing small scale industries has been viewed as an effective way of fostering the private sector's contribution to both the growth and the equity objectives of development. Small scale industries are found in existence in every country. They play a key role in the industrialization of developing country. This is because they provide immediate large-scale employment and have a comparatively higher labour-capital ratio, they have a shorter gestation period and relatively smaller markets to be economic, they need lower investments, offer a method of ensuring a more equitable distribution of national income and facilitate an effective mobilization of resources of capital and skill which might otherwise remained unutilized, and they stimulate the growth of industrial entrepreneurship and promote a more diffused pattern of ownership and location.

Small scale industries have been given an important place in the framework of Indian planning since beginning both for economic and ideological reasons. Today, India operates the largest and oldest programmes for the development of small scale industries in any developing country.[15] As a matter of fact, small sector has now emerged as a dynamic and vibrant sector for the Indian economy in the recent years.

There is no uniformity in the definition and meaning of small scale industry (SSI) from one country to another and from one time to another in the same country depending upon the pattern and stage of development. As a result, there are at least 50 different definitions of SSI's found and used in 75 countries.[16]

The Fiscal Commission, 1950[17], for the first time, defined a small scale industry as one which is operated mainly with hired labour usually 10 to 50 hands.

In order to promote small scale industries in the country, the Government of India has set up the Central Small Scale Industries Organization and the Small Scale Industries Board in 1954-55. The SSI Board at its first meeting held on January 5th and 6th, 1955, defined Small Scale Industry as a unit employing less than 50 employees, if using power, and less than 100 employees without the use of power and with a capital asset not exceeding Rs. 5 lakhs.

The various changes in the definitions of Small Scale Industry over a period in India is resumed in Table 1.1

As per the Abid Hussain Committee's recommendations on Small Scale Industries, the Government of India has, in March 1997, further raised investment ceiling to Rs. 3 crores for small scale industries and to Rs. 50 lakhs for tiny units.

The new policy initiative in 1999-2000 for the small scale sector has reduced the investment limit for small scale and ancillary undertakings from existing Rs.3 crores to Rs.1 crore.

An ancillary unit is one which sells not less than 50% of its products to one or more industrial units.

Table 1.1
Definitions of Small Scale Industry

Year	Investment Criterion		Employment Criterion
	SSI Unit	Ancillary Unit	
Upto 1958	Fixed capital investment upto Rs. 5 lakhs	Same as SSI Unit	Employment upto 50 workers if using power or upto 100 if not using power.
1959	The value of machine was taken as the original price paid irrespective of new or old machinery	Same as SSI Units	Employment upto 50 workers if using power or upto 100 if using power.
1960	The Gross value of fixed assets upto Rs. 5 lakhs	Gross value of fixed assets upto Rs. 10 lakhs	Employment criterion dropped
1966*	Rs. 7.5 lakhs	Rs. 10 lakhs	Employment criterion dropped
1975	Rs. 10 lakhs	Rs. 15 lakhs	Employment criterion dropped
1980	Rs. 20 lakhs	Rs. 25 lakhs	Employment criterion dropped
1985	Rs. 35 lakhs	Rs. 45 lakhs	Employment criterion dropped
1991	Rs. 60 lakhs	Rs. 75 lakhs	Employment criterion

Source : S.S. Khanka; Growth vis-a-vis Sickness in Small Scale Industries in India, *Productivity*, Vol. 35, No. 3, October – December, 1994, p.p. 488-493.

Note : Since 1996 investment limit applicable only to plant & machinery.
* The export units are those who export at least 30% of the annual production. The ceiling of investment shall be Rs. 75 lakhs for it.

For small scale industries, the Planning Commission of India uses terms 'village and small scale industries'. These include modern small scale industries and the traditional cottage and household industries.

Small scale industries are known and defined with different names and characteristics in different countries. In the USA, the manufacturing firm is officially a small business for Government procurement purposes, if it is not dominant in its field of operations and if it has fewer than 500 employees, or if it is certified as small by the small business administration for purposes fewer than 250 employees, depending on size and the standard set for different industries. In the UK, there is no demarcation between small and large industries. However, in books and treatises on industrial subjects, units employing less than 500 workers are generally referred to as small units.[18]

1.4 Role of Small Scale Industries in Economic Development

Small Scale Industries contribute significantly to social and economic development objectives such as labour absorption, income distribution, rural development, poverty eradication, regional balance and promotion of entrepreneurship. It generates immediate employment opportunities with relative low capital/investment, promotes more equitable distribution of national income, makes effective mobilization of untapped capital and human skills and leads to dispersal of manufacturing activities all over the country, leading to growth of villages, small towns and economically lagging regions.[19]

Particularly in developing countries, small labour intensive industries have been favoured basically to create employment opportunities in an economy with abundant unskilled labour even though such industries may not always be supported on grounds of economic efficiency. In addition, a low capital requirement, given an appropriate market environment, is believed to stimulate growth of numerous indigenous industries with wide regional dispersal. This helps to promote balanced growth, more equitable income distribution as well as diversification of the industrial structure which often leads to increased utilization of national resources. The process, if properly nurtured, can help the entrepreneurial class and boost capital formation as well as growth of industries in the small sector in urban and rural areas. Such a process creates the basis for transformation of technology management and paves the way for creative development while sustaining national heritage and skills. It will also pave the way for the growth of right type of entrepreneurship in the country.

Empirical studies have shown that small scale industries are important vehicles for meeting the growth and equity with social justice objectives of developing economics. Achievement of these objectives is seen as desirable in almost all developing countries, though the relative importance of these objectives varies from country to country, depending on the differences in the socio-economic and political complexes. In short, small enterprises sector help in generating large scale employment, wage goods and incomes in a fairly dispersed manner; mobilizing dormant skills and resources enhancing entrepreneurship; energising village economies aiding the process of backward area development and playing an important role in the overall process of industrialization.[20]

1.5 Evaluation of Small Scale Industries

The recent years have witnessed a dramatic expansion in the small scale sector in almost all parts of the world. It is not only in developing countries that have experienced such a phenomenon but a similar experience has also been gathered by a large number of industrially developed countries like Japan, U.K., Germany, U.S.A., Switzerland, etc.

Japan for instance, achieved rapid industrialization through the small scale sector in the latter half of the 19th century. The small scale sector in this country plays a catalytic and predominant role in the accelerated growth of the economy.

Even in the developed countries of Western Europe and United States of America, there is a recognition that small and rural industries play a significant role in complementing the large industry and in providing opportunities for creative energies of the skilled people. The watch industry in Switzerland - the largest in the world - is based on the work of a multitude of small, almost cottage industrial units.[21] So important were small firms considered in United Kingdom that a report (Boiton Committee, 1971) paradised the famous saying of Voltaire that. "if small business does not exist, it would be necessary to invent it", In the United States of America, small business administration, more than 30 years old, had been placed on a statutory footing reporting directly to the President.

1.6 Small scale Industries in India

The small scale industries are the hub of many economic activities in a developing country like India. The role played by these industries in the economic activity of advanced industrialized countries is also very significant. The socio-economic transformation of India cannot be achieved without paying adequate attention to the development of this labour intensive and capital sparing sector.

The most significant aspect of small industry development is that this sector has stimulated economic activity of a far reaching magnitude and has created a sense of confidence among a huge number of small entrepreneurs about their strength and validity. For example, the small scale industries have registered a phenomenal growth in their number, production, employment and exports over the years.[22] Their numbers have grown from 16000 in 1950 to 31.21 lakhs in 1998-99. While production has registered an increase of more than twenty times, employment grew by about three times over the period 1974-99. Growth in exports has been particularly commendable from mere Rs. 393 crores in 1973-74 to a mounting high figure of Rs. 57,488 crores in 1998-99. It is also encouraging to mention that the small scale enterprises account for 35% of the gross value of the output in the manufacturing sector, about 80% of the total industrial employment and about 40% of the total exports of the country.

The Government of India has also given important emphasis to the development of small scale industries in the country's Five Year Plans. The rationale behind such an approach is that small scale industries provide substantial scope for increasing employment as they are labour intensive and they require comparatively less capital. They have lesser gestation period and can easily be set up in rural areas or in backward areas. They need relatively small markets to be economical and hence they have advantage in being set up as ancillary units. They stimulate growth of entrepreneurship and promote a more decentralized pattern of ownership and location.

Since independence, these industries have made an all round effort to boost the economy. The traditional village and cottage industries provide a vital means of livelihood to village artisans. These industries create the scope of employment to the rural mass and by the way their act as a positive catalyst to ensure the quality of life to the village people. At the same time, these labour intensive industries are considered to be the important means of checking economic concentration in the hands of a few. Equitable distribution of national income is the thrust of our economic policy and towards this end, small scale industries play a crucial role. Employment generation, minimization of economic dispersal, development of backward areas, improvement of the quality of the village population are some of the many important dimensions of our pragmatic planning which always encourages the growth of small scale industries.

1.7 Manipur : Its Geographical Location

Manipur is a state on the eastern frontier of India, covering an area of 22,327 sq. kms. It is surrounded by Nagaland in the north, Myanmar in the east, Assam in the west and Mizoram in the south. It lies within a rectangle contained by 23.83N and 25.68N latitude and 93.03E and 94.78E longitude.[23] The area is visibly marked by two distinct regional peculiarities. They are the valley and the hills. The valley claims about 15% of the total state area and spreads over an area of 1843 sq.kms., accommodating about 65% of the total population. The density of population in the valley is 628 per sq.km. as per 2001 census. The hill region spreads over an extensive area of 20,513 sq.kms. Its small population representating 35% enjoys about 85% of the total area. The density of population in hill is only 49 per sq.kms. as per 2001 census.

1.8 Population of the state

According to the Census of India 2001, the population of the state of Manipur as on 31st March 2001 stood at 23,88.634 persons. This represents merely 0.23 percent of the total population of India which is about 1,027,015,247 persons as per 2001 figures. The population of the state among the different districts according to the Census of India 1991 and 2001 is given

Diagram 1.1
District-wise Population of the State in 1991 and 2001

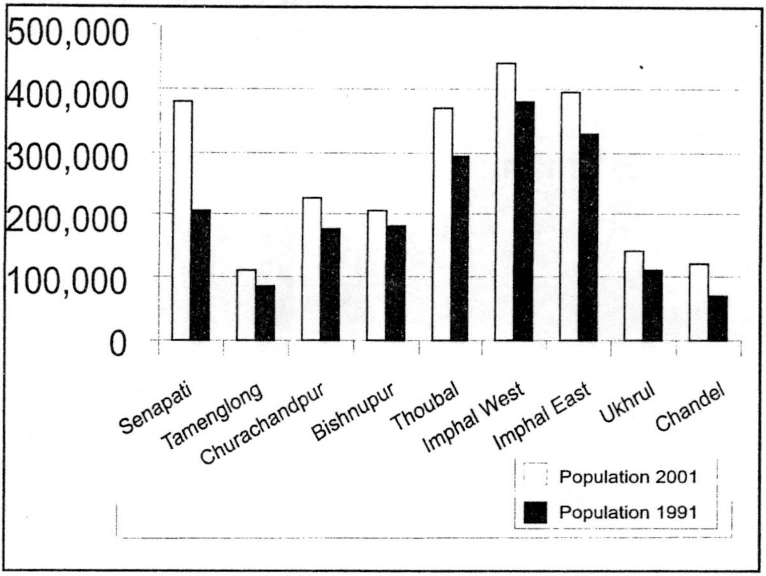

Source: Census of India, 2001. *Population of Manipur, Directorate of Census Operation, Manipur*

in Diagram No. 1.1 and percentage distribution of population in rural and urban is given in Diagram No. 1.2.

1.9 Industrial scenario of Manipur

Manipur is an industrially backward state. Economic reforms have failed to revive the down trend in industrialization. Manipur has practically no large scale industry which can produce a commodity in a large scale. The few small scale industries that are functioning are also not functioning optimally due to lack of availability of resources and the appropriate environment. The share of manufacturing in real Net State Domestic Product (NSDP) declined from 4.16% in 1980-81 to 3.37% in 1995-96. The growth rate of this sector in the 1990's was insignificant. The share of the tertiary sector

Diagram 1.2

Percentage of Distribution of Population Rural/Urban

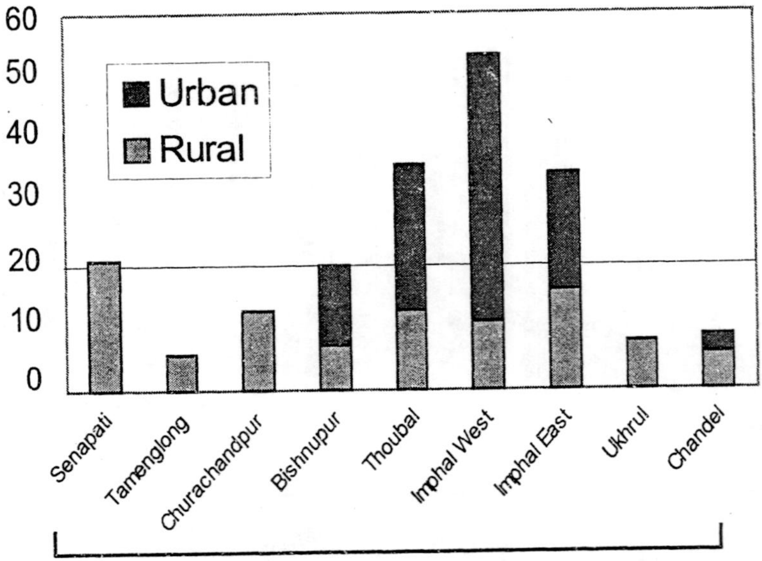

Source: Census of India 2001, *Population of Manipur, Directorate of Census Operations, Manipur.*

started dominating the economy without any significant relationship in the commodity producing sectors of the economy. Private sector employment constituted only 3% of organized sector employment. More than 4 lakhs people are registered in the live register of employment exchanges. Even though International Monetary Fund (IMF) studies categorize this state with 23 lakhs people (2001 census) as one of the fastest growing states in India, its per capita income has persistently fallen short of all India level.[24]

The district-wise number of registered industrial units, employment, investment and production since inception up to 31.3.2001 can be analyzed from the Table. 1.2

It can be observed from Table 1.2 that Imphal West District of Manipur has the largest number of industrial units totally 5185, Whereas Imphal East District has the lowest i.e. 137. The other 7 districts of Manipur have units numbering less than 1000 each.

1.10 Imphal East District and Imphal West District

The Imphal District is an offshoot of the then one district state of Manipur. Now, there are 9 (nine) Districts in Manipur i.e., 5 Hill Districts and 4 Valley Districts. The Imphal District has a total area of 1,201 sq.kms.

The Imphal District was bifurcated into 2 (two) Districts as Imphal West and Imphal East District with effect from 18th June, 1997. The Imphal East District has 4 (four) Sub-Divisions namely (1) Imphal East-I (Porompat), (2) Imphal East-II (Sawombung), (3) Keirao Bitra and (4) Jiribam Sub-Division and 5 (five) S.D.C. Circles. Likewise, the Imphal West District has 4 (four) Sub-Divisions namely (1) Imphal West –I (Lamphelpat) (2) Imphal West – II (Wangoi) (3) Lamsang Sub-division and (4) Patsoi Sub-Division and 10 S.D.C. Circles. Besides, Imphal East District have 3 (three) Community Development Blocks viz., (1) Imphal East – I, (2) Imphal West – II and (3) Jiribam and Imphal West District have 2 (two) of the same, viz., (1) Imphal West – I and (2) Imphal West – II for the implementation of development schemes.

1.11 Review of literature on entrepreneurship

Entrepreneurship, of late, has attracted much public interest. It may be noted that interest in the development of entrepreneurship arose only in the late fifties.[25] Here, an attempt has been made to make a review of the studies on entrepreneurship as many scholars have shown great interest in studying the various aspects of entrepreneurship in India.

Berna[26] made case studies of fifty medium size manufacturing firms engaged in various kinds of light engineering production in and around Madras and Coimbatore cities. He analyzed the entrepreneurs' origins and found that the initial entry into industry was open to persons of very different social standing and economic position. His basic finding goes against the popular belief that caste and tradition play an

Table 1.2

District-wise No. of the Registered, Industrial Units, Employment, Investment & Production since inception upto 31-03-2001

Sl. No.	Name of Districts	No. of Units			Production Unit			Investment			Employment		
		SIDO	Non-SIDO	Total	SIDO	Non-SIDO	Total	SIDO	Non-SIDO	Total	SIDO	Non SIDO	Total
1.	2	3	4	5	6	7	8	9	10	11	12	13	14
1.	Imphal West	2905	2280	5185	44.27	35.27	79.59	9.72	7.29	17.01	15083	11505	26588
2.	Ukhrul	670	105	775	9.73	2.07	11.80	2.70	0.43	3.13	3931	530	4461
3	Senapati	242	52	294	2.25	1.63	3.89	0.66	0.26	0.92	1056	252	1308
4	Churachandpur	425	109	534	3.73	3.39	7.12	1.86	0.33	2.19	2231	1085	3316
5	Tamenglong	277	208	485	1.07	5.16	6.23	0.31	0.87	1.18	564	1121	1775
6	Chandel	199	130	329	3.61	1.60	5.21	0.81	0.42	1.23	1157	648	1805
7	Thoubal	437	133	570	11.08	1.26	12.34	3.16	0.2	3.38	3123	746	3869
8	Bishnupur	507	175	682	11.21	1.14	12.35	2.32	0.36	2.68	3044	852	3896
9	Imphal East	117	20	137	4.67	0.43	5.10	1.27	0.05	1.32	666	250	916
	Total	**5779**	**3212**	**8991**	**91.63**	**51.95**	**143.63**	**22.81**	**10.21**	**33.04**	**30855**	**16989**	**47934**

Source : "Nucleus Cell", Directorate of Commerce & Industries, Manipur.

important role in the emergence of entrepreneurs. Berna further felt that the performance of the entrepreneurs would be improved and their contribution to industrial progress could be increased if certain help in techniques of production and management were provided to them.

McGary[27] studies seventeen small scale firms in Uttar Pradesh and focused his attention on the craftsman entrepreneur whom he regarded as a needed source of good industrial entrepreneurship. He analyzed the reasons for the high mortality rate and the lack of growth of their firms and made some policy recommendations for providing them an opportunity to grow especially through provision of capital.

Narain Singh[28] made a case study of 25 light engineering units in Agra. He classified the units on the basis of assets and employment and observed that (i) an increase in employment almost in proportion to the size of assets; (ii) dominance of Agarwal merchants and manufacturers; (iii) existence of profit as the main motivating factor; (iv) absence of relationship between the traditional business and the present manufacturing activity; and (v) absence of borrowing from Governments.

Thomas Timberg[29] analyzed the nature of entrepreneurship in Marawari community. He analyzed the theory of entrepreneurship with respect to the Marwari's success in business and their late entry into industry. He concluded that entrepreneurial Marwaris performed crucial roles in the development of industrial and commercial economy of Northern India.

The study made by **Pritam Singh**[30] focused on empirical findings relating to indigenous entrepreneurship after independence in the country as a whole. Both small scale and large scale entrepreneurs were evaluated in terms of their contribution to economic development. He contended that the entrepreneur need not necessarily be an innovator in the adoption of institutions which have been developed in other countries.

Shethy[31] focused the role of 'initiative' as opposed to innovative entrepreneur – managers in the new industrial countries. According to him, the small enterprises constitute the predominant form and such enterprises serve as the seed bed for spotting and nurturing much needed entrepreneurial talent.

Guha[32] reviewed historically the development of Parsi entrepreneurs during 1750-1850. The Parsis' success was attributed to their greater ability to adjust themselves to European power and their relative non-involvement in the earlier civil and military administration.

Gaikwad and **Tripathi**[33] studied the small entrepreneurs of Tanuku region of West Godavari district in Andhra Pradesh. The main focus of the study was on the manufacturing concerns belonging to the family of a leading industrial magnet Mullapudi Harischendra Prasad and their kith and kin. The study observed that all the entrepreneurs were persons with initiative drive and hard work, though the majority of the entrepreneurs had no technical knowledge. The traders, have realized the scope of industries in the region but hesitated to take up industrial entrepreneurship because, in their opinion, it required large capital outlay, high managerial skills and technical knowledge. They think that industrialists enjoy better status than the tradesmen. These findings of Gaikwad and Tripathi are very important for policy makes as the tradesmen are often looked upon as potential entrepreneurs.

Pathak[34] studies 12 units during 1969-70 to1970-71 with a view to evaluate entrepreneurship. The units were selected from industrial estates enjoying identical facilities and engaged in different lines of manufacture. He studies their problems at three different stages inception, operation and expansion/ diversification. He observes that factors like contacts, education and finance play an important role and the problems at the stage of inception received relatively more attention than the problems at the remaining two stages.

Ashish Nandy[35] carried on intensive study of an equal number of small scale entrepreneurs and non-entrepreneurs from an urban ward of Howrah in West Bengal to know and compare the enterprising and non-enterprising cultures. The study reveals that in an enterprising community, entrepreneur exposure themselves and contribute substantially to entrepreneurship and identified such a phenomenon as an important determinant of entry and survival in business.

Ramakrishnan[36] surveyed 94 small scale units employing five or more persons in eleven important industry groups in urban Delhi. He analyzed the social, educational and occupational backgrounds of the entrepreneurs, their motivations, expectations and reactions to schemes of assistance by the Government . He also collected information relating to the entrepreneurs who failed to commence production and those who dropped out after commencement of production.

The Small Industries Extension Training Institute (SIET)[37], Hyderabad, conducted a survey of small units situated in the twin cities of Hyderabad and Secunderabad. The study analyzed the reasons for starting industrial units by interviewing 61 entrepreneurs. The study revealed that "economic gain" was the most important reason for starting the small industrial units followed by "ambition" order. The study revealed "capital shortage" and "Government red-tapism" as the most discouraging factors. The study further showed that younger age, formal education, urban background, experience, risk taking and adoption propensity were some of the characteristics that were positively associated with the quality of entrepreneurship.

Sharma and **Harnak Singh**[38] explained inter-industry and inter-state pattern of entrepreneurial growth and analyzed the growth variables such as ethical values, need for achievement motivation, commitment of the political system etc. It has been observed that lack of inter-industry, inter-sectoral and inter-regional coordination is the major problem that needs to be tackled properly.

Choudury[39] made an attempt to review the entrepreneurial activity of the North-East region in order to find out its identity in terms of social, local occupational and product-wise variations. He collected data from 5,250 registered SSI Units in the region. He observes that in spite of abundant natural resources, the pace of industrial growth is slow not only because of the lack of basic facilities and financial institutions, but also due to untapped entrepreneurial talents in the region.

Sharma[40] made a study of entrepreneurs in Uttar Pradesh with respect to their entrepreneurial orientation, commitment and achievement. He found that entrepreneurs in Uttar Pradesh have higher entrepreneurial commitment and achievement.

Oomen[41] examined the development of entrepreneurship in the small scale sector of Kerala by studying the origin and growth of firms in the light engineering industry and the impact of Government programmes like industrial estates and rural industries project on entrepreneurship. The study was conducted on 45 entrepreneurs and it was found that engineers and technicians formed the single largest group of the entrepreneurs and most of the merchants who started industry were muslims.

Paul A. London's[42] study is an unusual study, because it focuses on rural merchants, a lively and enterprising group rarely mentioned in development literature. The study, based on nearly 200 interviews, shows that little noticed, often abused private shop keepers adapted remarkably to India's rural needs in the past decade by selling hundreds of millions of dollars worth of vital fertilizers and irrigation equipment. Their work helped make agricultural gains possible yet the Indian Government barely tolerates their continued existence in rural areas.

Vander Veen[43] differentiated and describes entrepreneurs with commercial and production orientation. He discussed the economic factors which favour the emergence of industrial entrepreneurs and delineated the "quantifying restrictions" method of implementing an import substitution strategy which reinforces their economic factors.

Gangadhara Rao's[44] study aimed at evaluating the impact of the programme of industrial estates on the emergence of entrepreneurship and growth of small units in Coastal Andhra. According to him, educational and income levels are important factors in motivating entrepreneurship.

Manohar Deshpande[45] surveyed 90 units in the Marathwada region (Maharastra). He evaluated the socio economic origins of entrepreneurs and problems faced by them at various stages. He established the relationship between performance and the causative factors. The study revealed that the upper strata of the society availed most of the economic benefits created by the Government agencies. The study stressed **"to get by the primary occupation"** is an important pre-condition for the development of entrepreneurship. It revealed that caste, family occupation and father's occupational status are important for entry into the business of manufacturing.

Ashok Kumar[46] studied the industrial estates in Visakhapatnam city of Andhra Pradesh. He selected 20 small industries each of the two industrial estates viz, Marripalem estate and Autonagar estate. He also evaluated the socio-economic origins of the entrepreneurs in the industrial estates, examine their motivations and ambitions, and offer suggestions for fostering entrepreneurship in small industry. The study revealed that education, entrepreneurship and development are interrelated. The government can also play effective role in fostering entrepreneurship in the estates.

Subbarao[47] conducted a study regarding the origin, growth and working of small scale industries in India, particularly in the state of Andhra Pradesh and in Vizianagaram, Srikakulam and Vishakhapatnam districts. The study covers a period from 1980-81 to 1995-96. The study revealed that growth in small scale industries in Andhra Pradesh in the recent past has been significant and the small entrepreneurs should develop a proper business plan before starting a unit.

1.12 Need of the present study

From the above review of literature, it can be understood that a lot of research work has been done with a focus on different dimensions of industrial entrepreneurship. However, research works on "Entrepreneurship in Small Scale Industries" particularly in the state of Manipur have to be considered as limited. In this regard, the study conducted by K.V.R. Choudhary may be considered as an important contribution towards entrepreneurial growth and development programme in North Eastern Region of India. But because of its wider scope to include the different registered small scale industries of the entire North-eastern states, the small scale industries of Manipur, particularly that of Imphal East and Imphal West Districts have not received the attention they deserved. Moreover, this study was conducted as far back as 1980 after which a number of development have taken place. The important one is that the rate of unemployment in Manipur is very high. At present, more than 4 lakhs people are registered in the live register of employment exchanges. With the ban in appointments in Government departments and downsizing process going on, the figure is likely to increase more. Being a land locked state, the scope of setting up large and medium size industries are also deemed. The only means for solving unemployment problem and tapping locally available resources is through fostering entrepreneurship in small scale industries in Manipur. It may also be pointed out that out of the 9 (nine) districts of Manipur, Imphal West District has the largest number of 5185 registered industrial units since inception upto 31.3.2001, while that of Imphal East District has 137. It has been observed that a large number of small scale industries are sick. It will be quite interesting to know as to why these two neighbouring districts show different industrial scenario. Of late, the state Government also is giving serious consideration for the development of small scale industries particularly through different self-employment schemes. In view of limited literature of entrepreneurship in small scale industries in Manipur and other developments that have taken place over a period of more than two decade after the study conducted by Mr. Choudary, it is felt necessary to focus attention on the entrepreneurship in Small Scale Industry coming up in Manipur, particularly in the districts of Imphal East and Imphal West.

1.13 Objectives

From the foregoing account, it is evident that small scale industries plays a significant role in the economic development of an underdeveloped state like Manipur. These industries meet the twin needs viz., solution of unemployment problem and checking the economic concentration in the hands of a few. And it is the entrepreneurs who are the central figure of any economic activity. Entrepreneurs are persons who initiate, organize, manage and control the affairs of a business unit. The first generation of entrepreneurs in a developing economy and their aspirations are important factors for its economic development. It is such entrepreneurs with whom this study is concerned.

The social groups from which the entrepreneurs are drawn, occupations pursued by them and their families earlier, their domiciliary background, the earnings at the time of their entry into industry, their ages and the level of education, the ambitions and compulsions that have led them to the conception of the idea to start an industrial enterprise and the difficulties encountered by them in the process are the factors greatly influencing the origin and evolution of entrepreneurship. As such, firstly the study is to enquire into what it that makes an entrepreneur.

Entrepreneurship can be definitely cultivated. There were few agriculturists and fewer tradesmen and industrialists in the earlier days. Had it not been possible to cultivate entrepreneurship, agriculture would not have become the primary occupation of millions and millions of people around the world. Trading has cut across the caste barrier and it is no more an exclusive privilege of a few communities traditionally known for trading. Likewise, entrepreneurship is undoubtedly a matter of nature and culture. The greater it is nurtured, the higher it is cultured. Successive generations of entrepreneurs create or usher in the industrial culture. Such an industrial culture nurtures, nourishes and multiply entrepreneurs.[48]

However, the predominance of certain communities in certain walks of life is neither insignificant nor it can be ignored. The underdeveloped countries have not yet reached a stage of development which can afford them either to discount or discard the notion that entrepreneurship is confined to few classes or communities. Therefore, it becomes a necessity to probe the genesis of entrepreneurship that may unravel the process of germination of entrepreneurship by establishing inter-relationship between socio-economic structures and entrepreneurship.

It is also necessary to make an evaluation of the role of small scale industries in promoting economic development. Their performance is to be evaluated by their growth and the problems faced by them are to be studied. If development of entrepreneurs is the prime need of present day underdeveloped countries, the type of entrepreneur who comes forward is also important. It makes a lot of difference to a country's rate of progress whether its industrialists take a 'short-term' approach to industry, regard the productive process as something fixed and static, are unwilling to tie up more than an absolute minimum of capital in plant and machinery, and remain pre-occupied with trade and quick turnover as the sole source of profit, or whether they exhibit a 'long-time' approach, are willing to plough back earning and wait for return, are anxious to improve technologically and are alert to new opportunities and willing to incur the risks involved and in exploiting them. It is not enough if a country develops an adequate supply of industrial entrepreneurs. It is also of vital importance that they should be of right type.

In view of the above, the study has the following specific objectives:

(i) To study the growth and development of small scale industries in Manipur.

(ii) To enquire into the socio-economic origins of the entrepreneurship emerging in the small scale industries of Manipur, particularly in the Imphal East and Imphal West Districts.

(iii) To examine the motivations and ambitions of the entrepreneurs.

(iv) To evaluate the entrepreneurial efforts and performance of enterprisers.

(v) To offer suggestions for fostering entrepreneurship in small scale industries of Manipur.

The study carried out with the above objectives is expected to throw light on some of the issues relating to entrepreneurship in small scale industries in Manipur that have remained dormant and come out with suggestions having policy implications at different levels for developing the right type of entrepreneurship required in a backward state like Manipur.

1.14 Research design

As a matter of fact, the small scale industries of Imphal East District and Imphal West District has gained a lot of significance on account of several factors particularly due to its large number of population and non-existence of other organized sector in absorbing the labour force. According to the population enumeration of the census of India 2001, the population of the state of Manipur as on 1st March 2001 stood at 23,88,635 persons.[4] Imphal West District accounts for 18.40% of the total population of the state whereas that of Imphal East Districts accounts for 16.49%. In this connection, it may be mentioned that the problems of unemployment and population growth has given impetus for the growth of small scale industries. There are 5185 and 137 industrial units in Imphal West and Imphal East District respectively as on 31.03.2001. Hence, the scope of the present study has been confined to these two districts of Manipur. It comprises 106 samples (estimated) of small scale industries which have been selected on random basis in such 56 samples from Imphal West Districts and the rest 50 from Imphal East District. The method of sampling adopted here is Stratified Random Sampling with proportional allocation in both stratum (two districts). The list of small scale industries is treated as sampling frame and the sample size is determined on the basis of a Pilot Survey (taking 10 small scale industries) say the mean ± S.D. of daily sales amount (in rupees) that is 2634.20 ± 2770.52 under the conditions that 95% degree of precision with 20% marginal error to the mean daily sales amount.

The formula used is

$$n = \frac{Z\alpha^2 \text{ x } s^2}{e^2}$$

Where,

n = sample size

e = marginal error/permissible error α

Zα = standard variate at "a" level

s = standard deviation.

In the selection of the sample units for the purpose of the study, those with less than 5 years' existence and not working at present have been completely ignored. It had also been ensured to give representation to different types of industries.

The data for the study have been collected mostly form the primary sources. An elaborate questionnaire was prepared for administering among the entrepreneurs. For the purpose of conversing the questionnaire one entrepreneur for each industry shall be selected irrespective of the fact that some are partnership firms and some are private limited companies.

Apart from these, secondary data has also been collected from different Government Department like Department of Commerce & Industries, District Industries Centers, Department of Economics and Statistics, Manipur Industrial Development Corporation etc. The data so collected will be tabulated and analyzed properly with the appropriate statistical tools and techniques.

1.15 Research questions

1. Entrepreneurship development in Small Scale Industries in Manipur is very slow and far below than the all India average.
2. The Industrial growth in the state has been on low growth path mostly due to more industrial failures in the small scale sector.
3. Lack of demand for products, scarcity of working capital and above all, infrastructure bottlenecks are the main factors for industrial backwardness in Manipur.
4. Improper project planning, lack of industrial conception, absence of entrepreneurial class adoptive to competitive and changing market forces and corrupt bureaucracy has also added to the problem of sickness in small scale industries in Manipur.

1.16 Scope and limitations of the study

The study conducted has the following scope and limitations.

(i) The scope of the present study has been confined in the two districts of Manipur viz, Imphal East District and Imphal West District.

(ii) Field survey was conducted during June-September, 2003.

(iii) As the findings and conclusions of this study are based on data collected from the selected entrepreneurs in the study area, it cannot be generalised for the entire state.

(iv) The methodology followed and tools employed in the analysis of the data involved certain merits as well as demerits of their own and also reflect the limitations of the data base.

(v) Data pertaining to sales, employment, capital, borrowings and time devoted by entrepreneurs were gathered from the selected entrepreneurs directly. There were no proper records maintained at the individual or firm level. Thus the information given by the sample units may not be accurate. However, utmost care was taken by the researcher to ensure accuracy, by adopting cross checking methods.

1.17 Presentation of the study

The study has been presented in seven chapters: Chapter I deals with the concept of entrepreneurship and its relationship with economic development, the emerging trends of small scale industry, objectives of the study and research design. Chapter II provides the socio-economic origins of entrepreneurs. Chapter III analyzes the entrepreneurial motivations and ambitions. The promotion of enterprises by the entrepreneurs are discussed in Chapter IV which is followed by Chapter V evaluating the performance and growth of enterprises. Problems encountered by enterprises are analyzed in Chapter VI. The last chapter is devoted for findings and suggestions of the whole study.

REFERENCES

1. George Herbertan Evens Jr., 'The Entrepreneur and Economic Theory', American Economic Review, 1949, p.338
2. Killy, Peter (Ed.), 'Entrepreneurship and Economic Development', The Free Press, New York, 1971, P.2
3. Cochran, T.C., Entrepreneurship, International Encyclopaedia of the Social Sciences,', Sills, D.L., (Ed.), The MacMillan Company and Free Press, P. 87

4. David Ricardo, The Principles of Political Economy and Taxation, J.M. Dent & Sons Ltd., London, 1962, P. 73
5. Joseph A. Sehumpeter, The Theory of Economic Development (translated by R. Opic), Oxford University Press, London, 1961, P.66
6. Web page: http//bus.colarado.edu/faculty/meyer/6700syl.htm
7. Ibid.
8. Schumpeter Joseph A., 'Economic Theory and Entrepreneurial History' in 'Exporations in Enterprise' Aitken, H.G.T (Ed.), Harvard University Press, Cambridge, 1955, pp. 51-52.
9. Dutta Aman, "Essays on Economic Development, Block Land Pvt. Ltd., Calcutta, 1961, p.23
10. Hans Singer, "Obstacles to Economic Development", Social Research, XX (Spring 1953) pp. 19-31.
11. Bhagwari Jugolish, "The Economics of Underdeveloped Countries", World University Library, London, 1966. p. 79.
12. Papanek, G.F., "The Development of Entrepreneurship, American Economic Review, Vol. LII May, 1962, p. 46.
13. Pieris, Ralph, "Studies in the Sociology of Development", Rotterdam University Press, 1969.
14. Galbraith, J.R. 'The New Industrial Estates', Oxford and IBM Publishing Company, Calcutta, 1969, pp. 71-72.
15. Ram K. Vepa : "Modern Small Industry in India: Problems and Prospects", Sage Publications, New Delhi, 1988, p. 18
16. An International Compilation of Small Scale Industry Definition (Mimeographed), Georgia Institute of Technology Engineering Experimental Station, Atlanta, Georgia, 1955.
17. Report of the Fiscal Commission, Government of India, New Delhi, 1950.
18. Desai, Vasant: Small Scale Industries and Enterpreneurship" Himalaya Publishing House, Mumbai, 2000, p. 26
19. Government of India : "Smal Scale Industries in India, Programmes and Institutional Support", New Delhi, March 1982. pp. 6-7
20. S.P. Kashyap : "Emerging Industrial Policy Reforms: Implications for Small Size Enterprises" *Productivity*, Vol. 36, No. 1, April – June, 1995, p. 16
21. P.S. Subbaro : Entrepreneurship and Small Business Management" Discovery Publishing House, New Delhi, 2001, p. 1

22. S.S. Khanka: "Entrepreneurial Development" ; S. Chand & Company Ltd., New Delhi, 2002, p. 79
23. S.S. Khanka: "Entrepreneurial Development" ; S. Chand & Company Ltd., New Delhi, 2002, p. 79
24. E. Nixon Singh, E. Bijoykumar Singh: "Entrepreneurship in Manipur; Problems & Prospects" Paper presented in the Vth Annual Conference of North Eastern Economic Association, 2002, Dec. 14-15, p.1
25. Udai Pareek and Rao, T.V., (Eds.), "Developing Entrepreneurship" New Delhi, 1978, p. I
26. Berna, J.J., "Industrial Entrepreneurship in Madras State", Asia Publishing House, Bombay, 1960
27. McGary, J.T., "Case Studies in Latent Industrial Potential: Small Industry in a North Indian Town", Ministry of Commerce and Industry, Government of India, New Delhi, 1976.
28. Narain Singh, B., "Pattern of Entrepreneurship in Agra", *The Indian Journal of Commerce*, Vol. B VII, Part III, NO. 69, September, 1964, pp. 205-13.
29. Thomas, A. Timberg, "Industrial Entrepreneurship Among the Trading Communities of India. How the Patten Differs?" Economic Development Report, No.126, 1969.
30. Pritam Singh, "Essays Concerning Some Types of Entrepreneurship in India," unpublished Ph.D. Dissertation, University of Michigan, 1963.
31. Shethy, M.C, "Entrepreneurship in Small Industry", *The Economic Weekly*, Vol., XVI, No. 22, May 1964, pp. 917.20.
32. Guha Amalendu, "Parsi Seths as Entrepreneurs" Economics and Political Weekly, Vol. V, No. 36, August, 29, 1970.
33. Gaikwad, V.R., and Tripathi, R.N., "Socio-Psychological Factors Influencing Industrial Entrepreneurship in Rural Areas, National Institute of Community Development, Hyderabad, May, 1970.
34. Pathak, H.N., "The Entrepreneur Technician and Manager in Small Scale Units," *Economic and Political Weekly*, Review of Management, Vol. VII, No. 48, November, 1972, pp. M 179 – M 187.
35. Ashish Nandy, "Entrepreneurial Cultures and Entrepreneurial Man"; *Economic and Political Weekly*, Review of Management, Vol. VIII, No. 47, November 24, 1973, pp.M98-M106.
36. Ramakrishnan, P., "New Entrepreneurship in small scale industry in Delhi; Economic and Scientific Research Foundation, New Delhi, July 1975, p. 179.

37. SIET, "Socio-Psychological Factors Influencing the Adaptation of the Innovation of Starting a Small Industrial Unit, SIET Institute, Hyderabad, 1974.

38. Sharma, K.L., and Harnak Singh, "Entrepreneurial Growth and Development Programme in Northern India," Abhinav Publications, New Delhi, 1980.

39. Choudury, K.V.R., "Entrepreneurial Activity in North Eastern Region, An Overview," SEDME, Vol. VIII, No. 1, March 1981 pp. 35 - 44.

40. Sharma, K.L., "Entrepreneurial Performance in Role Perspective," Abhinav Publications, New Delhi, 1975.

41. Oomen, M.A., "Small Industry in Indian Economic Growth-A case study of Kerala", S.B. Press, Trivendrum, 1972, pp.171-88.

42. Paul A. London, "Merchants a Promoters of Rural Development – An Indian Case study", Praeger Publishers, New York, 1978

43. Vander Veen, J.H., "Commercial Orientation of Industrial Entrepreneurs in India," Economic & Political Weekly, Vol, XIII. No. 3, Sept. 1975, pp. 318-30.

44. Gangadhara Rao, N., "Entrepreneurship and Growth of Enterprises in Industrial Estates," Deep and Deep Publications, New Delhi, 1986, P.21

45. Manohar U. Despande, "Entrepreneurship of Small Scale Industries' Deep and Deep Publications New Delhi, 1982.

46. Ashok Kumar, S, "Entrepreneurship in Small Industry" Discovery Publishing hose, New Delhi, 1990

47. Subbarao, P.S. "Entrepreneurship and Small Business Management" Discovery Publishing House, New Delhi, 2001.

48. G.B. Newalkar, Generation of Entrepreneurship in a Development Corporation Ltd., Bombay, undated, pp. 7-8.

49. Census of India, 2001 : Population of Manipur, Directorate of Census Operators, Manipur.

CHAPTER II

SOCIO-ECONOMIC ORIGINS OF ENTREPRENEURS

2.1 Introduction

Having analyzed the economic environment in which the entrepreneurs under study are operating, in the previous chapter, the emphasis now turns to the entrepreneurs themselves. It has been attempted in this Chapter to identify the sources of entrepreneurship by examining the socio-economic origins of the entrepreneurs in the two districts of Manipur under study viz., Imphal East and Imphal West Districts. It may be recognised that the entrepreneurship activity is dependent upon complex and varying combinations of the socio-economic, psychological and other factors like religion, occupation, educational level, earnings at the time of their entry into industry etc.

The post independence period has witnessed tremendous socio-economic and political changes in India. These changes had their effect on entrepreneurial activities in different regions of the country. It is also a fact that small scale industries play a pivotal role in the economic development of a region. Therefore, an analysis of factors which prompted the entrepreneurs of small scale industries under study may provide a clue to the influences to which these new and small entrepreneurs reacted to.

For the study, an entrepreneur is a person who is responsible for the establishment, management and development of the industrial unit. In the case of partnership firms, an active partner is taken as entrepreneur. The director or managing director is treated as entrepreneur in case of private limited companies. In almost all units under the present study, first generation entrepreneurs are found to be managing their units at the time of this survey except 21 entrepreneurs who were following the footsteps of their fathers who can be called second generation and only one third generation entrepreneur is there in the sample. Thus, in cases of change of ownership either by inheritance or acquisition, the person acquiring or inheriting the unit is deemed to be the entrepreneur. So no difficulty is experienced either in identifying the entrepreneurs or in contacting them. The socio-economic origins of entrepreneurs are discussed in the following paragraphs:

2.2 Generations of entrepreneurs

As briefly stated above, an attempt is made here to ascertain the generation in which the entrepreneurs under study belongs to. The generation of entrepreneurs were classified into three categories, namely (a) first generation, (b) second generation, and (c) third generation. The first generation refers to entrepreneurs who founded the industrial units. They took the first initiative and pain to start the business. By second generation, it means those entrepreneurs who inherited the unit from their fathers or acquired it from others. And lastly, by third generation, we mean those entrepreneurs who inherited the industrial units from their grandfathers.

No one can deny the fact that first generation entrepreneurs are risk takers who take every possible step to convert the idea to start business into action. They faced many obstacles in the beginning. Even though they are inexperienced, they gradually overcomes all these problems in successfully running their industrially units.

Second and third generation entrepreneurs are experienced entrepreneurs as they learnt the skills of business from their fathers or grandfathers. They faced less risk as compared to first generation entrepreneurs.

Table 2.1
Generation of Entrepreneurs : District-wise Classifications

Generation of Entrepreneurs		District		Both
		Imphal West	Imphal East	
First generation	Count	37	47	84
	% within Generation	44.0	56.0	100
	% within District	66.1	94.0	79.2
	% of Total	34.9	44.3	79.2
Second generation	Count	18	3	21
	% within Generation	85.7	14.3	100.0
	% within District	32.1	6.0	19.8
	% of Total	17.0	2.8	19.8
Third generation	Count	1		1
	% within Generation	100.0		100.0
	% within District	1.8		0.9
	% of Total	0.9		0.9
Total	**Count**	**56**	**50**	**106**
	% within Generation	**52.8**	**47.2**	**100**
	% within District	**100.0**	**100.0**	**100**
	% of Total	**52.8**	**47.2**	**100**

Source : Field Survey.

It can be seen from Table 2.1 that 79.2 per cent of entrepreneurs were first generation entrepreneurs, followed by 19.8 per cent second generation and 0.9 per cent third generation entrepreneurs.

Generation-wise, Imphal West District comprises 44 per cent of first generation entrepreneurs while it was 56 per cent in Imphal East District. However, second generation entrepreneurs constituted more in Imphal West District (85.7 per cent) than in Imphal East District (14.3 per cent). It is very interesting to note that only one third generation entrepreneur could be found in Imphal West District.

District-wise, first generation entrepreneurs formed 66.1 per cent in Imphal West District, followed by 32.1 per cent second generation and 1.8 per cent third generation entrepreneurs. In the Imphal East District, first generation formed 94.0 per cent and second generation 6.0 per cent.

It can be concluded that majority of the first generation entrepreneurs are from Imphal East District while majority of the second generation and third generation is from Imphal West District.

The fact that the sample respondents comprises of various generations initiates to analyze whether it has anything to do with their age, type of industry started, forms of organisation preferred etc.

(i) Age

It can be noticed from Table 2.2 that majority of the first generation entrepreneurs belongs to the age group 21-30 years (46.4 per cent), followed by age group 31-40 years (29.8 per cent), 41-50 years (14.3 per cent), 20 years and below (7.1 per cent) and 51 years and above (2.4 per cent).

Regarding second generation also, most of them are found in the age group 21-30 years (42.9 per cent) followed by the age-group 31-40 years (23.8 per cent) and 51 years and above (19.0 per cent). The third generation belong to 31-40 years age group.

(ii) Types of industry started

On analyzing the type of industry in which the various generations of entrepreneurs are venturing into, it can be noted from Table 2.3 that 19.0 per cent of the first generation entrepreneurs are in automobile and engineering works whereas it was 42.9 per cent in case of second generation entrepreneurs. It is worth mentioning that entrepreneurs in the handlooms and handicrafts industry are all first generation. The others type of industry consisting of arts, perfumery and detergents are also preferred by the first generation entrepreneurs only.

Table 2.2
Generation of Entrepreneurs : Age-wise Classification

Age of Entrepreneurs		Generation of Entrepreneurs			Total
		First	Second	Third	
20 years & below	Count	6	2		8
	% within Age	75.0	25.0		100
	% within Generation	7.1	9.5		7.5
	% of Total	5.7	1.9		7.5
21-30	Count	39	9		48
	% within Age	81.3	18.8		100
	% within Generation	46.4	42.9		45.3
	% of Total	36.8	8.5		45.3
31-40	Count	25	5.0	1	31
	% within Age	80.6	16.1	3.2	100
	% within Generation	29.6	23.8	100.0	29.2
	% of Total	23.6	4.7	0.9	29.2
41-50	Count	12	1		13
	% within Age	92.3	7.7		100
	% within Generation	14.3	4.8		12.3
	% of Total	11.3	0.9		12.3
51 years and above	Count	2	4		6
	% within Age	33.3	66.7		100
	% within Generation	2.4	19		5.7
	% of Total	1.9	3.8		5.7
Total	**Count**	**84**	**21**	**1**	**106**
	% within Age	**79.2**	**19.8**	**0.9**	**100.0**
	% within Generation	**100.0**	**100.0**	**100.0**	**100.0**
	% of Total	**79.2**	**19.8**	**0.9**	**100.0**

Source : Field Survey.

Table 2.3
Generation of Entrepreneurs : Type of Industry

Type of Industry		Generation of Entrepreneurs			Total
		First	Second	Third	
Food based	Count	15	2		17
	% within Type of Industry	88.2	11.8		100
	% within Generation	17.9	9.5		16
	% of Total	14.2	1.9		16
Metal based	Count	11	2	1	14
	% within Type of Industry	78.6	14.3	7.1	100
	% within Generation	13.1	9.5	100	13.2
	% of Total	10.4	1.9	0.9	13.2
Hand-looms & handicrafts	Count	8			8
	% within Type of Industry	100			100
	% within Generation	9.5			7.5
	% of Total	7.5			7.5
Plastics & Rubber based	Count	11	1		12
	% within Type of Industry	91.7	8.3		100
	% within Generation	13.1	4.8		11.3
	% of Total	10.4	0.9		11.3
Wood based	Count	10	5		15
	% within Type of Industry	66.7	33.3		100
	% within				

(contd.)

Type of Industry		Generation of Entrepreneurs			Total
		First	Second	Third	
	Generation	11.9	23.8		14.2
	% of Total	9.4	4.7		14.2
Printing and Stationery	Count	8	2		10
	% within Type of Industry	80	20		100
	% within Generation	9.5	9.5		9.4
	% of Total	7.5	1.9		9.4
Automobile and Engineering	Count	16	9		25
	% within Type of Industry	64	36		100
	% within Generation	19	42.9		23.6
	% of Total	15.1	8.5		23.6
Others (arts, perfumery and detergents)	Count	5			5
	% within Type of Industry	100			100
	% within Generation	6			4.7
	% of Total	4.7			4.7
Total	Count	84	21	1	106
	% within Type of Industry	79.2	19.8	0.9	100
	% within Generation	100	100	100	100
	% of Total	79.2	19.8	0.9	100

Coming to the industry-wise analysis of the various generation of entrepreneurs, 88.2 per cent of the food based industries are carried on by first generation entrepreneurs while the rest is carried by second generation. It was in the metal based industries that the lone third generation entrepreneur was interested (7.1 per cent). Plastics and rubber based industries, wood based industries, printing and stationery works are also some industries where majority of the first generation entrepreneurs are interested in.

(iii) Forms of organisation preferred

Here, an attempt is made to enquire into the forms of organisation of the enterprises across the generation of entrepreneurs.

Table 2.4 shows that 75.0 per cent of the private limited companies were established by first generation entrepreneurs as against 25.0 per cent by the second generation. In case of partnership firms, 75.0 per cent are carried on by first generation, followed by 16.7 per cent second generation and 8.3 per cent third generation.

With the exception of partnership firms, majority of the first and second generation entrepreneurs started their units as a sole proprietorship concerns. First generation accounted for 80.0 per cent of the sole proprietorship whereas 20.0 per cent by organised by second generation. The only third generation entrepreneur started his unit as a partnership firm.

2.3 Religion of entrepreneurs

Entrepreneurship is a socio-economic phenomenon. It cannot be denied that some social groups produce a large and capable body of entrepreneurs, while others do not because of the influence of prevailing social factors. This has been confirmed by Everett Hagen[1] who studied the origin and background of several countries and regions, including England, Western Europe, Soviet Union, Japan and Latin America. In several countries, entrepreneurs have emerged from a particular socio-economic class. In Britain, United States of America and Turkey, the ranks of entrepreneurs were largely filled from commerce.[2] It has often been suggested that certain religions and castes encourage the growth of entrepreneurial activity. It was the Samurai, in Japan, who turned to industry and kept their social structure in tact by the expedient of adopting vigorous young businessmen or taking them into the family through marriage.[3]

Table 2.4
Generation of Entrepreneurs : Forms of Organisation Preferred

Generation of Entrepreneurs		Forms of Organisation			Total
		Private Ltd. Co.	Partner-ship	Sole Proprietor-ship	
First	Count	3	9	72	84
	% within Generation	3.6	10.7	85.7	100
	% within Forms of Organisation	75	75	80	79.2
	% of Total	2.8	8.5	67.9	79.2
Second	Count	1	2	18	21
	% within Generation	4.8	9.5	85.7	100
	% within Forms of Organisation	25	16.7	20	19.8
	% of Total	0.9	1.9	17	19.8
Third	Count		1		1
	% within Generation		100		100
	% within Forms of Organisation		8.3		0.9
	% of Total		0.9		0.9
Total	Count	4	12	90	106
	% within Generation	3.8	11.3	84.9	100
	% within Forms of Organisation	100	100	100	100
	% of Total	3.8	11.3	84.9	100

Source : Field Survey.

The emergence of small scale firms in France is attributed to the social structure, especially to their family pattern.[4]

In India also, some religious communities like the Marwarees, Parsees and Sindhees seem to have an affinity for industrial activity though the available evidence is not conclusive on this point.[5] However, it is true that certain religions or communities have imbided in themselves a particular culture that fosters entrepreneurship. Hence, the religion factor should invariably be analysed while studying the origin of entrepreneurs.

It is, therefore, attempted here to examine the religious background of the entrepreneurs emerging in the small scale industries of Imphal East and Imphal West Districts under study. It may be seen from Table 2.5, the religious background of entrepreneurs. Hindus are the single largest group (90.6 per cent), whereas Christians stood as the smallest group (1.9 per cent).

In the district-wise classification, 53.1 per cent of the total Hindu entrepreneurs are in Imphal West District and that of 46.9 per cent in Imphal East District. Next to Hindus, Muslim entrepreneurs (5) accounted for 1.9 per cent in Imphal West District and 2.8 per cent in Imphal East District. However, Sikh entrepreneurs (3) formed 3.6 per cent in Imphal West District while it was only 2.0 per cent in Imphal East District.

It is thus clear from the above analysis that entrepreneurs in the two districts under study hailed mostly from Hindus, followed by Muslims, Sikhs and Christians respectively.

(i) Entry into entrepreneurship

(a)Time of entry : Table 2.6 (i) shows the time and age at which the respondents made an entry into the entrepreneurship. It is very interesting to note that 90.5 per cent of all the entrepreneurs who commenced their industrial units before 1980 were Hindus and 4.8 per cent each were Christians and Sikhs. Muslim entrepreneurs started entering into entrepreneurship during the period 1990-1995. Moreover, out of the total of 106, 27 entrepreneurs (25.5 per cent) started their units in 1990-95.

In Imphal West District as can be seen in Table 2.6 (ii), 26.8 per cent of the units were started before 1980 and 25.0 per cent were started between 1990 and 1995. Between 1985 and 1990 and 1995 and 2000, equal number of entrepreneurs started their units (17.9 per cent each).

Table 2.5
Entrepreneurs' Religion : District-wise Classification

Religion of Entrepreneurs		District		Total
		Imphal West	Imphal East	
Hindu	Count	51	45	96
	% within Religion	53.1	46.9	100
	% within District	91.1	90	90.6
	% of total	48.1	42.5	90.6
Muslim	Count	2	3	5
	% within Religion	40	60	100
	% within District	3.6	6	4.7
	% of total	1.9	2.8	4.7
Christian	Count	1	1	2
	% within Religion	50	50	100
	% within District	1.8	2	1.9
	% of total	0.9	0.9	1.9
Sikh	Count	2	1	3
	% within Religion	66.7	33.3	100
	% within District	3.6	2	2.8
	% of total	1.9	0.9	2.8
Total	Count	56	50	106
	% within Religion	52.8	47.2	100
	% within District	100	100	100
	% of total	52.8	47.2	100

Source : Field Survey.

Table 2.6 (i)

Entrepreneurs' Religions : Year of Commencement of Entrepreneurs

Entrepreneurs' Religion		Year of Commencement					Total
		Before 1980	1980-85	1985-90	1990-95	1995 -2000	
Hindu	Count	19	10	18	26	23	· 96
	% within Religion	19.8	10.4	18.8	27.1	24	100
	% within Year	90.5	90	85.7	88.5	88.5	90.6
	% of Total	17.9	9.4	17	24.5	21.7	90.6
Muslim	Count			2	1	2	5
	% within Religion			40	20	40	100
	% within Year			9.5	3.7	7.7	4.7
	% of Total			1.9	0.9	1.9	4.7
Christian	Count	1				1	2
	% within Religion	50				50	100

	% within Year	4.8				3.8	1.9
	% of Total	0.9				0.9	1.9
Sikh	Count	1	1	1			3
	% within Religion	33.3	33.3	33.3			100
	% within Year	4.8	9.1	4.8			2.8
	% of Total	0.9	0.9	0.9			2.8
Total	Count	21	11	21	27	26	106
	% within Religion	19.8	10.4	19.8	25.5	24.5	100
	% within Year	100	100	100	100	100	100
	% of Total	19.8	10.4	19.8	25.5	24.5	100

Source : Field Survey

Table 2.6 (ii)

Time of Entry into Entrepreneurship : District-wise Classification

Time of Entry		District		Total
		Imphal West	Imphal East	
Before 1980	Count	15	6	21
	% within Time of Entry	71.4	28.6	100
	% within District	26.8	12	19.8
	% of Total	14.2	5.7	19.8
1980-85	Count	7	4	11
	% within Time of Entry	63.6	36.4	100
	% within District	12.5	8	10.4
	% of Total	6.6	3.8	10.4
1985-90	Count	10	11	21
	% within Time of Entry	47.6	52.4	100
	% within District	17.9	22	19.8
	% of Total	9.4	10.4	19.8
1990-95	Count	14	13	27
	% within Time of Entry	51.9	48.15	100.05
	% within District	25	26	25.5
	% of Total	13.2	12.3	25.5
1995-2000	Count	10	16	26
	% within Time of Entry	38.5	61.5	100
	% within District	17.9	32	24.5
	% of Total	9.4	15.1	24.5

(contd.)

Time of Entry		District		Total
		Imphal West	Imphal East	
Total	Count	56	50	106
	% within Time of Entry	52.8	47.2	100
	% within District	100	100	100
	% of Total	52.8	47.2	100

Source : Field Survey.

On the other hand, in Imphal East District, 32.0 per cent of the entrepreneurs started their units between 1995 and 2000. As much as 26.0 per cent of the units were started between 1990 and 1995 and 22.0 per cent between 1985 and 1990. Only 12 per cent units were started before 1980. In view of this the industrial units in Imphal West District had greater length of existence than those in Imphal East Districts.

(b) Age of entry Vs religion : As can be seen from Table 2.7, the highest per centage of the entrepreneurs (45.3 per cent) entered into entrepreneurship at the age of 21-30 years. The average age of the entrepreneurs in this age group worked out to be 25.48 years. Only 5.7 per cent of them entered at the age group of 51 years and above (average age 58.83 years).

Religion-wise, 45.8 per cent of the Hindu entrepreneurs preferred the age group of 21-30 years to start the units while only 5.2 per cent of them entered into entrepreneurship at the age of 51 years and above. Among the Muslims also, 40.0 per cent started their units at the age of 21-30 years. The average age of the entrepreneurs in both the districts worked out to be 31.96 years. However, a slight difference was noticed between the two districts. In Imphal West District, it was only 31.89 years, whereas in Imphal East District, it was 32.04 years.

Religion-wise also, certain differences could be noticed. Christian entrepreneurs started units at the earlier age (average age 21.5 years) while the Muslim entrepreneurs started their units at a later stage (average age 36.8 years)

Table 2.7
Entrepreneurs' Religion : Age at the Time of Commencement

Age at the time of Commencement		Religion of Entrepreneurs				Total
		Hindu	Muslim	Christian	Sikh	
20 years & below	Count	7		1		8
	% within Age	87.5		12.5		100
	% within Religion	7.3		50		7.5
	% of Total	6.6		0.9		7.5
21-30	Count	44	2	1	1	48
	% within Age	91.7	4.2	2.1	21	100
	% within Religion	45.8	40	50	33.3	45.3
	% of Total	41.5	1.9	0.9	0.9	45.3
31-40	Count	29	1		1	31
	% within Age	93.5	3.2		3.2	100
	% within Religion	30.2	20		33.3	29.2
	% of Total	27.4	0.9		0.9	29.2

41-50	Count	11	1		1	13
	% within Age	84.6	7.7		7.7	100
	% within Religion	11.5	20		33.3	12.3
	% of Total	10.4	0.9		0.9	12.3
51 years & above	Count	5	1			6
	% within Age	83.3	16.17			100
	% within Religion	5.2	20			5.7
	% of Total	4.7	0.9			5.7
Total	Count	96	5	2	3	106
	% within Age	90.6	4.7	1.9	2.8	100
	% within Religion	100	100	100	100	100
	% of Total	90.6	4.7	1.9	2.8	100

Source : Field Survey

Moreover, the average age of the Hindu entrepreneurs (32.1 years) conformed nearly to the overall average age, whereas that of Christian (21.5 years) and Sikh (27.3 years) entrepreneurs were found to be less than that of Muslim entrepreneurs.

It can thus be concluded that in comparison with Hindu entrepreneurs, Christian and Sikh entrepreneurs entered into entrepreneurship at a younger age and Muslim entrepreneurs at an older age.

(ii) Type of industry chosen

Here, an attempt has been made to examine the type of industry preferred by the entrepreneurs. It may be seen from Table 2.8 that 23.6 per cent of the entrepreneurs started their industrial units in automobile and engineering works and 16 per cent of the entrepreneurs preferred food based industries. The third type of industry chosen by 14.2 per cent entrepreneurs was the wood-based industries while 13.2 per cent started their units in metal based industries. There were also few entrepreneurs who started units falling under the category of handlooms and handicrafts, plastics and rubber-based, printing and stationery etc.

Coming to the religion-wise analysis of the type of industry started by the entrepreneurs, 24.0 per cent of the Hindu entrepreneurs preferred automobile and engineering industries. It is very interesting to note here that 100.0 per cent of the handlooms and handicrafts industries and 'others' group of industries were undertaken by the Hindu entrepreneurs only. Among the Muslims, 60.0 per cent of them are associated with food based industries and metal based industries while 20.0 per cent each of them started their units in printing and stationery and automobile and engineering industries. Moreover, Christian entrepreneurs are equally interested in wood based and plastics and rubber based industries. Likewise, Sikh entrepreneurs are interested in metal based, plastics and rubber based and automobile and engineering industries.

(iii)Forms of organisation preferred

Sole proprietorship is the most popular of all the forms of organisation as could be seen in Table 2.9. 90 out of 106 (84.9

per cent) industrial units are run as sole proprietorship concerns. 12 out of 106 (11.3 per cent) are partnership firms. Only four are private limited companies.

Religion-wise, sole proprietorship concern as a form of organisation gained popularity among all the religion except Sikhs. Even among the Hindus, 83 out of 96 units (86.5 per cent) preferred sole proprietorship. It is worth mentioning that all the Muslim and Christian entrepreneurs run their units as sole trading concerns. Private limited companies were started only by the Hindu entrepreneurs.

2.4 Occupational background

However orthodox or traditional may be the way of living in India, the days of identifying occupations by castes, communities or religion is on the wane. It is no longer possible to identify the communities by occupation. Traditionally non –trading communities have started participating in trading and manufacturing activities in ever increasing numbers. Similarly, the trading communities are entering the manufacturing activities. Village artisans like weavers, blacksmiths and carpenters have started setting up their own tiny factory units which may ultimately become small or medium enterprises. The children of the farmers are migrating from villages to urban areas seeking better living. They are entering occupation entirely different from those of their parents and grand-parents. In view of the above change in behaviour, it would be interesting to enquire into the occupational background of entrepreneurs to have a broader understanding of the genesis of entrepreneurship. For this purpose, the occupation of the entrepreneurs before entering industry has been taken into consideration.

(i) An overview

Table 2.10 shows the district-wise earlier occupation of the entrepreneurs. 41.5 per cent were found to be students either coming out of schools or colleges or were unemployed.

While 30.2 per cent were having professional background related with the type of industry chosen, 20.8 per cent were found to be associated with some other business. Moreover, 4.7 per cent and 2.8 per cent were employed in Government service and agriculture respectively, prior to entering industry.

Table 2.8
Entrepreneurs' Religion : Type of Industry started

Type of Industry		Religion of Entrepreneurs				Total
		Hindu	Muslim	Christian	Sikh	
Food based	Count	16	1			17
	% within Type of Industry	94.1	5.9			100
	% within Religion	16.7	20			16
	% of Total	15.1	0.9			16
Metal based	Count	11	2		1	14
	% within Type of Industry	78.6	14.3		7.1	100
	% within Religion	11.5	40		33.3	13.2
	% of Total	10.4	1.9		0.9	13.2
Handlooms & handicrafts	Count	8				8
	% within Type of Industry	100				100
	% within Religion	8.3				7.5
	% of Total	7.5				7.5

Plastics & rubber based	Count	10		1	1	12
	% within Type of Industry	83.3		8.3	8.3	100
	% within Religion	10.4		50	33.3	11.3
	% of Total	9.4		0.9	0.9	11.3
Wood based	Count	14		1		15
	% within Type of Industry	93.3		6.7		100
	% within Religion	14.6		50		14.2
	% of Total	13.2		0.9		14.2
Printing & stationery	Count	9	1			10
	% within Type of Industry	90	10			100
	% within Religion	9.4	20			9.4
	% of Total	8.5	0.9			9.4
Automobile & engineering	Count	23	1		1	25
	% within Type of Industry	92	40		4	100
	% within Religion	24	20		33.3	23.6
	% of Total	21.7	0.9		0.9	23.6

(contd.)

Table 2.8 ***(contd.)***

Type of Industry		Religion of Entrepreneurs				Total
		Hindu	Muslim	Christian	Sikh	
Other (arts, perfumery & detergents	Count		5			5
	% within Type of Industry	100				100
	% within Religion	5.2				4.7
	% of Total	4.7				4.7
Total	Count	96	5	2	3	106
	% within Type of Industry	90.6	4.7	1.9	2.8	100
	% within Religion	100	100	100	100	100
	% of Total	90.6	4.7	1.9	2.8	100

Source : Field Survey

Table 2.9
Entrepreneurs' Religion : Forms of Organisation

Forms of Organisation		Religion of Entrepreneurs				Total
		Hindu	Muslim	Christian	Sikh	
Pvt. Ltd Co.	Count	4				4
	% within Organisation	100				100
	% within Religion	4.2				3.8
	% of Total	3.8				3.8
Partnership	Count	9			3	12
	% within Organisation	75			25	100
	% within Religion	9.4			100	11.3
	% of Total	8.5			2.8	11.3
Sole Proprietorship	Count	83	5	2		90
	% within Organisation	92.2	5.6	2.2		100

(contd.)

Forms of Organisation		Religion of Entrepreneurs				Total
		Hindu	Muslim	Christian	Sikh	
	% within Religion	86.5	100	100		84.9
	% of Total	78.3	4.7	1.9		84.9
Total	Count	96	5	2	3	106
	% within Organisation	90.6	4.7	1.9	2.8	100
	% within Religion	100	100	100	100	100
	% of Total	90.6	4.7	1.9	2.8	100

Source : Field Survey

Table 2.10
Entrepreneurs Occupational Background : District-wise Classification

Earlier Occupation of Entrepreneurs		District		Total
		Imphal West	Imphal East	
Business	Count	12	10	22
	% within Occupation	54.5	45.5	100
	% within District	21.4	20	20.8
	% of Total	11.3	9.4	20.8
Agriculture	Count	1	2	3
	% within Occupation	33.3	66.7	100
	% within District	1.8	4	2.8
	% of Total	0.9	1.9	2.8
Govt. service	Count	3	2	5
	% within Occupation	60	40	100
	% within District	5.4	40	4.7
	% of Total	2.8	1.9	4.7
Students	Count	26	18	44
	% within Occupation	59.1	40.9	100
	% within District	46.4	36	41.5
	% of Total	24.5	17	41.5
Profession	Count	14	18	32
	% within Occupation	43.8	56.3	100
	% within District	25	36	30.2
	% of Total	13.2	17	30.2
Total	Count	56	50	106
	% within Occupation	52.8	47.2	100
	% within District	100	100	100
	% of Total	52.8	47.2	100

Source : Field Survey.

Table 2.11
Entrepreneurs' Occupational Background : Age at the Time of Entry

Age at the Time of Entry		Earlier Occupation of Entrepreneurs					Total
		Business	Agriculture	Govt. Service	Student	Profession	
20 & below	Count	2			3	3	8
	% within Age	25			27.5	27.5	100
	% within Occupation	9.1			6.8	9.4	7.5
	% of Total	1.9			2.8	2.8	7.5
21-30	Count	6	1	2	30	9	48
	% within Age	12.5	2.1	4.2	62.5	18.8	100
	% within Occupation	27.3	33.3	40	68.2	28.1	45.3
	% of Total	5.7	0.9	1.9	28.3	8.5	45.3
31-40	Count	5		2	11	13	31
	% within Age	16.1		6.5	35.5	71.9	100
	% within Occupation	22.7		40	25	40.6	29.2
	% of Total	4.7		1.9	10.4	12.3	29.2

41-50	Count	7		1		5	13
	% within Age	53.8		7.7		38.5	100
	% within Occupation	31.8		20		15.6	12.3
	% of Total	6.6		0.9		4.7	12.3
51 & above	Count	2	2			2	6
	% within Age	33.3	33.3			33.3	100
	% within Occupation	9.1	66.7			6.3	5.7
	% of Total	1.9	1.9			1.9	5.7
Total	Count	22	3	5	44	32	106
	% within Age	20.8	2.8	4.7	41.5	30.2	100
	% within Occupation	100	100	100	100	100	100
	% of Total	20.8	4.7	4.7	41.5	30.2	100

Source : Field Survey.

Table 2.12
Entrepreneurs' Occupational Background : Type of Industry Opted

Type of Industry		Earlier Occupation of Entrepreneurs					Total
		Business	Agriculture	Govt. Service	Student	Profession	
Food based	Count	9	1		6	1	17
	% within Industry	5.29	5.9		35.3	5.9	100
	% within Occupation	40.9	33.3		13.6	3.1	16
	% of Total	8.5	0.9		5.7	0.9	16
Metal based	Count	2	1	2	4	5	14
	% within Industry	14.3	7.1	14.3	28.6	35.7	100
	% within Occupation	9.1	33.3	40	9.1	15.6	7.5
	% of Total	1.9	0.9	1.9	3.8	4.7	7.5
Handlooms & handicrafts	Count				5	3	8
	% within Industry				62.5	37.5	100
	% within Occupation				11.4	9.4	11.3
	% of Total				4.7	2.8	11.3
Plastics & rubber based	Count	4			5	3	12
	% within Industry	33.3			41.7	25	100
	% within Occupation	18.2			11.4	9.4	11.3
	% of Total	3.8			4.7	2.8	11.3

Wood based	Count	3		1	9	2	15
	% within Industry	20		6.7	60	13.3	100
	% within Occupation	13.6		20	20.5	6.3	14.2
	% of Total	2.8		0.9	8.5	1.9	14.2
Printing & stationery	Count	1	1	1	3	4	10
	% within Industry	10	10	10	30	40	100
	% within Occupation	4.5	33.3	20	6.8	12.5	9.4
	% of Total	0.9	0.9	0.9	2.8		9.4
Automobile & engineering	Count	3		1	8	3.8	25
	% within Industry	12		4	32	52	100
	% within Occupation	13.6		20	18.2	40.6	23.6
	% of Total	2.8		0.9	7.5	12.3	23.6
Others (arts, perfumery & detergents)	Count				4	1	5
	% within Industry				80	20	100
	% within Occupation				9.1	3.1	4.7
	% of Total				3.8	0.9	4.7
Total	Count	22	3	5	44	32	106
	% within Industry	20.8	2.8	4.7	41.5	30.2	100
	% within Occupation	100	100	100	100	100	100
	% of Total	20.8	2.8	4.7	41.5	30.2	100

Source : Field Survey

District-wise, Imphal West District has 46.4 per cent entrepreneurs having students background while professional background accounted for 25.0 per cent. On the other hand, Imphal East District has 36.0 per cent entrepreneurs having student and professional background. It may also be noticed that entrepreneurs whose occupational background was business, government service and students constituted a greater percentage in Imphal West District, whereas in Imphal East District, those from agriculture and professional background formed a greater per centage

It may be concluded that more people from students, professional and business background were attracted towards industrial entrepreneurship than those occupied in government service and agriculture.

(ii) Occupational background and age of entry into entrepreneurship

It is sought to examine here the entrepreneurs' age at the time of their entry into industry across their occupational background. Table 2.11 reveals that 68.2 per cent of the entrepreneurs with student background, 40.0 per cent with government service background, 33.3 per cent with agricultural background and 28.1 per cent with professional background made their entry into industrial entrepreneurship at the age of 21-30 years. On the other hand, 31.8 per cent of the entrepreneurs with business background entered at a later age of 41-50 years. Among them all, 21-30 years is the most preferred age group to start their units while 51 years and above age group is preferred by the majority of the entrepreneurs having agricultural background. Among all, students or unemployed youth made an entry relative at a younger age (average age 26.41 years).

(iii) Occupational background and type of industry chosen

On examining the type of industry chosen by the entrepreneurs having different occupational background at the time of entry into entrepreneurship, Table 2.12 shows that most of the entrepreneurs who were having professional background started industries falling under the category of automobile and engineering works (40.6 per cent), followed by those with student background (18.2 per cent). Those whose occupational background was agriculture were found uniformly in food based, metal based and printing and stationery industries.

On the other hand, entrepreneurs with business background were found in all the industrial groups except handlooms and handicrafts industries. Moreover, entrepreneurs coming from govt. service background started metal based industries (40.0 per cent), wood based, printing and stationery and automobile and engineering industries (20.0 per cent each).

(iv) Occupational background and forms of organisation

It is attempted here to ascertain how earlier occupation of entrepreneurs influences on the form of organisation of industries they opted.

It is interesting to observe from Table 2.13 that private limited companies were started by the highest per centage of the entrepreneurs who were having professional background (75.0 per cent) and followed by those who were either unemployed or students (25.0 per cent). Partnership firms were preferred by majority of the entrepreneurs having business background (50.0 per cent), followed by equal number of entrepreneurs having students and professional background (25.0 per cent each). Out of the entrepreneurs who owned sole proprietorship concerns, those with students background formed the majority (44.4 per cent), followed by those with professional background (28.9 per cent), business background (17.8 per cent), government service (5.6 per cent) and agricultural background (3.3 per cent). Majority of the entrepreneurs started units as sole proprietorship concerns.

It can be deducted that entrepreneurs having agricultural and government service background preferred only the sole proprietorship concerns.

2.5 Educational background

Educationists have long been aware of the importance of education in the development of human resources. It may also be noted that education, entrepreneurship and

Table 2.13

Entrepreneurs' Occupational Background : Forms of Organisation

Forms of Organisation		Earlier Occupation of Entrepreneurs					Total
		Business	Agriculture	Govt. Service	Student	Profession	
Pvt. Limited Company	Count				1	3	4
	% within Organisation				25	75	100
	% within Occupation				2.3	9.4	3.8
	% of Total				0.9	2.8	3.8
Partnership	Count	6			3	3	12
	% within Organisation	50			25	25	100
	% within Occupation	27.3			6.8	9.4	11.3
	% of Total	5.7			2.8	2.8	11.3
Sole Proprietorship concern	Count	16	3	5	40	26	90
	% within Organisation	17.8	3.3	5.6	44.4	28.9	100

	% within Occupation	72.7	100	100	90.9	81.3	84.9
	% of Total	15.1	2.8	4.7	37.7	24.5	84.9
Total	Count	22	3	5	44	32	106
	% within Organisation	20.8	2.8	4.7	41.5	30.2	100
	% within Occupation	100	100	100	100	100	100
	% of Total	20.8	2.8	4.7	41.5	30.2	100

Source : Field Survey

development are inter-related. For example, Frederick Harbition and Charles A. Myers[6] points out that if one rejects the notion that investment in education must be productive, then he should also be prepared to reject the goal of rapid economic progress. Education is the best means of developing man's resourcefulness which encompasses different dimensions of entrepreneurship. Thus, formal education is always considered an important asset of an individual in building an occupational career. The formal education is expected to increase the supply of entrepreneurs by making available more skills necessary to entrepreneurial endeavour. It is attempted in this study to ascertain the educational qualification of the entrepreneurs. Entrepreneurs' education at the time of entry into entrepreneurship can be seen and analysed in Table 2.14.

It is interesting to note that majority of them (49 out of 106) were graduates and post-graduates, particularly some in engineering and other technical disciplines. While undergraduates constituted 26.4 per cent, matriculates accounted for 16.0 per cent. It is worthwhile to mention that 11.3 per cent of the total entrepreneurs were under-matriculates. In other words, a low level of education has not thus deterred the under-matriculates to be ahead of others in industrial entrepreneurship.

District-wise, it was found that graduates and post-graduates constituted 48.2 per cent in Imphal West District and 44.0 per cent in Imphal East District. Under-graduate entrepreneurs were 30.4 per cent in Imphal West District while they constitute 22.0 per cent in Imphal East District. Only 8.9 per cent and 14.0 per cent were under-matriculates in Imphal West and Imphal East Districts respectively.

Qualification-wise, out of the entrepreneurs with graduate qualification, 53.8 per cent and 46.2 per cent respectively were in Imphal West and Imphal East Districts. Even among the post-graduates, Imphal West District constituted 60.0 per cent and Imphal East Districts 40.0 per cent. While Imphal West District accounted for 41.7 per cent under-matriculates, Imphal East District accounted for 58.3 per cent of the same.

It is thus clear that a large majority of the respondents in both the districts were educated upto under-graduation and graduation.

Table 2.14
Entrepreneurs' Education : District-wise Classification

Educational Qualification of Entrepreneurs	District		Total
	Imphal West	Imphal East	
Under-matriculate			
Count	5	7	12
% within Qualification	41.7	58.3	100
% within District	8.9	14	11.3
% of Total	4.7	6.6	11.3
Matriculate			
Count	7	10	17
% within Qualification	41.2	58.8	100
% within District	12.5	20	16
% of Total	6.6	9.4	16
Under-graduation			
Count	17	11	28
% within Qualification	60.7	39.3	100
% within District	30.4	22	26.4
% of Total	16	10.4	26.4
Graduate			
Count	21	18	39
% within Qualification	53.8	46.2	100
% within District	37.5	36	36.8
% of Total	19.8	17	36.8
Post-graduate			
Count	6	4	10
% within Qualification	60	40	100
% within District	10.7	8	9.4
% of Total	5.7	3.8	9.4
Total			
Count	**56**	**50**	**106**
% within Qualification	**52.8**	**47.2**	**100**
% within District	**100**	**100**	**100**
% of Total	**52.8**	**47.2**	**100**

Source : Field Survey

(i) Educational qualification of entrepreneurs and their age at the time of entry

An enquiry made on the educational level of entrepreneurs across their age at the time of starting their industrial units can highlight whether there is any influence to push them into industrial entrepreneurship by their level of education.

It may be observed from Table 2.15 that out of the entrepreneurs who entered industry at the age group of 21-30 years, graduates formed the highest (41.7 per cent). 60.0 per cent and 40.0 per cent of the post-graduates entered at the age of 21-30 and 31-40 years respectively.

On the other hand, 50.0 per cent of the entrepreneurs who started their units in the age group of 51 & above years were only educated upto under-matric. At the same time, 7.1 per cent under-graduate and 2.6 per cent graduate entrepreneurs were cautions enough to enter industry at this later age of 51 & above years. Altogether there are only 6 entrepreneurs in the age group for 51 & above. It is under-matriculates who are the majority (50 per cent) in this age group.

It was found that matriculates made an entry into industrial entrepreneurship at the youngest age (average age : 27.29 years) followed by post-graduates (average age : 31.10 years) and under-graduates (average age : 32.21 years). It is worthwhile to mention here that under-matriculates made an entry into entrepreneurship at a later age (average age: 36.25 years).

These observations make necessarily one feel that education plays a pivotal role to the cause of the furtherance of entrepreneurship. Educated people who have joined the industry in their prime age can do lot of good work in the development of nation. It is that age where people can face challenges boldly with more determination and seize the opportunity offered to them. Hence, it can be concluded that people with higher educational levels are finding their entry into industry earlier.

(ii)Entrepreneurs' education and their generation

An attempt is here made to examine whether there is any relationship between entrepreneurs' education and the generation they belongs to.

Table 2.16 observes that 76.9 per cent graduate entrepreneurs were first generation while the rest are second generation. It is very interesting to note that all the post-graduate entrepreneurs are first generation entrepreneurs. On the other hand, the only third generation entrepreneur is educated upto twelve standard. It can thus be concluded that higher the level of education the greater is the chance to start industry as a first generation entrepreneur.

(iii) Entrepreneurs' education and their religion

Table 2.17 demonstrates that the spread of schooling has cut across the business of religion. It may be noticed that majority of the graduates and all of the post-graduates were Hindu. It seems none of the entrepreneurial religions are placed in a disadvantageous position by comparison. But the levels of education, religion-wise, shown in the table gives scope for one or two influences. The educational level of Muslim entrepreneurs is below graduates and that of all Sikhs is under-graduates. Only 9.4 per cent of Hindu entrepreneurs were under-matriculates. Among the under-matriculates, 75.0 per cent are Hindus and 25.0 per cent are Muslims. Out of 2 Christians, one is matriculate and the other is graduate. Comparatively lower level of education has not deterred the Muslims to follow the footsteps of others in industrial entrepreneurship.

(iv) Entrepreneurs' educational qualification and type of industry chosen

It is enquired here to know how education influenced entrepreneurs' choice of the particular type of industry. Table 2.18 shows that majority of the graduates and under-graduates (23.1 per cent and 25.0 per cent respectively) opted for automobile and engineering industries. 30.0 per cent of the post graduates also preferred automobile and engineering industries whereas under-matriculates were very fond of metal based industries (50.0 per cent) and followed by automobile and engineering industries (16.7per cent). Among the matriculates, equal number of entrepreneurs opted metal based, plastics and rubber based and automobile and engineering industries (23.5 per cent each).

Table 2.15
Entrepreneurs' Education : Age at the Time of Entry

Age at the Time of Entry	Educational Qualification of Entrepreneurs					Total
	Under-Matriculate	Matri-culate	Under-Matriculate	Graduate	Post-Graduate	
20 & above						
Count	2	5	1			8
% within Age	25	62.5	12.5			100
% within Qualification	16.7	29.4	3.6			7.5
% of Total	1.9	4.7	0.9			7.5
21-30						
Count	3	6	13	20	6	48
% within Age	6.3	12.5	27.1	41.7	12.5	100
% within Qualification	25	35.3	46.4	51.3	60	45.3
% of Total	2.8	5.7	12.3	18.9	5.7	45.3
31-40						
Count	1	4	10	12	4	31
% within Age	3.2	12.9	32.3	38.7	12.9	100

% within Qualification	8.3	23.5	35.7	30.8	40	12.3
% of Total	0.9	3.8	9.4	11.3	3.8	12.3
41- 50						
Count	3	2	2	6		13
% within Age	23.1	15.4	15.4	46.2		100
% within Qualification	25	11.8	7.1	1.4		12.3
% of Total	2.8	1.9	1.9	5.7		12.3
51 years & above						
Count	3		2	1		6
% within Age	50		33.3	16.7		100
% within Qualification	25		7.1	2.6		5.7
% of Total	2.8		1.9	0.9		5.7
Total						
Count	12	17	28	39	10	106
% within Age	11.3	16	26.4	36.8	9.4	100
% within Qualification	100	100	100	100	100	100
% of Total	11.3	16	26.4	36.8	9.4	100

Source : Field Survey

Table 2.16
Entrepreneurs' Education : Generation of Entrepreneurs

Educational Qualification of Entrepreneurs	Generation of Entrepreneurs			Total
	First	Second	Third	
Under-Matriculates				
Count	10	2		12
% within Qualification	83.3	16.7		100
% within Generation	11.9	8.5		11.3
% of Total	9.4	1.9		11.3
Matriculates				
Count	14	3		17
% within Qualification	82.4	17.6		100
% within Generation	16.7	14.3		16
% of Total	13.2	2.8		16
Under-graduates				
Count	20	7	1	28
% within Qualification	71.4	25.1	3.6	100

% within Generation	16.7	33.3	100	26.4
% of Total	18.9	6.6	0.9	26.4
Graduates				
Count	30	9		39
% within Qualification	76.9	23.1		100
% within Generation	35.7	42.9		36.8
% of Total	28.3	8.5		36.8
Post-graduates				
Count	10			10
% within Qualification	100			100
% within Generation	11.9			9.4
% of Total	9.4			9.4
Total				
Count	84	21	1	106
% within Qualification	79.2	19.8	0.9	100
% within Generation	100	100	100	100
% of Total	79.2	19.8	0.9	100

Source : Field Survey

Table 2.17
Entrepreneurs' Education : Entrepreneurs' Religions

Educational Qualification of Entrepreneurs	Religion of Entrepreneurs				Total
	Hindu	Muslim	Christian	Sikh	
Under-Matriculate					
Count	9	3			12
% within Qualification	75.1	25			100
% within Religion	9.4	60			11.3
% of Total	8.5	2.8			11.3
Matriculates					
Count	15	1	1		17
% within Qualification	88.2	5.9	5.9		100
% within Religion	15.6	20	50		16
% of Total	14.2	0.9	0.9		16
Under-graduates					
Count	24	1		3	28
% within Qualification	85.7	3.6		10.7	100
% within Religion	25	20		100	26.4
% of Total	22.6	0.9		2.8	26.4
Graduates					
Count	38		1		39
% within Qualification	97.4		2.6		100
% within Religion	39		50		36.8
% of Total	35.80%		0.9		36.8
Post-graduates					
Count	10				10
% within Qualification	100				100
% within Religion	10.4				9.4
% of Total	9.4				9.4
Total					
Count	96	5	2	3	106
% within Qualification	90.6	4.7	1.9	2.8	100
% within Religion	100	100	100	100	100
% of Total	90.6	4.7	1.9	2.8	100

Source : Field Survey

Industry-wise, metal based industries were not opted by graduate and post-graduate entrepreneurs. On the other hand, 46.7 per cent of the wood based industries were opted by the graduates. At the same time, majority of the printing and stationery industries (60.0 per cent) were preferred by the graduates.

It can be concluded that entrepreneurs with high educational levels preferred automobile and engineering industries whereas that of with low educational levels opted for metal based industries.

(v) Entrepreneurs' educational qualification and form of organisation preferred

It can be noted from Table 2.19 that graduates and post-graduates (75.0 per cent) preferred private limited companies whereas most of the under-matriculates, matriculates and under-graduates held sole proprietorship concerns. Among those who started partnership firms, under-graduates, graduates and post-graduates accounted for 50.0, 41.7 and 8.3 per cent respectively.

Moreover, sole proprietorship concern is most popular in all the levels of entrepreneurs' education. All the under-matriculates had preferred sole proprietorship while 94.1 per cent of the matriculates and 78.6 per cent of the under-graduates runs their units as sole proprietorship concerns.

Among the graduates and post-graduates also, sole proprietorship is the most popular form of ownership.

It may thus be concluded that private limited company and partnership as a form of organisation is not yet popular in Manipur. But education can play a greater role in the choice of form of organisation in the days to come.

2.6 Parental occupation of entrepreneurs

The parental occupation of the entrepreneurs were analysed and shown in Table 2.20. Government service was the parental occupation of the highest per centage of the entrepreneurs (31.1 per cent) followed by agriculture (26.4 per cent). Next to agriculture, 21.7 per cent of the entrepreneurs have a parental occupation of profession, followed by 20.8 per cent in business.

Table 2.18

Entrepreneurs' Education : Type of Industry Opted

Type of Industry		Educational Qualification of Entrepreneurs					Total
		Under-Matriculate	Matriculate	Under-Graduate	Graduate	Post-Graduate	
Food based	Count	1	2	5	8	1	17
	% within Industry	5.9	11.8	29.4	47.1	5.9	100
	% within Qualification	8.3	11.8	17.9	20.5	10	16
	% of Total	0.9	1.9	4.7	7.5	0.9	16
Metal based	Count	6	4	4			14
	% within Industry	42.9	28.6	28.6			100
	% within Qualification	50	23.5	14.3			13.2
	% of Total	5.7	3.8	3.8			13.2
Handlooms & Handicrafts	Count	1		2	3	2	8
	% within Industry	12.5		25	37.5	25	100
	% within Qualification	8.3		7.1	7.7	20	7.5
	% of Total	0.9		1.9	2.8	1.9	7.5
Plastics and rubber based	Count		4	3	3	2	12
	% within Industry		33.3	25	25	16.7	
	% within Qualification		23.5	10.7	7.7	20	11.3
	% of Total		3.8	2.8	2.8	1.9	11.3

Wood based	Count	1	3	3	7	1	15
	% within Industry	6.7	20	10	46.7	6.7	100
	% within Qualification	8.3	17.6	10.7	17.9	10	14.2
	% of Total	0.9	2.8	2.8	6.6	0.9	14.2
Printing & stationery	Count	1		2	6	1	10
	% within Industry	10		20	60	10	100
	% within Qualification	8.3		7.1	15.4	10	9.4
	% of Total	0.9		1.9	5.7	0.9	9.4
Automobile & engineering	Count	2	4	7	9	3	25
	% within Industry	8	16	28	36.10	12	100
	% within Qualification	16.7	23.5	25	23.1	30	23.6
	% of Total	1.9	3.8	6.6	8.5		23.6
Others (arts, perfumery & detergents)	Count			2	3	2.8	5
	% within Industry			40	60		100
	% within Qualification			7.1	7.7		4.7
	% of Total			1.9	2.8		4.7
Total	Count	12	17	28	39	10	106
	% within Industry	11.3	16	26.4	36.8	9.4	100
	% within Qualification	100	100	100	100	100	100
	% of Total	11.3	16	26.4	36.8	9.4	100

Source : Field Survey.

Table 2.19

Entrepreneurs' Education : Forms of Organisation preferred

Forms of Organisation		Educational Qualification of Entrepreneurs					Total
		Under-Matriculate	Matriculate	Under-Graduate	Graduate	Post-Graduate	
Pvt. Limited Company	Count		1		1	2	4
	% within Organisation		25		25	50	100
	% within Qualification		5.9		2.6	20	3.8
	% of Total		0.9		0.9	1.9	3.8
Partnership	Count			6	5	1	12
	% within Organisation			50	41.7	8.3	100
	% within Qualification			21.4	12.8	10	11.3
	% of Total			5.7	4.7	0.9	11.3
Sole Proprietorship	Count	12	16	22	33	7	90
	% within Organisation	13.3	17.8	24.4	36.7	7.8	100

	% within Qualification	100	94.1	78.6	84.6	70	84.9
	% of Total	11.3	15.1	20.8	31.1	6.6	84.9
Total	Count	12	17	28	39	10	106
	% within Organisation	11.3	16	26.4	36.8	9.4	100
	% within Qualification	100	100	100	100	100	100
	% of Total	11.3	16	26.4	36.8	9.4	100

Source : Field Survey

Table 2.20
Parental Occupation of Entrepreneurs : District-wise Classification

Parental Occupation of Entrepreneurs		District		Total
		Imphal West	Imphal East	
Business	Count	12	10	22
	% within Occupation	54.5	45.5	100
	% within District	21.4	20	20.8
	% of Total	11.3	9.4	20.8
Agriculture	Count	12	16	28
	% within Occupation	42.9	57.1	100
	% within District	21.4	32	26.4
	% of Total	11.3	15.1	26.4
Government service	Count	21	12	33
	% within Occupation	63.6	36.4	100
	% within District	37.5	24	31.1
	% of Total	19.8	11.3	31.1
Profession	Count	11	12	23
	% within Occupation	47.8	52.2	100
	% within District	19.6	24	21.7
	% of Total	10.4	11.3	21.7
Total	Count	56	50	106
	% within Occupation	52.8	47.2	100
	% within District	100	100	100
	% of Total	52.8	47.2	100

Source : Field Survey.

District-wise, it can be observed that agriculture was the pre-dominant parental occupation in Imphal East District (32.0 per cent), while government service was the dominant occupation in the Imphal West District (37.5 per cent). The entrepreneurs with business and professions parental occupation were found almost equally in the two districts of Manipur.

(i) Parental occupation of entrepreneurs and age at the time of entry

The parental occupation and the entrepreneurs' age at the time of starting their industry were enquired into and shown in Table 2.21.

Majority of the entrepreneurs whose parental occupation were agriculture, government service and profession entered the industry at the age of 21-30 years.

On the other hand, a good number of entrepreneurs whose parental occupation was business entered into the entrepreneurial activity either at the age of 21-30 years or 31-40 years. It was found that of all the entrepreneurs who started their units when they are 41 or more years, those with agriculture as parental occupation formed the highest. Moreover, the average age of entrepreneurs having profession as parental occupation was 30.17 years while that of business was 45.55 years.

(ii) Parental occupation of entrepreneurs and type of industry preferred

The parental occupation of the entrepreneurs and the type of industry preferred by them were analysed and shown in Table 2.22.

Majority of the entrepreneurs, irrespective of their parental occupation, started their units related to automobile and engineering industries. Among them, entrepreneurs whose parental occupation was agriculture, government service and profession formed the highest (28.0 per cent each) followed by business (16.0 per cent). Next to automobile and engineering industries, most of the units relate to food based industries were started mainly by the entrepreneurs whose parental occupation was business and government service (35.3 per cent each).

Occupation-wise, 31.1 per cent of the entrepreneurs were found to be having a parental occupation of government service, followed by agriculture (26.4 per cent), profession (21.7 per cent) and business (20.8 per cent).

Table 2.21

Parental Occupation of Entrepreneurs : Age at the Time of Entry

Age at the Time of Entry		Parental Occupation of Entrepreneurs				Total
		Business	Agriculture	Govt. service	Profession	
20 & below	Count	2	2	1	3	8
	% within Age	25	25	12.5	27.5	100
	% within Occupation	9.1	7.1	3	13	7.5
	% of Total	1.9	1.9	0.9	2.8	7.5
21-30	Count	8	11	17	12	48
	% within Age	16.7	22.9	35.4	25	100
	% within Occupation	36.4	39.9	51.5	52.2	45.3
	% of Total	7.5	10.4	16	11.3	45.3
31-40	Count	9	7	12	3	31
	% within Age	29	22.6	38.7	9.7	100
	% within Occupation	40.9	25	36.4	13	29.2
	% of Total	8.5	6.6	11.3	2.8	29.2

41-50	Count	2	5	3	3	13
	% within Age	15.4	38.5	23.1	23.1	100
	% within Occupation	9.1	17.9	9.1	13	12.3
	% of Total	1.9	4.7	2.8	2.8	12.3
51 & above	Count	1	3		2	6
	% within Age	16.7	50		33.3	100
	% within Occupation	4.5	10.7		8.7	5.7
	% of Total	0.9	2.8		1.9	5.7
Total	Count	22	28	33	23	106
	% within Age	20.8	26.4	31.1	21.7	100
	% within Occupation	100	100	100	100	100
	% of Total	20.8	26.4	31.1	21.7	100

Source : Field Survey

Table 2.22

Parental Occupation of Entrepreneurs : Type of Industry Opted

Type of Industry		Parental Occupation of Entrepreneurs				Total
		Business	Agriculture	Govt. service	Profession	
Food based	Count	6	3	6	2	17
	% within Industry	35.3	17.6	35.3	11.8	100
	% within Occupation	27.3	10.7	18.2	8.7	16
	% of Total	5.7	2.8	5.7	1.9	16
Metal based	Count	1	6		7	14
	% within Industry	7.1	42.9		50	100
	% within Occupation	4.5	21.4		30.4	13.2
	% of Total	0.9	5.7		6.6	13.2
Handlooms & handicrafts	Count	3	1	3	1	8
	% within Industry	37.5	12.5	37.5	12.5	100
	% within Occupation	13.5	3.6	9.1	4.3	7.5
	% of Total	2.8	0.9	2.8	0.9	7.5
Plastics & rubber based	Count	2	3	6	1	12
	% within Industry	16.7	25	50	8.3	100
	% within Occupation	9.1	10.7	18.2	4.3	11.3
	% of Total	1.9	2.8	5.7	0.9	11.3

Printing & stationery	Count	1	5	3	1	10
	% within Industry	10	50	30	10	100
	% within Occupation	4.5	17.9	9.1	4.3	9.4
	% of Total	0.9	4.7	2.8	0.9	9.4
Automobile & engineering	Count	4	7	7	7	25
	% within Industry	16	28	28	28	100
	% within Occupation	18.2	25	21.2	30.4	23.6
	% of Total	3.8	6.6	6.6		23.6
Others (arts, perfumery & detergents)	Count	1	1	3	6.6	5
	% within Industry	20	20	60		100
	% within Occupation	4.5	3.6	9.1		4.7
	% of Total	0.9	0.9	2.8		4.7
Total	Count	22	28	33	23	106
	% within Industry	20.8	26.4	31.1	21.7	100
	% within Occupation	100	100	100	100	100
	% of Total	20.8	26.4	31.1	21.7	100

Source : Field Survey

2.7 Parental education of entrepreneurs

Like character, education as such is impossible to be measured. It is not intended to measure the educational background of the entrepreneurs' parents in the present study. What is proposed here is only to ascertain the educational level of the entrepreneurs' parents by the examinations they have passed or the degrees or diplomas they have obtained from the schools and colleges. And then it is proposed to examine the inter-relationship between this characteristic and other characteristics of socio-economic background.

The parental education of the entrepreneurs were enquired and shown in Table 2.23.

It is interesting to note that majority of the entrepreneurs' parents were under-matriculates (38.7 per cent). While graduates constituted 12.3 per cent, post-graduates accounted for only 1.9 per cent. It is worthwhile to mention here that 23.6 per cent (25 out of 106) of the entrepreneurs' parents were illiterates. In other words, the above analysis interprets that low level of education of entrepreneurs' parents need be no roadblock on the way to entrepreneurship since majority of them (91 out of 106) are educated only upto under-graduation.

District-wise, it was found that graduates and post-graduates constituted only 14.2 per cent in Imphal West District. While graduates accounted for 14.0 per cent, in Imphal East District, parental education of post-graduate are not found. Parental education of matriculates were 25.0 per cent in Imphal West District while they constituted 12.0 per cent in Imphal East District. 21.4 per cent and 26.0 per cent were illiterates in Imphal West and Imphal East Districts respectively.

Qualification-wise, out of the parents who were illiterates, 48.0 per cent were in Imphal West District while 52.0 per cent were in Imphal East District. Even among the under-matriculates, Imphal West District accounted for 32.1 per cent and Imphal East District 46.0 per cent. While Imphal West District constituted for 70.0 per cent matriculates, Imphal East District accounted for 30.0 per cent of the same.

It is thus clear that a majority of the entrepreneurs' parents posses only low or medium qualifications. It will be interesting to know and examine whether parental education of entrepreneurs has anything to influence on age of entrepreneurs to enter into industry, type of industry chosen, forms of organisation preferred etc.

Table 2.23
Parental Education of Entrepreneurs : District-wise Classification

Parental Education of Entrepreneurs		District		Total
		Imphal West	Imphal East	
Illiterates	Count	12	13	25
	% within Education	48	52	100
	% within District	21.4	26	23.6
	% of Total	11.3	12.3	23.6
Under-Matriculates	Count	18	23	41
	% within Education	43.9	56.1	100
	% within District	32.1	46.1	38.7
	% of Total	17	21.7	38.7
Matriculates	Count	14	6	20
	% within Education	70	30	100
	% within District	25	12	18.9
	% of Total	13.2	5.7	18.9
Under-Graduates	Count	4	1	5
	% within Education	80	20	100
	% within District	7.1	2	4.7
	% of Total	3.8	0.9	4.7
Graduates	Count	6	7	13
	% within Education	46.2	534.8	100
	% within District	10.7	14	12.3
	% of Total	5.7	6.6	12.3

(contd.)

Table 2.23 *(contd.)*

		Imphal West	Imphal East	Total
Post-Graduates	Count	2		2
	% within Education	100		100
	% within District	3.6		1.9
	% of Total	1.9		1.9
Total	Count	56	50	106
	% within Education	52.8	47.2	100
	% within District	100	100	100
	% of Total	52.8	47.2	100

Source : Field Survey.

(i) Parental education and entrepreneurs' age at the time of entry

It can be seen from Table 2.24 that out of the entrepreneurs who entered industry at the age of 21-30 years, parental education of under-matriculates formed the highest per centage (37.5 per cent) followed by matriculates (20.8 per cent) and illiterates (16.7 per cent).

It was found that 53.8 per cent of the entrepreneurs having a parental education of graduate preferred the age group of 21-30 years, followed by 38.5 per cent entrepreneurs having the same parental education preferring the age group of 31-40 years to start industry. For the parental education of post-graduate, 21-30 years is the chosen age group to enter into entrepreneurship.

Further, it is observed that those who started industry at the later stage of 41-50 years, illiterate parents formed the highest (61.5 per cent) followed by under-matriculates (15.4 per cent), matriculates (15.4 per cent) and under-graduates (7.7 per cent). After 50 years, majority of the parents were under-matriculates (66.7 per cent) when their wards entered into industrial entrepreneurship.

It indicates that higher level of parental education induces entrepreneurs to make an early entry into industrial entrepreneurship.

(ii) Parental education and entrepreneurs' education

An attempt is made here to examine whether parental education of entrepreneurs has any impact on the entrepreneurs' education which is detrimental for the growth of entrepreneurship.

As can be seen from Table 2.25, majority of the graduate entrepreneurs were having a parental education of under-matric (35.9 per cent) while those of post-graduate entrepreneurs were graduate (60.0 per cent). It is interesting to note that 23.1 per cent (9 out of 39) graduate entrepreneurs were having illiterate parents. It was also the same in case of 10.0 per cent post-graduate entrepreneurs.

Parental education-wise, 36.0 per cent of the graduate entrepreneurs were having illiterate parents (9 out of 25) while it was 20.0 per cent each in case of under-matric, matric and under-graduate entrepreneurs (5 each out of 25).It was the parental education of under-matric that majority of the graduate (34.1 per cent), under-graduate (31.7 per cent), matriculates (19.5 per cent) and under-matriculates (12.2 per cent) entrepreneurs were influenced to start industry.

It can thus be concluded that almost all the entrepreneurs under study are not only first generation entrepreneurs but also they are first among the generation that are educated. But it does not mean that the low level of parental education proves hindrance to entrepreneurship as majority of the entrepreneurs were having parental education upto matriculation only.

(iii) Parental education and religion

An attempt is made here to ascertain the parental education of entrepreneurs across their religions. It may be seen from Table 2.26 that the parental education of under-graduation, graduation and post-graduation were found only for the Hindu entrepreneurs. For the Muslim entrepreneurs, their parents were educated upto matriculation whereas it was only upto under-matriculation for the Christian and Sikh entrepreneurs.

Religion-wise, 35.4 per cent (34 out of 96) Hindu entrepreneurs were having a parental education of under-

Table 2.24

Parental Education of Entrepreneurs : Age at the time of Entry

Parental Education of Entrepreneurs		Age at the time of Entry					Total
		20 & below	21-30	31-40	41-50	50 & above	
Illiterate	Count	1	8	7	8	1	25
	% within Education	4	32	28	32.05	4	100
	% within Age	12.5	16.7	22.6	61.5	16.7	23.6
	% of Total	0.9	7.5	6.6	7.5	0.9	23.6
Under-Matriculate	Count	4	18	13	2	4	41
	% within Education	9.8	43.9	31.7	4.9	9.8	100
	% within Age	50	37.5	41.9	15.4	66.7	38.7
	% of Total	3.8	17	12.3	1.9	3.8	38.7
Matriculate	Count	2	10	5	2	1	20
	% within Education	10	50	25	10	5	100
	% within Age	25	20.8	16.1	15.4	16.7	18.9
	% of Total	1.9	9.4	4.7	1.9	0.9	18.9

Under-Graduate	Count		3	1	1		5
	% within Education		60	20	20		100
	% within Age		6.3	3.2	7.7		4.7
	% of Total		2.8	0.9	0.9		4.7
Graduate	Count	1	7	5			13
	% within Education	7.7	53.8	38.5			100
	% within Age	12.5	14.6	16.1			12.3
	% of Total	0.9	6.6	4.7			12.3
Post-Graduate	Count		2				2
	% within Education		100				100
	% within Age		4.2				1.9
	% of Total		1.9				1.9
Total	Count	8	48	31	13	6	106
	% within Education	7.5	29.2	29.2	12.3	5.7	100
	% within Age	100	100	100	100	100	100
	% of Total	7.5	45.3	29.2	12.3	5.7	100

Source : Field Survey

Table 2.25
Education : Parents Vs Entrepreneurs

Parental Education	Educational Qualification of Entrepreneurs	Under-Matriculate	Matriculate	Under-Graduate	Graduate	Post-Graduate	Total
Illiterate	Count	5	5	5	9	1	25
	% within Parents	20	20	20	36	4	100
	% within Entrepreneurs	41.7	29.4	17.9	23.1	10	23.6
	% of Total	4.7	4.7	4.7	8.5	0.9	23.8
Under-Matriculate	Count	5	8	13	14	1	41
	% within Parents	12.2	19.5	31.7	34.1	2.4	100
	% within Entrepreneurs	41.7	47.1	46.4	35.9	10	38.7
	% of Total	4.7	7.5	12.3	13.2	0.9	38.7
Matriculate	Count	2	2	6	9	1	20
	% within Parents	10	10	30	45	5	100
	% within Entrepreneurs	16.7	11.8	21.4	23.1	10	18.9
	% of Total	1.9	1.9	5.7	8.5	0.9	18.9

Under-Graduate	Count			1	3	1	5
	% within Parents			20	60	20	100
	% within Entrepreneurs			3.6	7.7	10	4.7
	% of Total			0.9	2.8	0.9	4.7
Graduate	Count		2	2	3	6	13
	% within Parents		15.4	15.4	23.1	46.2	100
	% within Entrepreneurs		11.8	7.1	7.7	60	12.3
	% of Total		1.9	1.9	2.8	0.9	12.3
Post-Graduate	Count			1	1		2
	% within Parents			50	50		100
	% within Entrepreneurs			3.6	2.6		1.9
	% of Total			0.9	0.9		1.9
Total	Count	12	17	26	39	10	106
	% within Parents	11.3	16	26.4	36.85	9.4	100
	% within Entrepreneurs	100	100	100	100	100	100
	% of Total	11.3	16	26.4	36.8	9.4	100

Source : Field Survey

matriculation, followed by illiterates (24.0 per cent) matriculation (19.8 per cent), graduates (13.5 per cent), under-graduation (5.2 per cent) and post-graduation (2.1 per cent). On the other hand, 80.0 per cent of the Muslim entrepreneurs were having a parental education of under-matriculation as against 20.0 per cent matriculates. It can thus be concluded that Hindu entrepreneurs are more educated than others as regards their parental education.

Table 2.26
Parental Education of Entrepreneurs : Religion-wise Classification

Parental Education of Entrepreneurs	Religion of Entrepreneurs				
	Hindu	Muslim	Christian	Sikh	Total
Illiterates					
Count	23		1	1	25
% within Education	92		4	4	100
% within Religion	24		50	33.3	23.6
% of Total	21.7		0.9	0.9	23.6
Under-Matriculates					
Count	34	4	1	2	41
% within Education	82.9	9.8	2.4	4.9	100
% within Religion	35.4	80	50	66.7	38.7
% of Total	32.1	3.8	0.9	1.9	38.7
Matriculates					
Count	19	1			20
% within Education	95	5			100
% within Religion	19.8	20			18.9
% of Total	17.9	0.9			18.9
Under-Graduates					
Count	5				5
% within Education	100				100

(contd.)

	Hindu	Muslim	Christian	Sikh	Total
% within Religion	5.2				4.7
% of Total	4.7				4.7
Graduates					
Count	13				13
% within Education	100				100
% within Religion	13.5				12.3
% of Total	12.3				12.3
Post-Graduates					
Count	2				2
% within Education	100				100
% within Religion	2.1				1.9
% of Total	1.9				1.9
Total					
Count	96	5	2	3	106
% within Education	90.6	4.7	1.9	2.8	100
% within Religion	100	100	100	100	100
% of Total	90	4.7	1.9	2.8	100

Source : Field Survey

(iv) Parental education and type of industry opted

It is enquired here to find out how parental education of entrepreneurs influenced entrepreneurs' choice of the particular type of industry. Table 2.27 reveals that out of all the entrepreneurs whose parental education were upto under-matriculation, majority of them opted for automobile & engineering units (22.0 per cent) followed by food based (19.5 per cent), metal based (17.1 per cent), wood based and printing and stationery (12.2 per cent each). Even among the entrepreneurs having illiterate parents, automobile and engineering industries are opted commonly (40.0 per cent) followed by wood and metal based (16.0 per cent each) and plastics & rubber based industries (12.0 per cent). For the entrepreneurs having parental education

Table 2.27

Parental Education of Entrepreneurs : Type of Industry opted

Parental Education of Entrepreneurs		Type of Industry				
		Food based	Metal based	Handlooms & Handicrafts	Plastics & rubber based	Wood based
	0	1	2	3	4	5
Illiterates	Count	2	4	1	3	4
	% within Education	8	16	4	12	16
	% within Industry	11.8	28.8	12.5	25	26.7
	% of Total	1.9	3.8	0.9	2.8	3.8
Under-matriculates	Count	8	7	2	3	5
	% within Education	19.5	17.1	4.9	7.3	12.2
	% within Industry	47.1	50	25	25	33.3
	% of Total	7.5	6.6	1.9	2.8	4.7
Matriculates	Count	3	2	3	3	3
	% within Education	15	10	15	15	15
	% within Industry	17.6	14.3	37.5	25.5	20
	% of Total	2.8	1.9	2.8	2.8	2.8

Under-graduates	Count	2	1	1		
	% within Education	40	20	20		
	% within Industry	11.8	7.1	12.5		
	% of Total	1.9	0.9	0.9		
Graduates	Count	2		1	3	2
	% within Education	15.4		7.7	23.1	15.4
	% within Industry	11.8		12.5	25	13.3
	% of Total	1.9		0.9	2.8	1.9
Post-graduates	Count					1
	% within Education					50
	% within Industry					6.7
	% of Total					0.9
Total	Count	17	14	8	12	15
	% within Education	16	13.2	7.5	11.3	14.2
	% within Industry	100	100	100	100	100
	% of Total	16	13.2	7.5	11.3	14.2

Source : Field Survey

(contd.)

Table 2.27 *(contd.)*

Parental Education of Entrepreneurs		Type of Industry			Total
		Printing & Stationeries	Automobile & Engineerng	Others	
	0	6	7	8	9
Illiterates	Count	1	10		25
	% within Education	4	40		100
	% within Industry	10	40		23.6
	% of Total	0.9	9.4		23.6
Under-Matriculate	Count	5	9	2	41
	% within Education	12.2	22	4.9	100
	% within Industry	50	36	40	38.7
	% of Total	4.7	8.5	1.9	38.7
Matriculate	Count	2	2	2	20
	% within Education	10	10	10	100
	% within Industry	20.05	8	40	18.9
	% of Total	1.9	1.9	1.9	18.9

Under-Graduate	Count	1			5
	% within Education	20			100
	% within Industry	10			4.7
	% of Total	0.9			4.7
Graduate	Count	1	3	1	13
	% within Education	7.7	23.1	7.7	100
	% within Industry	10	12	20	12.3
	% of Total	0.9	2.8	0.9	12.3
Post-Graduates	Count		1		2
	% within Education		50		100
	% within Industry		4		1.9
	% of Total		0.9		1.9
Total	Count	10	25	5	106
	% within Education	9.4	23.6	4.7	100
	% within Industry	100	100	100	100
	% of Total	9.4	23.6	4.7	100

upto matriculation, almost all the different types of industries are uniformly preferred.

On the other hand, wood based and automobile and engineering units are equally common among the entrepreneurs having parental education upto post-graduation. Similar is the case among the entrepreneurs having parental education upto graduation where automobile and engineering unit are the chosen type of industry along with printing & stationery units, wood based and food based units.

It can thus be concluded that automobile and engineering units are opted by majority of the entrepreneurs having different parental education except those having upto under-graduation, followed by food based and wood based industries.

(v) Parental education and forms of organisation

It can be observed from Table 2.28 that 42.2 per cent of the sole proprietorship concerns are started by those entrepreneurs having parental education only upto under-matriculation. On the other hand, private limited companies are equally started by those entrepreneurs having parents who were illiterates and educated upto post-graduation. So far as partnership firms are concerned, majority of them are run by those entrepreneurs whose parents are illiterates.

It can thus be concluded that less parental education has not deterred the entrepreneurs to start units either on company form or partnership form rather than the ordinary sole proprietorship concerns.

(vi) Parental education and generation of entrepreneurs

It is attempted here to analyse the generation of entrepreneurs across their parental education. Table 2.29 reveals that 34.5 per cent of the first generation entrepreneurs had parents educated only upto under-matriculation. Likewise, majority of the second generation entrepreneurs were having parental education upto under-matriculation.

On the other hand, parental education of graduation induced 92.3 per cent of their wards to start industry as first generation entrepreneurs while that of post-graduation influenced all of their wards to become first generation entrepreneurs.

Table 2.28
Parental Education of Entrepreneurs : Forms of Organisation preferred

Parental Educaticn of Entrepreneurs	Forms of Organisation preferred			Total
	Pvt. Ltd Co.	Partner-ship	Sole Prop-rietorship	
Illiterate				
Count	2	5	18	25
% within Education	8	20	72	100
% within Organisation	50	41.7	20	23.6
% of Total	1.9	4.7	17	23.6
Under-matriculate				
Count		3	38	41
% within Education		7.3	92.7	100
% within Organisation		25	42.2	18.9
% of Total		2.8	35.8	18.9
Matriculate				
Count			20	20
% within Education			100	100
% within Organisation			22.2	18.9
% of Total			18.9	18.9
Under-graduate				
Count		1	4	5
% within Education		20	80	100
% within Organisation		8.3	4.4	4.7
% of Total		0.9	3.8	4.7

(contd.)

Parental Education of Entrepreneurs	Forms of Organisation preferred			Total
	Pvt. Ltd Co.	Partner-ship	Sole Proprietorship	
Graduate				
Count	2	2	9	13
% within Education	15.4	15.4	69.2	100
% within Organisation	50	16.7	10	12.3
% of Total	1.9	1.9	8.5	12.3
Post-graduates				
Count		1	1	2
% within Education		50	50	100
% within Organisation		16.7	10	1.9
% of Total		1.9	8.5	1.9
Total				
Count	4	12	90	106
% within Education	3.8	11.3	84.9	100
% within Organisation	100	100	100	100
% of Total	3.8	11.3	84	100

Source : Field Survey.

Thus, it can be concluded that higher the parental education, the greater is the chance to become entrepreneurs as first generation

2.8 Economic status of entrepreneurs

The economic status of the entrepreneurs at the time of starting the industrial unit has been studied. For this purpose, the monthly income of the entrepreneurs from different sources were taken into consideration.

Table 2.30 observes that 40.6 per cent of the entrepreneurs earned a monthly income ranging upto Rs. 5000 forming the highest group followed by those entrepreneurs (12.3 per cent)

with monthly income ranging between Rs. 5000 – Rs. 10,000. It is worthwhile to mention here that 41.5 per cent of the entrepreneurs were unemployed or students whose particulars are not available. The average monthly income of the entrepreneurs was Rs. 2689.01.

Table 2.29
Parental Education of Entrepreneurs: Generation of Entrepreneurs

Parental Education of Entrepreneurs	Generation of Entrepreneurs			Total
	First	Second	Third	
Illiterate				
Count	20	5		25
% within Education	80	20		100
% within Generation	23.8	23.8		23.6
% of Total	18.9	4.7		23.6
Under-Matriculate				
Count	29	11	1	41
% within Education	70.7	26.8	2.4	100
% within Generation	34.5	52.4	100	38.7
% of Total	27.4	10.4	0.9	38.7
Matriculate				
Count	17	3		20
% within Education	85	15		100.05
% within Generation	20.2	14.3		18.9
% of Total	16	2.8		18.9
Under-Graduate				
Count	4	1		5
% within Education	80	20		100
% within Generation	4.8	4.8		4.7
% of Total	3.8	0.9		4.7

(contd.)

Table 2.29 *(contd.)*

Parental Education of Entrepreneurs	Generation of Entrepreneurs			Total
	First	Second	Third	
Graduate				
Count	12	1		13
% within Education	92.3	7.75		100
% within Generation	14.3	4.8		12.3
% of Total	11.3	0.9		12.3
Post-Graduate				
Count	2			2
% within Education	100			100
% within Generation	2.4			1.9
% of Total	1.9			1.9
Total				
Count	**84**	**21**	**1**	**106**
% within Education	**79.2**	**19.8**	**0.9**	**100**
% within Generation	**100**	**100**	**100**	**100**
% of Total	**79.2**	**19.8**	**0.9**	**100**

Source : Field Survey.

District-wise, as seen in Table 2.31, the average monthly income of entrepreneurs of Imphal West District is Rs. 2951.79 while that of Imphal East District is Rs. 2394.70.

There is no difference in monthly income of entrepreneurs between Imphal West District and Imphal East District which is proved by T-value say 0.634 with P-value 0.527 (> p = 0.05).

Religion-wise, it can be seen from Table 2.32 that the average monthly income of Hindu entrepreneurs were found to be the highest followed by Muslim, Sikh and Christian entrepreneurs. Moreover, there is no statistically difference among the average monthly income of entrepreneurs as regards to their religion which is witnessed by analysis of variance (ANOVA) i.e., F-value say .289 with P-value 0.834 (> 0.05).

Table 2.30
Monthly Income of Entrepreneurs at the Time of Starting the Enterprises

Monthly Income (Rs.)	Imphal West District	Imphal East District	Both
Upto 5000	19 (33.9)	24 (48)	43 (40.6)
5000-10000	7 (12.5)	6 (12)	13 (12.3)
10000-15000	1 (1.8)	2 (4)	3 (1.9)
15000-20000	2 (3.6)	-	2 (1.9)
20000 & above	1 (1.8)	-	1 (0.9)
Particulars not available	26 (46.4)	18 (36)	44 (41.5)
Total	56 (100.00)	50 (100.00)	106 (100.00)

Source : Field Survey
Note : Figures in parentheses indicate per centages to total.

Table 2.31
District-wise Average Monthly Income of Entrepreneurs

District	No. of Cases	Average Monthly Income (Rs.)	Standard Deviation (Rs.)
Imphal West District	56	295.79	5318.61
Imphal East District	50	2394.70	3395.37

Source : Field Survey
$T = 0.634$, $d.f = 104$, $p = 0.527 > p = 0.05$

Table 2.32
Religion-wise Average Monthly Income of Entrepreneurs

Religion	No. of Cases	Average Monthly Income (Rs.)	Standard Deviation (Rs.)
Hindu	96	2811.8	4673.4
Muslim	5	1800	2196.6
Christian	2	500	707.11
Sikh	3	1700	2858.3

Source : Field Survey.

2.9 Rural/urban background of entrepreneurs

The entrepreneurs under study are classified into two categories, namely, urban and rural applying the criteria where the entrepreneur has lived during the last ten years preceding the time of setting up one's unit. Such an enquiry may enable us to find out the rural-urban background of entrepreneurs and whether the urban experience is a precondition of entrepreneurship.

As can be seen from Table 2.33, majority of the entrepreneurs under study had rural background (60.4 per cent) while entrepreneurs with urban background formed 39.6 per cent. It may also be seen that Imphal West District had 50.00 per cent each of entrepreneurs with urban and rural background whereas in Imphal East District, entrepreneurs with urban background accounted for 28.0 per cent only. Thus, it can be concluded that urban experience is not a precondition of industrial entrepreneurship.

(i) Rural/urban background and type of industry preferred

Table 2.34 reveals that the highest per centage of the entrepreneurs with rural background started automobile and engineering units (29.7per cent) followed by metal based units (15.6 per cent) and food based units (14.1 per cent). Those with urban background, who started food based units constituted the highest (19.0 per cent) followed by handlooms and handicrafts units and wood based units (16.7 per cent each).

Table 2.33
Rural/Urban Background of Entrepreneurs : District-wise Classification

Background of Entrepreneurs	Districts		
	West	East	Total
Urban			
Count	28	14	42
% within Background	66.7	33.3	100
% within District	50	28	39.6
% of Total	26.4	13.2	39.6
Rural			
Count	28	36	64
% within Background	43.8	56.3	100
% within District	50	72	60.4
% of Total	26.4	34	60.4
Total			
Count	56	50	106
% within Background	52.8	47.2	100
% within District	100	100	100
% of Total	52.8	47.2	100

Source : Field Survey

(ii) Rural/urban background and form of organisation

It can be noted from Table 2.35 that private limited company and partnership form of organisation was preferred by the entrepreneurs hailing from rural and urban background in the ratio 1:3. As regards the sole proprietorship form of organisation, 42.2 per cent had come from urban background whereas 57.8 per cent had rural background.

Table 2.34

Rural/Urban Background of Entrepreneurs : Type of Industry Opted

Type of Industry	Background of Entrepreneurs		
	Urban	Rural	Total
Food Based			
Count	8	9	17
% within Industry	47.1	52.9	100
% within Background	19	14.1	16
% of Total	7.5	8.5	16
Metal Based			
Count	4	10	14
% within Industry	28.6	71.4	100
% within Background	9.5	15.6	13.2
% of Total	3.8	9.4	13.2
Handlooms & Handicrafts			
Count	7	1	8
% within Industry	87.5	12.5	100
% within Background	16.7	1.6	7.5
% of Total	6.6	0.9	7.5
Plastics & Rubber Based			
Count	5	7	12
% within Industry	41.7	58.3	100
% within Background	11.9	10.9	11.3
% of Total	4.7	6.6	11.3
Wool Based			
Count	7	8	15
% within Industry	46.7	53.3	100
% within Background	16.7	12.5	14.2
% of Total	6.6	7.5	14.2

(contd.)

Type of Industry	Background of Entrepreneurs		
	Urban	Rural	Total
Printing & Stationery			
Count	4	6	10
% within Industry	40	60	100
% within Background	9.5	9.4	9.4
% of Total	3.8	5.7	9.4
Automobile & Engineering			
Count	6	19	25
% within Industry	24	76	100
% within Background	14.3	29.7	23.6
% of Total	5.7	17.9	23.6
Others (Arts, perfumery, detergents)			
Count	1	4	5
% within Industry	20	80	100
% within Background	2.4	6.3	4.7
% of Total	0.9	3.8	4.7
Total			
Count	42	64	106
% within Industry	39.6	60.4	100
% within Background	100	100	100
% of Total	39.6	60.4	100

Source : Field Survey.

Background-wise, 90.5 per cent entrepreneurs having urban background, preferred sole proprietorship concern while only 2.4 per cent opted for the private limited company form of organisation. On the other hand, 81.3 per cent entrepreneurs having rural background preferred sole proprietorship concern while 14.1 per cent opted for partnership form of organisation. As to the company form of organisation, 4.7 per cent entrepreneurs having rural background opted for it.

Table 2.35
Rural/Urban Background of Entrepreneurs: Forms of Organisation Preferred

Forms of Organisation	Background of Entrepreneurs		
	Urban	Rural	Total
Pvt. Limited Company			
Count	1	3	4
% within Organisation	25	75	100
% within Background	2.4	4.7	3.8
% of Total	0.9	2.8	3.8
Partnership			
Count	3	9	12
% within Organisation	25	75	100
% within Background	7.1	14.1	11.3
% of Total	2.8	8.5	11.3
Sole Proprietorship			
Count	38	52	90
% within Organisation	42.2	57.8	100
% within Background	90.5	81.3	84.9
% of Total	35.8	49.1	84.9
Total			
Count	42	64	106
% within Organisation	39.6	60.4	100
% within Background	100	100	100
% of Total	39.6	60.4	100

Source : Field Survey

(iii) Rural/urban background and generation of entrepreneurs

As can be seen from Table 2.36, 76.2 per cent of the entrepreneurs hailing from urban background are first generation entrepreneurs, followed by 21.4 per cent second and 2.4 per cent third generation entrepreneurs. On the other hand, entrepreneurs having rural background are 81.3 per cent first and 18.8 per cent second generation entrepreneurs.

Table 2.36
Rural/Urban Background of Entrepreneurs: Generation of Entrepreneurs

Generation of Entrepreneurs	Background of Entrepreneurs		
	Urban	Rural	Total
First			
Count	32	52	84
% within Generation	38.1	61.9	100
% within Background	76.2	81.3	79.2
% of Total	30.2	49.1	79.2
Second			
Count	9	12	21
% within Generation	42.9	57.1	100
% within Background	21.4	18.8	19.8
% of Total	8.5	11.3	19.8
Third			
Count	1		1
% within Generation	100		100
% within Background	2.4		0.9
% of Total	0.9		0.9
Total			
Count	42	64	106
% within Generation	39.6	60.4	100
% within Background	100	100	100
% of Total	39.6	60.4	100

Source : Field Survey

Generation-wise, first generation entrepreneurs consist of 38.1 per cent entrepreneurs having urban background and 61.9 per cent having rural background. At the same time, second generation entrepreneurs consists of urban and rural background entrepreneurs in the ratio 3:4. It is interesting to note that the only third generation hails from urban background.

2.10 Pattern of families

The families of the entrepreneurs are categorised into two, namely, joint life family and nuclear family. Such an analysis may enable us to find out the pattern of families of the entrepreneurs at the time of starting their units and whether independent decision making under nuclear family pattern has any direct relationship with the growth of entrepreneurship.

Table 2.37
Type of Entrepreneurs' Families : Religion-wise Classification

Religion of Entrepreneurs	Type of Families		
	Joint	Nuclear	Total
Hindu			
Count	76	20	96
% within Religion	79.2	20.8	100
% within Families	90.5	90.9	90.6
% of Total	71.7	18.9	90.6
Muslim			
Count	3	2	5
% within Religion	60	40	100
% within Families	3.6	9.1	4.7
% of Total	2.8	1.9	4.7
Christian			
Count	2		2
% within Religion	100		100
% within Families	2.4		1.9
% of Total	1.9		1.9

(contd.)

Religion of Entrepreneurs	Type of Families		
	Joint	Nuclear	Total
Sikh			
Count	3		3
% within Religion	100		100
% within Families	3.6		2.8
% of Total	2.8		2.8
Total			
Count	84	22	106
% within Religion	79.2	20.8	100
% within Families	100	100	100
% of Total	79.2	20.8	100

Source : Field Survey.

Table 2.38
Type of Entrepreneurs' Families: District-wise Classification

District	Type of Families		
	Joint	Nuclear	Total
Imphal West			
Count	45	11	56
% within Religion	80.4	19.6	100
% within Families	53.6	50	52.8
% of Total	42.5	10.4	52.8
Imphal East			
Count	39	11	50
% within Religion	78	22	100
% within Families	46.4	50	47.2
% of Total	36.8	10.4	47.2

(contd.)

District	Type of Families		Total
	Joint	Nuclear	
Total			
Count	84	22	106
% within Religion	79.2	20.8	100
% within Families	100	100	100
% of Total	79.2	20.8	100

Source : Field Survey

Table 2.37 shows the religion-wise distribution of the type of entrepreneurs' families. 84 of the total entrepreneurs (79.2 per cent) were in joint life families at the time of starting their units and 22 (20.8 per cent) were in nuclear families.

Religion-wise, all the Christian and Sikh entrepreneurs were in joint families. Among the Hindu entrepreneurs, 79.2 per cent were from joint life families as against 20.8 per cent from nuclear families. The ratio of joint life family and nuclear family in respect of Muslim entrepreneurs is 3:2.

District-wise (Table 2.38), 53.6 per cent of the joint families were found in the Imphal West District whereas only 46.4 per cent of the same were found in the Imphal East District. On the other hand, both the two districts have equal distribution of nuclear families.

REFERENCES

1. Everett, Hagen , "The Economics of Development", Homewood, III, Richard D. Irwin, 1968, PP. 7-15.
2. Kindel Berger, "Economic Development", McGraw Hill, New York, 1961, P. 86.
3. Hery, M.J., "Contrasting Factors in the Modernisation of China and Japan", Simon Kuzents, el. al., (Eds), "Economic Growth: Brazil, India, Japan", N.C. Duke University Press, Durham, 1965, P. 6.
4. Landes, D.S., "French Entrepreneurship and Industrial Growth in the Nineteenth Century, Journal of Economic History, May, 1949, PP. 45-61.

5. Gangadhara Rao, N., "Entrepreneurship and Growth of Enterprise in Industrial Estates" Deep and Deep Publications, New Delhi, 1986, P. 83.
6. Frederick Harbition and Charles A. Myers, "Education, Manpower and Economic Growth", Oxford and BH Publishing Co. Calcutta, 1968, P. 13.

CHAPTER III

ENTREPRENEURIAL MOTIVATION AND AMBITIONS

3.1 Introduction

The socio-economic origins of the entrepreneurs are discussed in the last chapter. Now it is proposed to analyse the factors that have motivated and facilitated the entrepreneurship development in the two districts selected for study. What makes a man is mostly his environment and his attitudes. The prevailing socio-economic, psychological and the cultural factors naturally influence a man and act as a source of inspiration to make a successful living in the society.

Environment and attitudes are not two different separable entities. The former influences the latter and vice versa. But the attitudes of people exert more influence on the environment. Sometimes, man becomes a prisoner of the environment of which he is the creator. Here again, the attitudes of man are not static. They are ever changing. Man constantly endeavours to conceive new and better ideas and indulges in experimenting on them. This process guides to changed attitudes and changed environments.

The level of economic development differs from one country to another country because the people of these countries are placed in different socio-economic setting with different attitudes. Wytinsky remarks that if it was possible to transplant overnight all the factories of Michigan, Ohio and Pennsylvania to India without changing the economic attitudes of the people, two decades later, the country would be as poor as it is now. He felt that the main source of India's weakness lies in the human factor. What is lacking is not innate abilities or technical skills in her people but it is the lack of initiative or interest in improving their economic status.[1]

The paradox of the abundance of innate abilities, the lack of enterprising qualities in India is well exemplified by Ram K. Vepa. He cited the example of Bihar, Orissa, Assam and Madhya Pradesh which are endowed with rich natural resources and have, in the past, produced amazing achievements both artistic and cultural. He cited the temples at Konark, Bhubaneshwar and Khajuraho which speak volumes about the skills of the master-craftsmen and the culture of the people of those areas in the past but which remained backward. Even today, these states remained backward despite massive investment in public sector projects there since the beginning of the era of planning in India.[2]

As such, of all the attitudes, innovation, risk taking and future planning is the most important from the point of view of industrial development. It is the entrepreneur who acts as a 'spark plug' to transform the economic scene and brings a sense of dynamism into it.[3] **Entrepreneurs like any other careerists are not born but they are made.** Career depends upon several factors other than the attitudes of the careerist himself. The attitudes of others like his family members, friends and relatives and the government would exert influence the career making. Entrepreneurship is no exception. Entrepreneurs are not only a product of their ambitions, but also those of the aspirations of their family members, friends and the nation.

Certain compulsions also, at times, push them to the entrepreneurial roles. The encouragement and help received from Government and non-governmental agencies are some of the important factors instrumental to the emergence of entrepreneurship. It is proposed in this chapter to enquire into the entrepreneurs' ambitions, the compelling forces, the sources of motivation, the facilitating factors, etc.

3.2 Entrepreneurs' ambitions

Ambitions motivate men. Ambition is an index of one's own resourcefulness. It activise men, broaden their vision and make the life more meaningful. Ambition is not something which is akin to greed or windfall. Greed results in disaster and windfall makes one a speculator. Like an individual, a nation or a region may have their own ambitions or aspirations which speak of their resourcefulness. **"The people are poor because they prefer it that way".** This is one of the causes of poverty attributed by Galbraith for the backwardness of many Asian and African nations. Galbraith further explained that because the people of those nations are lacking in ambition, they are lagging behind others in development."[4]

Ambition is the wrench of all motives. The intentions and initiative of a man are motivated by his ambitions. The importance of ambition in life can be justified by the common saying **"aimless life is a goal less game."** Hence, their aspirations and means to reach their goal is much more important than the man himself. However, ambitions differ from one person to another person depending upon the characteristics, priorities etc. which they have set for themselves. Sometimes, personal ambitions may come in the way of achieving national aspirations. Well conceived notions, careful planning, calculated risk taking, timely decision-making and swift execution make the ambition meaningful and fruitful and hence the achievement of nation's economic growth and development.

As regards the entrepreneurs' ambitions under the present study, the entrepreneurs were asked to rank in the order of importance, any three of five given ambitions. The ambitions marked by them were ranked by weighted score by according three points to the ambition ranked first, two points to the ambition ranked second and one point to the ambition ranked third. On the basis of the per centage of total weighted score each ambition, overall ranking is made.[5] As can be observed from Table 3.1, the ambition of gaining independent living or self-employment was ranked first in Imphal West District (40.5 per cent) as well as in Imphal East District (42.0 per cent). In both the districts put together, 'to make money' received second rank (23.1 per cent). 'To gain social prestige' was the third ranked ambition in Imphal East District while it was 'to make money' in the case of Imphal West District.

Table 3.1
Entrepreneurs' Ambitions

Ambitions	Imphal West District					Rank	Imphal East District					Both			Rank
	Entrepreneurs' Ranking			Weighted score	Rating (%)		Entrepreneurs' Ranking			Weighted	Rating (%)	Rank	Weighted score	Rating (%)	
	One	Two	Three				One	Two	Three						
To make money	10	8	18	64	20.7	3	6	16	22	72	25.6	2	136	23.1	2
To gain independent living (self-employment)	30	16	3	125	40.5	1	30	13	2	118	42	1	243	41.2	1
To fulfil the desire of myself/my father/my wife	6	10	12	50	16.2	4	2	12	10	40	14.2	4	90	15.3	4
To gain social prestige	9	14	10	65	21	2	11	6	3	48	17.1	3	113	19.2	3
Others*	1	1	-	5	1.6	5	1	-	-	3	1.1	5	8	1.4	5
No response	-	7	13	0	-	-	-	3	13	0	-		0	-	-
Total	56	56	56	309	100		50	50	50	281	100		590	100	

Source : **Field Survey**

* 'Others' **ambitions includes the desire to do something new or creative, self-employment to youths, etc.**

"To fulfill the desire of myself/my father/my wife" was the fourth ranked ambition in both the districts. The "other" ambition ranked fifth in both in districts which includes the desire to do something new or creative, self- employment to youths, etc. It is clear from the above analysis that the entrepreneurs in the two districts had mainly the ambition of gaining independent living or self-employment, making money, gaining social prestige and fulfilling the desires of himself and his family. It is also to be noted that basically there was only a slight, just an inter-changing, difference in the ambitions of entrepreneurs in Imphal West district and those in Imphal East District in respect of the top three ambitions.

3.3 Reasons compelling entrepreneurs to enter industry

Sometimes the compulsion rather than the ambition leads the man to success. At times, the initial aspirations and the opportunities may clash with each other. Then the destiny is shaped none other than by the compulsions encountered by the individual. Sometimes, one may be thrown out of his job all of a sudden or he may remain unemployed for long time after his education. There are also cases of people who start tiny industry as a diversification of economic interests and ultimately making lakhs of rupees and providing employment to others in hundreds. Such is the importance of the element of compulsion in everyday life. Hence, it is thought appropriate to examine the reasons that might have compelled the entrepreneurs to pursue entrepreneurship.

Table 3.2 shows that the compulsion number one that have compelled the entrepreneurs in both the districts was the diversification of economic interests (31.3 per cent). 'Unemployment' was the number two compulsion of the Imphal West District that has driven 24.7 per cent of the entrepreneurs to the industry whereas 'dissatisfaction' with the previous job held' has shaped the destiny of 25.7 per cent of the entrepreneurs to become industrialists in Imphal East District. 18.3 per cent of the Imphal West District entrepreneurs ranked 'dissatisfaction with the previous job held' as number three compelling reason while 22.0 per cent of the Imphal East District entrepreneurs mentioned 'unemployment' as the

Table 3.2
Reasons Compelling Entrepreneurs to Enter Industry

Ambitions	Imphal West District					Rank	Imphal East District					Both			Rank
	Entrepreneurs' Ranking			Weigh-ted score	Rat-ing (%)		Entrepreneurs' Ranking			Weigh-ted	Rat-ing (%)	Rank	Weight-ted score	Rat-ing (%)	
	One	Two	Three				One	Two	Three						
Unemployment	17	3	5	62	24.7	2	9	10	1	48	22	3	110	23.5	2
Dissatisfaction with the previous job held	9	9	1	46	18.3	3	13	8	1	56	25.7	2	102	21.8	3
To make use of idle funds	3	12	4	37	14.7	4	3	6	1	22	10.1	4	59	12.6	4
Diversification of economic interests	17	9	7	76.	30.3	1	17	4	12	71	32.6	1	147	31.3	1
Others*	8	1	4	30	12	5	4	4	1	21	9.6	5	51	10.9	5
No compelling reasons	2	22	45	0	-	-	4	18	34	0	-	-	0	-	-
Total	56	56	56	251	100		50	50	50	218	100		469	100	

Source : Field Survey
* 'Others' **includes maintenance of large families, revival of sick unit started by father etc.**

number three. Compelling reason that ranked fourth in both the districts is making use of idle funds (12.6 per cent).

It may be interesting to note that 6 entrepreneurs, 2 from Imphal West District and 4 from Imphal East District, had no compelling reason to start industry. Moreover, 40 entrepreneurs, 22 from Imphal West District and 18 from Imphal East District had not mentioned any number two compelling reason. Likewise, 35 entrepreneurs of the Imphal West District and 34 entrepreneurs of the Imphal East District didn't find any number three compelling reason to start industry.

It is not an easy task to differentiate between one's ambition and compulsion. What is an ambition for one entrepreneur may be a compulsion for another. It is the entrepreneurs' attitudes that ultimately make the difference.

3.4 Factors facilitating entrepreneurship

Ambitions or compulsions alone may not make an entrepreneur. Sometimes, the encouragement he got from his family members or his friends and relatives, the experience he gained in employment, the skills he acquired or inherited etc., also facilitate the exercise of entrepreneurship. Many factors may comes up in the way of starting an industry. For example, encouragement of the family elders is very much needed in the process of starting an unit. If they are reluctant, quite naturally, it is difficult to expect support from others including entrepreneur's wife. Moreover, first generation entrepreneurs generally face strong opposition from their parents as occupation pursued by the family so far is different from what is going to be done by the entrepreneur. Therefore, an attempt has been made to examine whether there were any such facilitating factors.

Table 3.3 demonstrates the factors facilitating the emergence of entrepreneurship. Previous experience in manufacturing was rated highest (33.2 per cent) of all the facilitating factors in both the two districts. The next important factor facilitating entrepreneurship was the encouragement of family members/relatives/friends (26.5 per cent). Success stories of entrepreneurs were ranked as the third important factor (15.6 per cent). Closely followed, acquired or inherited professional and technical skills was rated as the fourth factor facilitating the entrepreneurship. This is the overall position in both the districts.

It is clear from the above analysis that there are at least two important factors facilitating entrepreneurship apart from a few others. They are previous experience in manufacturing and encouragement of family members/ relatives / friends. These two were ranked first and second most important factor in both the Imphal West District and Imphal East District.

3.5 Expectations of entrepreneurs

Expectations of the entrepreneurs which stimulated their desire to jump into entrepreneurship and the degree of fulfillment of such expectations is enquired in this section. It is quite natural that many of the entrepreneurs expect a lot from the state government and other non-government agencies. Whether these expectations get fulfilled or not, they initiate a useful function in stimulating the desire of the entrepreneur to start an industry.

In this study, a long list of possible expectations or aspirations are given to the entrepreneurs and asked to mark any expectation or expectations that had stimulated their desire to enter industry. Table 3.4 shows the distribution of the expectations. Even though a long list of expectations are given to the entrepreneurs, 19.6 per cent (11 out of 56 entrepreneurs) of the Imphal West District and 28 per cent (14 out of 50 entrepreneurs) of the Imphal East District entrepreneurs admitted that they had no expectations as such. Many of the entrepreneurs (73 out of the total 106) expected financial assistance from State Government, Manipur Industrial Development Corporation (MANIDCO) and other state and national agencies. Expectation of getting technical assistance from the government/non-government agencies ranked second in Imphal East District (6.0 per cent) as well as in Imphal West District (8.9 per cent). Whereas in Imphal West District, expectation of availability of skilled labour was ranked as equal as the expectation of getting technical assistance (8.9 per cent). Only 3 entrepreneurs in Imphal West District and 1 in Imphal East District expected getting of anciliary relation with large firms.

Table 3.3
Factors Facilitating Entrepreneurship

Ambitions	Imphal West District					Rank	Imphal East District						Both			Rank
	Entrepreneurs' Ranking			Weigh-ted score	Rat-ing (%)		Entrepreneurs' Ranking			Weigh-ted	Rat-ing (%)	Rank	Weight-ted score	Rat-ing (%)		
	One	Two	Three				One	Two	Three							
Success stories of entrepreneurs	11	6	2	47	15.4	3	10	7 -	-	44	15.8	3	91	15.6		3
Previous experience in manufacturing	27	6	-	93	30.5	1	31	4	-	101	36.2	1	194	33.2		1
Previous employment in industry	-	3	1	7	2.3	7	1	1	-	4	1.4	6	11	1.9		6
Property-inherited/ acquired/wife's	4	6	1	25	8.2	5	1	4	1	12	4.3	5	37	6.3		5
Encouragement of family members/ relatives/friends	8	25	5	79	25.9	2	5	28	5	76	27.2	2	155	26.5		2

Acquired or inherited professional and technical skills	3	5	24	43	14.1	4	1	3	33	42	15.1	4	85	14.6	4
Others*	2	-	5	11	3.6	6	-	-	-	-	-	-	11	1.9	6
No. of entrepreneurs not responding	1	5	18	0	-	-	1	3	11	0	-	-	0		
Total	56	. 56	56	305	100		50	50	50	279	100		584	100	

Source : Field Survey

* **'Others'** includes availability of raw material, nearness to markets, existence of similar units in the locality etc.

Table 3.4
Distribution of Expectations Stimulating the Entrepreneurs' Desire to Start Industry

Expectations	District		Both
	Imphal West	Imphal East	
1. Allotment of plot/shed in industrial estate.	1 (1.8)	-	1 (0.9)
2. Financial corporations from State Govt./Financial corporations and other state agencies	40 (71.4)	33 (66.0)	73 (68.9)
3. Technical assistance from the Govt./non-government agencies.	5 (8.9)	3 (6.0)	8 (7.6)
4. Government assistance in machinery and raw material.	1 (1.8)	-	1 (0.9)
5. Ancillary relation with large firms	3 (5.3)	1 (2.0)	4 (3.8)
6. Availability of skilled labour	5 (8.9)	2 (4.0)	7 (6.6)
7. Support of dependable partners/ shareholders	3 (3.6)	-	3 (2.8)
8. Others*	2 (3.6)	-	2 (1.9)
9. No. of entrepreneurs not responding.	11 (19.6)	14 (28)	25 (23.6)
Total	56 (100.00)	50 (100.00)	106 (100.00)

Source : Field Survey
Note: Figures in parentheses indicate per centages to total.

And 2 entrepreneurs of the Imphal West District had 'others' expectations which includes financial assistance from moneylenders, government assistance in the sale of finished products, securing favours at political or official level etc.

This analysis draws the following conclusions: State agencies like the MANIDCO, the nationalised banks and more particularly, the self-employment schemes initiated by the central Government are stimulating agents of entrepreneurship. Considerable assistance is also expected from the government agencies as regards technical aspects. What is expected from partners and shareholders, government assistance in machinery and raw-material are the least.

3.6 Entrepreneurs' expectations and its fulfillment

Here, the expectations of the entrepreneurs is sought to be self-assessed by the entrepreneurs themselves. Table 3.5 demonstrates the degree of fulfillment of the entrepreneurs' expectations.

Table 3.5
The Degree of Fulfillment of Entrepreneur's Expectations

Degree of Fulfillment	District		Both
	Imphal West	Imphal East	
Fulfilled	12 (21.4)	13 (26.0)	25(23.6)
Party fulfilled	20 (35.7)	11 (22.0)	31(29.3)
Unfulfilled	13 (23.2)	12 (24.0)	25 (23.6)
No. of Entrepreneurs having no expectations	11 (19.6)	14 (28.0)	25 (23.6)
Total	56 (100.0)	50 (100.0)	106 (100.0)

Source : Field Survey.
Note: Figures in parentheses indicate per centage to total.

Only 21.4 per cent of the Imphal West District (12 out of 56) and 26.0 per cent of the Imphal East District (13 out of 50) entrepreneurs fulfilled their expectations. The expectations of 29.3 per cent of the total entrepreneurs (31 out of 106) are partly fulfilled. Again, 13 entrepreneurs of the Imphal West District remained unfulfilled as regards their expectations. It was 12 in the case of Imphal East District. As pointed out earlier, 25 entrepreneurs had no prior expectations to enter into entrepreneurship. This explains the realistic attitude of the entrepreneurs in general. The expectancy gap is broader perhaps because many of them have the expectation of getting financial assistance from government or other sources.

3.7 Discouraging factors in the process of setting up/commencement of the unit.

After the unit has been located at the selected district, here an enquiry is made to ascertain whether there had been any reason or factors which slowed down the process of setting up or commencement of their units by the entrepreneurs. As regards this, Table 3.6 observed that the major problem of the entrepreneurs was the shortage of working capital which was rated as rank one in both the districts (31.5 per cent). Another second important discouraging factor was delay in commencement of production which arises due to want of materials, skilled workmen, power connection etc. (20.3 per cent). Delay in construction of shed was also another reason which slowed down the process of commencement of the unit (10.7 per cent). But, it is interesting to note that 39.3 per cent (22 out of 56) entrepreneurs of Imphal West District started their units without having any discouraging headache at the beginning.

The above analysis proves that the main factor responsible for slow commencement of the industrial unit was shortage of working capital. This automatically points to the inadequate banking facilities in the state or poor banking habits of the entrepreneurs.

3.8 Friend, philosopher and guide of the entrepreneur

The entrepreneur might have come up on his own or on being shaped, encouraged and motivated by somebody else. The person whoever has an instrumental role in making the entrepreneur is described as his friend, philosopher and guide. The meaning of the term is taken in the sense of a motivator, not its literal one. The main interest is to find the man responsible for infusing the spirit of enterprise in the entrepreneur. With this objective, the sample respondents were asked to indicate the persons who have encouraged them to venture towards entrepreneurship.

Entrepreneurs' responses are shown in Table 3.7. 51.9 per cent of the entrepreneurs (55 out of 106) gave the names of either their family members or relatives as friend, philosopher and guide. While 20.8 per cent of the entrepreneurs were motivated by their friends, 15.1per cent were encouraged by institutional agencies' advice to start industries. Among the institutions, Small Industries Service Institute, Takyelpat (SISI), Imphal, All Manipur Entrepreneurs' Association (AMEA), Institute of Co-operative Management (ICM), Imphal etc. can be mentioned. However, there were 10.4 per cent of the entrepreneurs not motivated by any outside individual but they received the motivation from within. Only 1.9 per cent of them didn't give response as to who encouraged and shaped their destiny as entrepreneur.

It is worth mentioning that self motivated entrepreneurs constituted 63.6 per cent in Imphal West District while they were 36.4 per cent in Imphal East District. In contrast, entrepreneurs motivated by friends were more in Imphal East District (54.5 per cent) than in Imphal West District (45.5 per cent).

The analysis below (Table 3.7) signifies that less number of entrepreneurs were self-motivated. As majority of them are motivated by family and relatives, it is to be seen in later chapter whether their ventures are a success or failure.

3.9 Satisfaction with location of unit

The enquiry is limited only to the citing aspects of Imphal West and Imphal East Districts. The interest is confined to ascertain the pulse of the entrepreneurs about the site where their industrial unit is located. Another important consideration taken for evaluation of satisfaction with location of unit is the common facilities found in the two districts. These facilities include banks, post-office, water, electricity, raw-material servicing ventures, testing laboratories for raw-materials and products etc.

Table 3.8 shows the entrepreneurs' assessment of the satisfaction with location of their units in the two districts. 58.9 per cent (33 out of 56) entrepreneurs of Imphal West District expressed their thorough satisfaction with the location of their units while that was only 8.0 per cent (4 out of 50) in Imphal East District. In the overall situation, 34.9 per cent (37 out of 106) entrepreneurs expressed thorough satisfaction.

Table 3.6
Factors Discouraging the Process of Selling up/Commencement of the Unit

Ambitions	Imphal West District					Rank	Imphal East District					Both			Rank
	Entrepreneurs' Ranking			Weighted score	Rating (%)		Entrepreneurs' Ranking			Weighted	Rating (%)	Rank	Weighted score	Rating (%)	
	One	Two	Three				One	Two	Three						
Delay in allotment of plot	4	-	-	12	8.9	5	2	1	-	8	5.5	4	20	6.9	5
Delay in construction of shed	5	1	-	17	11.7	3	3	2	1	14	9.6	3	31	10.7	3
Delay in erection of machinery	2	4	-	14	9.7	4	1	5	1	14	9.6	3	28	9.6	4
Delay in commencement of production	6	7	1	33	22.8	2	7	2	1	26	17.8	2	59	20.3	2
Shortage of working capital	14	6	1	55	37.9	1	17	11	-	73	50	1	128	44	1
Lack of technical guidance	1	-	3	6	4.1	7	1	2	-	7	4.8	5	13	4.5	6
Others	2	1	-	8	5.5	6	-	2	-	4	2.7	6	12	4.1	7

No. of entrepreneurs having no discouraging factors.	22	37	51	0	-	-	19	25	47	0	-	-	0	-	-
Total	56	56	56	145	100		50	50	50	146	100		291	100	

Source : Field Survey

* **'Others'** includes delayed clearance by the Dept. of industries or other govt. agencies, want of installation of machinery etc.

In addition 37.7 per cent (40 out of 106) entrepreneurs are satisfied. Thus, the per centage of entrepreneurs who are either thoroughly satisfied or satisfied in both the districts is over 72.0 per cent (77 out of 106). Other entrepreneurs (24 out of 106) are either not satisfied (19.8 per cent) or never seriously thought about the location of their units (2.8 per cent). It is interesting to note that the number of entrepreneurs not responding in this regard is 5 in Imphal West District while there is none in Imphal East District.

Table 3.7
Persons Who Shaped the Destiny of Entrepreneurs

Persons	District		Total
	Imphal West	Imphal East	
Friend			
Count	10	12	22
% within Persons	45.5	54.5	100
% within District	17.9	24	20.8
% of total	9.4	11.3	20.8
Self			
Count	7	4	11
% within Persons	63.6	36.4	100
% within District	12.5	8	10.4
% of total	6.6	3.8	10.4
Family and relatives			
Count	28	27	55
% within Persons	50.9	49.1	100
% within District	50	54	51.9
% of total	26.4	25.5	51.9
Institutional agencies' advice			
Count	9	7	16
% within Persons	56.3	43.8	100
% within District	16.1	14	15.1
% of total	8.5	6.6	15.1

(contd.)

Persons	District		Total
	Imphal West	Imphal East	
No. of entrepreneurs not responding			
Count	2		2
% within Persons	100		100
% within District	3.6		1.9
% of total	1.9		1.9
Total			
Count	56	50	106
% within Persons	52.8	47.2	100
% within District	100	100	100
% of total	52.8	47.2	100

Source : Field Survey

Table 3.8
Satisfaction of Location of Unit

Entrepreneurs' Assessment	District		Both
	Imphal West	Imphal East	
Thoroughly satisfied	33 (58.9)	4 (8.0)	37 (34.9)
Satisfied	3 (5.4)	37 (74.0)	40(37.7)
Not satisfied	12 (21.4)	9 (18.0)	21 (19.8)
Never seriously thought about it	3 (5.4)	-	3 (2.8)
No. of entrepreneurs not responding	5 (8.9)	-	5 (4.7)
Total	56 (100.0)	50 (100.0)	106 (100.0)

Source: Field Survey
Note: Figures in parentheses indicate per centage to total.

Thus, it is found that majority of the entrepreneurs under study are satisfied with the location of their units. It will go hand-in-hand with the development of entrepreneurship in small scale industries.

Table 3.9
Reasons for Dissatisfaction with the Location of Unit

Ambitions	Imphal West District					Rank	Imphal East District					Both			Rank
	Entrepreneurs' Ranking			Weigh-ted score	Rat-ing (%)		Entrepreneurs' Ranking			Weigh-ted	Rat-ing (%)	Rank	Weight-ted score	Rat-ing (%)	
	One	Two	Three				One	Two	Three						
Inaccessibility to raw-materials	1	-	-	3	7.3	4	-	-	-	-	-	-	3	4.3	4
Inaccessibility of markets	2	2	-	10	24.4	2	-	1	-	2	6.9	2	12	17.1	2
Non-availability of skilled labour	2	-	-	6	14.6	3	-	-	-	-	-	-	6	8.6	3
Inadequate common facilities	7	-	1	22	53.7	1	9	-	-	27	93.1	1	49	70	1
No. of entrepreneurs not responding	-	10	11	0	-	-	-	8	9	0		-			
Total	12	12	12	41	100		9	9	9	29	100		70	100	

Source : Field Survey

Reasons for dissatisfaction from 21 entrepreneurs who are not satisfied with the location of their unit are solicited. Table 3.9 observed the reasons for their dissatisfaction. Inadequate common facilities were rated highest as reason number one by 7 out of 12 dissatisfied entrepreneurs of Imphal West District. The dissatisfaction reason number one specified by all the 9 entrepreneurs of Imphal East District was also the same. To be more precise, lack of water supply, erratic power condition and more specially, lack of testing laboratory for raw-materials and products are some of the inadequate common facilities availed by the entrepreneurs. The second reason was inaccessibility to markets. It was rated 24.4 per cent by Imphal West District entrepreneurs whereas 6.9 per cent rating was given by Imphal East District entrepreneurs.

REFERENCES

1. Wytinsky, India : The Awakening Giant, P. 187
2. Ram K. Vepa, "Entrepreneurship for Development of Backward Areas," National Productivity Council, New Delhi, 1973, PP. 14 -15.
3. Ibid., P. 16.
4. John Kenneth Galbraith, "Economic Development' Havard University Press, Cambridge, 1969, P. 15.
5. Data relating to reasons compelling entrepreneurs to enter industry, factors facilitating entrepreneurship, entrepreneurs choice of type of industries etc. is also elicited and evaluated similarly in the ensuing sections of this chapter.

CHAPTER IV

PROMOTION OF ENTERPRISES

4.1 Introduction

Promotion of an enterprise involves a long process, having different stages. Apart from being complicated with legal requirements, these stages need various non-legal formalities to be satisfied for the starting of an industrial unit. Right from the conception of an idea to start an unit until its registration, crucial decisions need to be taken by the entrepreneur at various stages. For example, where the industrial unit is to be located? What type of industry is to be started? Is there any feasibility study to be undertaken? How much capital should be invested? Where and how to acquire entrepreneurial skills? etc., are some of the sensitive areas where important decisions are required to be taken. Once a wrong decision is made in this context, huge losses are to be incurred by the entrepreneur in the days to come. Hence, the task of promoting an enterprise can be considered an issue of utmost concern for the entrepreneur.

Taking into consideration the starting of an industrial unit as an important stage of entrepreneurship, this chapter attempted to analyze in detail the promotional efforts of the sample respondents in starting their respective units.

4.2 Feasibility study of the enterprise

Nowadays, every business is surrounded by so many risks. Before starting an industrial unit, the feasibility study is usually carried out in order to confront such risks or uncertainties. Whether there will be enough demand for the product desired to be produced? If so, how long will the demand last? Whether the necessary technology will be available locally or not? If it is to be obtained from outside the state or country, will it be possible to purchase or import? Whether the necessary raw-material will be available or not? What kind of human resource will be required? Whether skill labour will be available or not? What will be the labour cost? Is there any specific government policy regarding the type of industry proposed to be started? etc., are some of the uncertainties confronted with the entrepreneur at the stage of floating a business. The entrepreneur needs clear answers to these questions before making his efforts to start the business. A crucial decision whether to go ahead with the proposal or to drop it is made at this stage. A weak decision either way will ultimately make the prospects of the entrepreneur depressing. Thus, two things are to be clearly established at this stage-whether the proposed industry will be profitable or not and whether it will be feasible or not. For establishing it, the market conditions and the prevailing situation should be elaborately studied by the entrepreneur himself or through other experienced agencies in this field. This is called as feasibility study of the project. An attempt is made here to find out whether the entrepreneurs under study have undertaken any feasibility study or not? If so, whose help they have sought? Who are the entrepreneurs undertaking the feasibility study through other agencies? In what type of industry, the feasibility study has been undertaken, etc.

Table 4.1 shows the district-wise feasibility study undertaken by the sample respondents. 55.6 per cent of the entrepreneurs undertook feasibility study of their projects while the rest had not undertaken any kind of feasibility study. Out of these, 26.4 per cent (28 out of 106) conducted the study themselves whereas 29.2 per cent (31 out 106) took the help of other outside agencies in undertaking the study.

Individually, however, it can be observed that 30.0 per cent (15 out of 50) entrepreneurs of Imphal East District conducted the study themselves whereas it was only 23.2 per cent (13 out of 56) in Imphal West District. Besides, the table shows that greater dependence upon outside agencies could be noticed in Imphal West District (33.9 per cent) than in Imphal East District (24.0 per cent).

Table 4.1
Feasibility Study : District-wise Classification

Feasibility study	District		Total
	Imphal West	Imphal East	
Conducted by self			
Count	13	15	28
% within Feasibility study	46.4	53.6	100
% within District	23.2	30	26.4
% of Total	12.3	14.2	26.4
Conducted through outside agencies			
Count	19	12	31
% within Feasibility study	61.3	38.7	100
% within District	33.9	24	29.2
% of Total	17.9	11.3	29.2
Study not undertaken			
Count	24	23	47
% within Feasibility study	51.1	48.9	100
% within District	42.9	46	44.3
% of Total	22.6	21.7	44.3
Total			
Count	**56**	**50**	**106**
% within Feasibility study	**52.8**	**47.2**	**100**
% within District	**100**	**100**	**100**
% of Total	**52.8**	**47.2**	**100**

Source : Field Survey.

The agencies who helped the entrepreneurs in undertaking feasibility study of the project were the District Industries Centre, Manipur, financial institutions like Manipur Industrial Development Corporation (MANIDCO), commercial banks and also the family members/relatives.

It can be concluded that more than half of the entrepreneurs under study undertook feasibility study of their respective projects. While some carried out the study themselves, others took the help of outside agencies. The fact that some entrepreneurs undertook feasibility study themselves and some through outside agencies prompts us to verify whether it has anything to do with their age, education, religion, rural/urban background, type of industry, etc.

(i) Age of entrepreneurs

As seen in Table 4.2, 46.4 per cent (13 out of 28) entrepreneurs who had conducted feasibility study themselves were found in the age group of 21-30 years whereas that of 35.7 per cent (10 out of 28) were found in the age group of 31-40 years. Only 3.6 per cent and 14.3 per cent conducted their feasibility study themselves in the age group of 20 & below and 41-50 years.

Table 4.2
Age of Entrepreneurs Vs Undertaking of Feasibility Study

Age of Entrepreneurs	Feasibility Study			
	Conducted by Self	Conducted through other agencies	Not under-taken	Total
20 years & below				
Count	1		7	8
% within age of entrepreneurs	12.5		87.5	100
% within Feasibility study	3.6		14.9	7.5
% of Total	0.9		6.6	7.5
21-30 years				
Count	13	14	21	48
% within age of entrepreneurs	27.1	29.2	43.8	100
% within Feasibility study	46.4	45.2	44.7	45.3
% of Total	12.3	13.2	19.8	45.3

(contd.)

Table 4.2 *(contd.)*

Age of Entrepreneurs	Feasibility Study			
	Conducted by Self	Conducted through other agencies	Not under-taken	Total
31-40 years				
Count	10	12	9	31
% within age of entrepreneurs	32.3	38.7	29	100
% within Feasibility study	35.7	38.7	19.1	29.2
% of Total	9.4	11.3	8.5	29.2
41-50 years				
Count	4	5	4	13
% within age of entrepreneurs	30.8	38.5	30.8	100
% within Feasibility study	14.3	16.1	8.5	12.3
% of Total	3.8	4.7	3.8	12.3
51 years & above				
Count			6	6
% within age of entrepreneurs			100	100
% within Feasibility study			12.8	5.7
% of Total			5.7	5.7
Total				
Count	28	31	47	106
% within age of entrepreneurs	26.4	29.2	44.3	100
% within Feasibility study	100	100	100	100
% of Total	26.4	29.2	44.3	100

Source : Field Survey.

Moreover, it has been noticed that with the increase in the age of entrepreneurs starting from 21-30 years group, less number of entrepreneurs depends upon outside agencies for conducting their feasibility study. The maximum dependence is found in the age group of 21-30 years (45.2 per cent) whereas the minimum is found in 41-50 years (16.1 per cent). More interestingly, all the entrepreneurs in the 51 & above years group didn't conduct any feasibility study. It is, perhaps, due to the difference in the maturity level of entrepreneurs.

(ii) Educational level of entrepreneurs

Table 4.3 observed that more educated entrepreneurs undertook the feasibility study through other experienced agencies and less educated entrepreneurs mostly took the study themselves.

Table 4.3
Educational Qualification of Entrepreneurs Vs Undertaking of Feasibility Study

Educational level of Entrepreneurs	Feasibility Study			
	Conducted by Self	Conducted through other agencies	Not under-taken	Total
Under -Matriculates				
Count	1		11	12
% within Educational level	8.3		91.7	100
% within Feasibility study	3.6		23.4	11.3
% of Total	0.9		10.4	11.3
Matriculates				
Count	4	2	11	17
% within Educational level	23.5	11.8	64.7	100
% within Feasibility study	14.3	6.5	23.4	26.4
% of Total	3.8	1.9	10.4	26.4
Under-Graduates				
Count	8	5	15	28
% within Educational level	28.6	17.9	53.6	100
% within Feasibility study	28.6	16.1	31.9	26.4
% of Total	7.5	4.7	14.2	26.4

(contd.)

Table 4.3 *(contd.)*

Educational level of Entrepreneurs	Feasibility Study			
	Conducted by Self	Conducted through other agencies	Not under-taken	Total
Graduates				
Count	12	17	10	39
% within Educational level	30.8	43.6	25.6	100
% within Feasibility study	42.9	54.8	21.3	36.8
% of Total	11.3	16	9.4	36.8
Post -Graduates				
Count	3	7		10
% within Educational level	30	70		100
% within Feasibility study	10.7	22.6		9.4
% of Total	2.8	6.6		9.4
Total				
Count	28	31	47	106
% within Educational level	26.4	29.2	44.3	100
% within Feasibility study	100	100	100	100
% of Total	26.4	44.3	44.3	100

Source : Field Survey.

For example, out of 31 entrepreneurs who carried out the study through other agencies, 17 are graduates (54.8 per cent) and 7 are post-graduates (22.6 per cent), whereas nearly half of the entrepreneurs who undertook the feasibility study themselves were only upto under graduation (46.5 per cent).

It is also interesting to note that the number of entrepreneurs who never conducted any feasibility study decreases with the increase in the educational level of the entrepreneurs. For example, 91.7 per cent (11 out of 12) of the under matriculate entrepreneurs didn't conduct any feasibility study whereas only 25.6 per cent (10 out of 39) graduate entrepreneurs didn't find any reason to conduct the study. Hence, it can be concluded that education of entrepreneurs has a direct relation with the undertaking of feasibility study of the project.

(iii) Religion of entrepreneurs

In respect of religion, its has been found that 26.0 per cent (25 out of 96) Hindu entrepreneurs carried out the feasibility study themselves and that of 31.3 per cent (30 out of 96) have gone in for outside agencies (Table 4.4). In case of Muslim entrepreneurs, only 20.0 per cent (1 out of 4) conducted the study themselves. It was in the case of Sikh entrepreneurs that two-thirds conducted the study either themselves or through other agencies.

Table 4.4
Religion of Entrepreneurs and Feasibility Study

Religion of Entrepreneurs	Feasibility Study			
	Conducted by Self	Conducted through other agencies	Not under-taken	Total
Hindu				
Count	25	30	41	96
% within Religion	26	31.3	42.7	10
% within Feasibility study	89.3	96.8	87.2	90.6
% of Total	23.6	28.3	38.7	90.6
Muslim				
Count	1		4	5
% within Religion	20		80	100
% within Feasibility study	3.6		8.5	1.9
% of Total	9		3.8	1.9

(contd.)

Table 4.4 *(contd.)*

Religion of Entrepreneurs	Feasibility Study			Total
	Conducted by Self	Conducted through other agencies	Not undertaken	
Christian				
Count	1		1	2
% within Religion	50		50	100
% within Feasibility study	3.6		2.1	1.9
% of Total	0.9		0.9	1.9
Sikh				
Count	1	1	1	1
% within Religion	33.3	33.3	33.3	100
% within Feasibility study	3.6	3.2	2.1	2.8
% of Total	0.9	0.9	0.9	2.8
Total				
Count	28	31	47	106
% within Religion	26	29.2	44.3	100
% within Feasibility study	100	100	100	100
% of Total	26.4	29.2	44.3	100

Source : Field Survey.

(iv) Rural / urban background of entrepreneurs

It may be expected that in comparison with entrepreneurs having rural background, those having urban background can carry out feasibility study themselves or through other agencies. But this expectation has not come true in the present study. For example, out of the 64 entrepreneurs with rural background, 26.6 per cent (17 entrepreneurs) conducted the study themselves and 34.4 per cent (22 entrepreneurs) conducted the study through other agencies. On the other hand, out of 42 entrepreneurs with urban background, only 26.2 per cent (11 entrepreneurs) conducted the study themselves and

21.4 per cent (9 entrepreneurs) depended on outside agencies for conducting the study (Table 4.5).

Table 4.5
Rural / Urban Background of Entrepreneurs and Feasibility Study

Background of Entrepreneurs	Feasibility Study			
	Conducted by Self	Conducted through other agencies	Not under-taken	Total
Urban				
Count	11	9	22	42
% within Background	26.2	21.4	52.4	100
% within Feasibility Study	39.3	29	46.8	39.6
% of Total	10.4	8.5	20.8	39.6
Rural				
Count	17	22	25	64
% within Background	26.6	34.4	39.1	100
% within Feasibility Study	60.7	71	53.2	60.4
% of Total	16	20.8	23.6	60.4
Total				
Count	28	31	47	106
% within Background	26.4	29.2	44.3	100
% within Feasibility Study	100	100	100	100
% of Total	26.4	29.2	44.3	100

Source : Field Survey.

Thus, we can conclude that rural background cannot be a disadvantage to the entrepreneurs in carrying out the feasibility study.

(v) Type of industry

It may be seen from Table 4.6 that those who started plastic and rubber based industries had not undertaken any feasibility study by themselves. 75.0 per cent (9 out of 12) of them depended on outside agencies for conducting the study. On the other hand, 21.4 per cent (3 out of 14) of the entrepreneurs who started metal based industries conducted the feasibility study by themselves, leaving no room for outsiders.

The highest per centage of entrepreneurs who conducted the study themselves were found in the automobile and engineering works (7.5 per cent) whereas that of entrepreneurs who depended on outside agencies were found in plastic & rubber based industries (8.6 per cent).

Table 4.6
Type of Industry and Feasibility Study

Type of Industry	Feasibility Study			
	Conducted by Self	Conducted through other agencies	Not under-taken	Total
Food based				
Count	3	8	6	17
% within Industry	17.6	47.1	35.3	100
% within Feasibility Study	10.7	25.8	12.8	15
% of Total	2.8	7.5	5.7	16
Metal based				
Count	3		11	14
% within Industry	21.3		78.6	100
% within Feasibility Study	10.7		23.4	13.2
% of Total	2.8		10.4	13.2
Handlooms & handicrafts				
Count	3	1	4	8
% within Industry	37.5	12.5	50	100
% within Feasibility Study	10.7	3.2	8.5	7.5
% of Total	2.8	0.9	3.8	7.5
Plastics & rubber based				
Count		9	3	12
% within Industry		75	25	100
% within Feasibility Study		29	6.4	11.3
% of Total		8.5	2.8	11.3

(contd.)

Type of Industry	Feasibility Study			
	Conducted by Self	Conducted through other agencies	Not under-taken	Total
Wood based				
Count	4	3	8	15
% within Industry	26.7	20	53.3	100
% within Feasibility Study	14.3	9.7	17	14.2
% of Total	3.8	2.8	7.5	14.2
Printing & stationery				
Count	5	3	2	10
% within Industry	50	30	20	100
% within Feasibility Study	17.9	9.7	4.3	9.4
% of Total	4.7	2.8	1.9	9.4
Automobiles & engineering				
Count	8	6	11	25
% within Industry	32	24	44	100
% within Feasibility Study	28.6	19.4	23.4	23.6
% of Total	7.5	5.7		23.6
Others				
Count	2	1	10.4	5
% within Industry	40	20	40	100
% within Feasibility Study	7.1	3.2	4.3	4.7
% of Total	1.9	0.9	1.9	4.7
Total				
Count	28	31	47	106
% within Industry	26.4	29.4	44.3	100
% within Feasibility Study	100	100	100	100
% of Total	26.4	29.2	44.3	100

Source : Field Survey.

(vi) Generation of entrepreneurs

Generation of entrepreneurs also influences the conduct of feasibility study. It may be observed from Table 4.7 that third generation entrepreneurs conduct the study only by themselves.

The first generation entrepreneurs depended mostly on outside agencies for conducting feasibility study (34.5 per cent) while 26.2 per cent conducted the same by themselves. The scene is just the opposite in case of second generation entrepreneurs. 23.8 per cent of them have faith in themselves for conducting the study whereas only 9.5 per cent carried out the study through other agencies.

Table 4.7
Generation of Entrepreneurs and Feasibility Study

Generation of Entrepreneurs	Feasibility Study			
	Conducted by Self	Conducted through other agencies	Not under-taken	Total
First				
Count	22	29	33	84
% within Generation	26.2	34.5	39.3	100
% within Feasibility Study	78.6	93.5	70.2	79.2
% of Total	20.8	27.4	31.1	79.2
Second				
Count	5	2	14	21
% within Generation	23.8	9.5	66.7	100
% within Feasibility Study	17.8	6.5	29.8	19.8
% of Total	4.7	1.9	13.2	19.8
Third				
Count	1			1
% within Generation	100			100
% within Feasibility Study	3.5			0.9
% of Total	0.9			0.9

(contd.)

Generation of Entrepreneurs	Feasibility Study			Total
	Conducted by Self	Conducted through other agencies	Not under-taken	
Total				
Count	28	31	47	106
% within Generation	26.4	29.2	44.3	100
% within Feasibility Study	100	100	100	100
% of Total	26.4	29.2	44.3	100

Source : Field Survey.

It is, perhaps, due to the difference in the degree of self-confidence of entrepreneurs.

(vii) Forms of organization

It has been observed that forms of organization also have an impact on the undertaking of feasibility study. Table 4.8 shows that all the entrepreneurs who started their units as private limited companies conducted the study either by themselves (50.0 per cent) or through other agencies (50.0 per cent).

Table 4.8
Forms of Organization and Feasibility Study

Forms of Organization	Feasibility Study			Total
	Conducted by Self	Conducted through other agencies	Not under-taken	
Private Ltd. Co				
Count	2	2		4
% within Organization	50	50		100
% within Feasibility Study	7.1	6.5		3.8
% of Total	1.9	1.9		3.8

(contd.)

Table 4.8 *(contd.)*

Forms of Organization	Feasibility Study			
	Conducted by Self	Conducted through other agencies	Not under-taken	Total
Partnership				
Count	2	6	4	12
% within Organization	16.7	50	33.3	100
% within Feasibility Study	7.1	19.4	8.5	11.3
% of Total	1.9	5.7	3.8	11.3
Sole Proprietorship				
Count	24	23	43	90
% within Organization	26.7	25.6	47.8	100
% within Feasibility Study	85.7	74.2	91.5	84.9
% of Total	22.6	21.7	40.6	84.9
Total				
Count	28	31	47	90
% within Organization	26.4	29.2	44.3	100
% within Feasibility Study	100	100	100	100
% of Total	26.4	29.2	44.3	100

Source : Field Survey.

50 per cent of the entrepreneurs who formed partnership firms conducted the study through outside agencies as against 16.7 per cent who conducted it by themselves. Regarding entrepreneurs who started units as sole proprietorship, more than half of them conducted the study either by themselves or through other agencies.

4.3 Choice of type of industry

Types of industries chosen by the entrepreneurs are explained in the previous chapter. But the reasons therefore are yet to be examined. In fact, selection of an industry type is not easy task. This task, perhaps, may lead to success or failure of an entrepreneur. The skillfulness of an entrepreneur is analysed in such selection. No other decision may be so important as this. The preference of a particular type of industry and the choice of suitable location are inter-related affairs. The expertise of professional guidance is required in such type of decision making. Once a mistake is committed, entrepreneurs can least afford to shift to another type of industry or location. As can be seen from Table 4.9, the ease with which previous employment in the industry (related or otherwise) influenced the entrepreneurs much in their preference of type of industries. 19.1 per cent of the total entrepreneurs have listed this as number one reason that influenced them. While this is the overall position in both the districts, individually there are some interesting aspects to be noted. In Imphal West District, it was listed as reason number two by 15.9 per cent entrepreneurs of the District. 17.5 per cent of the said District ranked reasons related to profession or occupation so far persued as number one reason influencing them to choose their types of industries. As regards to Imphal East District, 19.2 per cent of the entrepreneurs ranked reasons related to the profession or occupation persued so far as number two reason. The third important reason influencing the entrepreneurs to opt for a particular industry was 'no difficulty in securing machinery/raw-materials/skilled workmen'. 11.7 per cent of the Imphal West District and 17.7 per cent of the Imphal East District entrepreneurs ranked it as third reason. 11.7 per cent of the Imphal West District entrepreneurs, at the same time, ranked 'no difficulty in securing technical know-how' as the third reason, influencing them in choosing the industry type. The other important reasons cited by the entrepreneurs are 'no competition' (10.5 per cent), 'no difficulty in securing technical know-how' (9.8 per cent), 'previous employment in a related trade' (8.1 per cent). It is interesting to note that only 4.0 per cent of the total entrepreneurs choose industries which are easy to set up. Moreover, many of the entrepreneurs are not lured by the consideration of high margin of profits, which is rated 3.1 per cent and ranked last of the ten ranks. 'Others' reason was rated as 6.9 per cent and ranked seventh. It includes assured market, father's experience in related industry or trade, revival of sick unit, advice of family members, friends, relatives, etc.

Table 4.9

Reasons of Choosing Entrepreneurs' Types of Industry

Ambitions	Imphal West District					Rank	Imphal East District					Both			Rank
	Entrepreneurs' Ranking			Weighted score	Rating (%)		Entrepreneurs' Ranking			Weighted	Rating (%)	Rank	Weighted score	Rating (%)	
	One	Two	Three				One	Two	Three						
Easy to set up	5	1	3	20	6.5	7	-	1	3	3	1.1	10	23	4	8
High margin of profit	2	2	3	13	4.2	8	1	-	2	5	1.9	9	18	3.1	10
No difficulty in securing machinery/ raw-materials/ skilled workmen	3	9	9	36	11.7	3	2	13	16	48	17.7	3	84	14.5	3
Previous employment in the industry (related or otherwise)	15	1	2	49	15.9	2	20	1	-	62	22.9	1	111	19.1	1
Previous employment in a related trade	6	2	2	24	7.8	5	6	2	1	23	8.5	5	47	8.1	6
No competition	6	7	1	33	10.7	4	6	4	2	28	10.3	4	61	10.5	4

Related to the profession or occupation perused so far	11	9	3	54	17.5	1	9	12	1	52	19.2	2	106	18.3	2
No difficulty in securing technical know-how	-	13	10	36	11.7	3	-	7	7	21	7.8	6	57	9.8	5
Existence of similar industry in the neighbourhood	2	4	8	22	7.1	6	1	4	-	11	4.1	8	33	5.7	8
Others	6	1	2	22	7.1	6	1	4	-	18	6.6	7	40	6.9	7
No. of entre-preneurs not giving the reason	-	7	13	0	-	-	-	5	17	0	-	-	0	-	-
Total	56	56	56	309	100		50	50	50	271	100		580	100	

Source : Field Survey

* **'Others'** ambitions includes the desire to do among new or creative self-employment to youths, etc.

Entrepreneurs are not tempted by the existence of similar units in the neighborhood (only 5.7 per cent). May be they are afraid of competition. The reason 'no competition' influencing the preference of industry types, which is ranked fourth, support this view.

Selecting an industry type on reason like easy to set up or easy availability of technical know-how or easy availability of machinery or raw-materials are weaknesses of entrepreneurs. Banking on initial easiness is not enterprising. They may face problems in the future if they hesitate to take more pains in the beginning. But, it does not mean that choosing industries on such grounds will err the entrepreneurs in all the cases.

4.4 Reasons influencing entrepreneurs to locate their unit in the district

After discussing entrepreneurs' reasons for preference of their types of industries, here an attempt is made to examine entrepreneurs' reasons for the choice of the district as a location for their units. As observed in Table 4.10, the consideration of the hometown or nearness to native place ranked highest in the selection of the district as a suitable location of the industrial unit. 30.1 per cent of the Imphal West District and 33.0 of Imphal East District entrepreneurs rated this as number one rank. Overall idealness of the place for the industry was rated as number two rank by 22.8 per cent of the Imphal West District entrepreneurs whereas 23.0 per cent of the Imphal East District entrepreneurs rated nearness to markets as number two rank. While these are the individual situations in the two districts, nearness to markets (21.3 per cent) and overall idealness of the place for the industry (21.0 per cent) was rated as rank two and three respectively in the overall situation in both the two districts. The other major considerations that influenced the entrepreneurs in the order of importance (rating are given within brackets) are: nearness to raw materials (15.2 per cent), availability of plot/shed in the industrial estate (3.2 per cent), others (1.8 per cent) and existence of similar units in the neighbourhood (0.7 per cent). The top three reasons are rated 73.7 per cent. Of these, the first reason alone i.e., hometown or nearness to native place, is rated 31.5 per cent. Thus hometown or nearness to native place is more important than other reasons and the rating of other reasons are nowhere nearer to it.

To be concluded, the above analysis indicates that the entrepreneurs are very much reluctant to move away from their hometowns or native place or the district under consideration provides an ideal place for the industry chosen by them.

4.5 Time lag between commencement of production and other stages of promotion

In fact, there are some certain stages involved in the promotion of enterprises and complying with every stage of promotion involves some amount of time. It may be observed from Table 4.11 that between commencement of production and conception of idea to start unit in the Imphal West District, 32.1 per cent entrepreneurs reported a time lag of less than one year, 25.0 per cent a time lag of 1-2 years, 16.1 per cent 2-3 years, 8.9 per cent 3-4 years and 3.6 per cent 4 and above years. There was no time lag involved in respect of 14.3 per cent entrepreneurs in this district as their units were already established by their fathers. While 69.6 per cent of the entrepreneurs reported a time lag of less than one year between commencement of construction of shed and production, 82.1 per cent took less than one year between completion of construction of shed and commencement of production. Again, between installation of equipment and machinery and commencement of production, almost all the entrepreneurs (85.7 per cent) suffered a delay for less than one year. Quite a few (1.8 per cent each) suffered 1-2 years and 2-3 years between completion of construction of shed and commencement of production.

On the other hand, in Imphal East District, between conception of idea to start unit and commencement of production, a time lag of less than one year was reported by 46.0 per cent of the entrepreneurs, while 1-2 years was reported by another 26 per cent. 2-3 years delay was reported by 16 per cent and 3-4 years delay was reported by 4.0 per cent. 6.0 per cent reported a delay of 4.0 years & above. No time lag was reported by 2.0 per cent of the entrepreneurs. Between commencement of construction of shed and production, 86.0

Table 4.10
Reasons for Locating the Unit in the District

Ambitions	Imphal West District					Rank	Imphal East District					Both			Rank
	Entrepreneurs' Ranking			Weigh-ted score	Rat-ing (%)		Entrepreneurs' Ranking			Weigh-ted	Rat-ing (%)	Rank	Weight-ted score	Rat-ing (%)	
	One	Two	Three				One	Two	Three						
Availability of plot/ shed in the industrial estate.	5	1	1	18	5.5	6	-	1	-	2	0.7	8	20	3.2	6
Overall idealness of the place for the industry	19	7	4	75	22.8	2	13	7	2	55	18.9	3	130	21	3
Nearness to markets	3	14	28	65	19.8	3	6	14	21	67	23	2	132	21.3	2
Nearness to raw materials	1	16	8	43	13.1	4	1	17	14	51	17.5	4	94	15.2	4
Hometown or nearness to native place	23	13	4	99	30.1	1	29	3	3	96	33	1	195	31.5	1

Good transport facilities	3	4	5	22	6.7	5	-	4	4	12	4.1	5	34	5.5	5
Existence of similar units in the neighbourhood	-	-	1	1	0.3	8	-	1	1	3	1	7	4	0.7	8
Others*	2	0	-	6	1.8	7	1	1	-	5	1.7	6	11	1.8	7
No. of entre-preneurs not giving the reason	-	1	5	0	-		-	2	5	0	-	-	0	-	-
Total	56	56	56	329	100		50	50	50	291	100		620	100	

Source : Field Survey
* **'Others'** includes advice from family, relatives and friends, earlier job experience etc.

per cent of the entrepreneurs suffered a delay of less than one year and 4.0 per cent each reported a delay of 1-2 years, 2-3 years and 4 years & above. 92.0 per cent took less than one year between completion of construction of shed and commencement of production. Once equipment and machinery was installed, almost all of them (98.0 per cent) started production of their units within one year.

4.6 Financing the enterprises

In the promotion of an enterprise, the availability of enough finance is the most important factor, without it, the idea to start business or industry will always remain a simple wish. Even if the necessary finance is available, there are many obstacles in financing the small scale industries. These obstacles are always rated as high risks. In fact, the risk element is present in every industrial financing. But more significantly, a special[1] type of risk is associated with the small industry finance. This is because (a) Small firms have a limited pool of management capabilities and business experience, (b) Small firms are highly vulnerable to environment pressure and (c) Small firms are not always able to provide sufficient collateral to comply with assured repayment. Hence, financing a small scale industry is indeed a totally different problem in nature. Besides, the small units cannot enter the capital market on account of its organizational limitations. At the same time, the small entrepreneur is handicapped in his efforts to organize risk capital because his own savings are limited and his capacity to approach capital market is strictly limited. Therefore, he has to depend upon institutional and non-institutional sources for financing his unit.

(i) Initial capital invested

Regarding the initial capital invested in the enterprises, it may be seen from Table 4.12 that in both the districts, an amount upto Rs.2 lakhs were invested in the highest per centage of the enterprises (69.8 per cent).

Capital of more than Rs.10 lakhs was invested in 8.5 per cent of the units. District-wise, it may be observed that greater amount of capital was invested in units in Imphal West District (average capital Rs.3.5 lakhs) than in the units of Imphal East District (average capital Rs.3.2 lakhs).

Table 4.11

Time Lag between Commencement of Production and other Stages of Promotion

Stages of Promotion	Time Leg						
	< than a year	1-2 years	2-3 years	3-4 & above	4 years	No. appli-cability	Total
Imphal West District							
1. Conception of idea to start unit	18 (32.1)	14 (25.0)	9 (16.1)	5 (8.9)	2 (3.6)	8 (14.3)	56 (100.0)
2. Commencement of construction of shed	39 (69.6)	6 (10.7)	2 (3.6)	1 (1.8)	-	8 (14.3)	56 (100.0)
3. Completion of construction of shed	46 (82.1)	1 (1.8)	1 (1.8)	-	-	8 (14.3)	56 (100.0)
4. Installation of equipment & machinery	48 (85.7)	-	-	-	-	8 (14.3)	56 (100.0)
Imphal East District							
1. Conception of idea of start unit	23 (46.0)	13 (26.0)	8 (16.0)	2 (4.0)	3 (6.0)	1 (2.00	50 (100.0)
2. Commencement of construction of shed	43 (86.0)	2 (4.0)	2 (4.0)	-	2 (4.0)	1 (2.0)	50 (100.0)
3. Completion of construction of shed	46 (92.0)	2 (4.0)	1 (2.0)	-	-	1 (2.0)	50 (100.0)
4. Installation of equipment & machinery	49 (98.0)	-	-	-	-	1 (2.0)	50 (100.0)

Source : Field Survey.

Table 4.12
Initial Capital Invested in the Enterprises

Capital Invested (Rs. in lakhs)	Imphal West District	Imphal East District	Both
Upto 2	39 (69.6)	35 (70.0)	74 (69.8)
2-4	6 (10.7)	8 (16.00)	14 (13.2)
4-6	5 (8.9)	2 (4.0)	7 (6.6)
6-8	-	-	-
8-10	1 (1.8)	1 (2.0)	2 (1.9)
10 & >	5 (8.9)	4 (8.0)	9 (8.5)
Total	56 (100.0)	50 (100.0)	106 (100.0)

Source : Field Survey
Note : Figures in parenthesis indicate per centages to total.

(ii) Entrepreneurs' own capital

Table 4.13 shows the entrepreneurs' own share in the total initial capital invested in their units.

Table 4.13
Entrepreneurs' own share in the Initial Total Capital Structure

Per centage share of own capital	Imphal West District	Imphal East District	Both
Upto 25	12 (21.4)	11 (22.0)	23 (21.7)
25-50	11 (19.6)	8 (16.0)	19 (17.9)
50-75	6 (10.7)	3 (6.0)	9 (8.5)
75-100	27 (48.2)	28 (56.0)	55 (51.9)
Total	56 (100.0)	50 (100.0)	106 (100.0)

Source : Field Survey.
Note : Figures in parenthesis indicate per centages to total.

It can be noted that the highest per centage (51. 9 per cent) invested their own capital to extent ranging from 75-100 followed by those (21.7 per cent) who invested own capital ranging upto 25.0 per cent. Only a few entrepreneurs invested own capital ranging from 50-75 per cent (8.5 per cent).

District-wise, it can be seen that 19.6 per cent of the sample respondents had invested their own capital ranging from 25-50 per cent in Imphal West District, whereas in Imphal East District, such respondents formed only 16.0 per cent. Further, it can be observed that more entrepreneurs in Imphal East District invested own capital even beyond 75.0 per cent of the total initial capital.

It can thus be concluded that more than half of the total entrepreneurs started their industrial units at their own risks, depending less on institutional finance.

(iii) Sources of initial capital

It would be very interesting to enquire about the sources from where the entrepreneurs raised the initial capital. Table 4.14 shows the multiple responses given by the sample respondents, indicating the sources of initial capital. It reveals that the respondents depended more on family income as a source of initial capital. While as many as 50.0 per cent of the entrepreneurs in Imphal West District raised initial capital from family income, it was 62.0 per cent in Imphal East District. Next after family income, government agencies and commercial banks proves as another important source of initial capital. While this is the overall position, district-wise the position is a little different. Almost equal number of entrepreneurs depended on government agencies (16.0 per cent) for initial capital in both the two district. However, commercial banks plays a more important role as source of initial capital in Imphal West District (21.4 per cent) than in Imphal East District (8.0 per cent). Apart from these sources, the sources like employment, friends and relatives, sale of properties etc. were also depended upon for raising initial capital.

4.7 Skills of business – entrepreneurship development programmes (EDPs)

Running a business, whether large or small, requires the managerial skill. Since a small entrepreneur cannot employ management experts to manage his/her business, he/she needs to be imparted basic and essential managerial skills in the functional areas like finance, production and marketing.

Table 4.14
Sources of Initial Capital

Source	Imphal West District N-56 Multiple Responses	Imphal East District N-50 Multiple Responses	Both N= 106 Multiple Responses
Agriculture	1 (1.8)	-1 (0.0)	
Industry/trade	3 (5.4)	1 (2.0)	4 (3.8)
Salaries/Employment	4 (7.1)	3 (6.0)	7 (6.6)
Family Income	28 (50.0)	31 (62.0)	59 (55.7)
Sale of Land	1 (1.8)	3 (6.0)	4 (3. 8)
Sale of Business	2 (3.6)	1 (2.0)	3 (2.8)
Sale of Other Properties	2 (3.6)	2 (4.0)	4 (3.8)
Government Agencies	9 (16.1)	8 (16.0)	17 (16.0)
Commercial Banks	12 (21,4)	4 (8.0)	16 (15.1)
Friends & Relatives	4 (7.4)	3 (6.0)	7 (6.6)
Money Lenders	2 (3.6)	1 (2.0)	3 (2.8)

Source : Field Survey
Note : Figures in parentheses indicate per centage to total.

Developing entrepreneurship has become a movement in India in the recent years. In fact, it was the Kakinanda Experiment[2] that made people appreciate the need for and importance of the entrepreneurial training, now popularly known as EDP (Entrepreneurship Development Programme), to induce motivation and competence among the young and prospective entrepreneurs. At present, hundreds of EDPs are conducted by some 686 organizations to impart entrepreneurship training to participants in thousands.[3]

Keeping the importance of EDPs in the development of entrepreneurship in view, an attempt is here, made to evaluate the entrepreneurial quality or skills of the sample respondents. As can be seen from Table 4.15, 36.8 per cent of the entrepreneurs undertook training under EDPs conducted by various agencies like District Industry Centre of the Government, Small Industry Service Institute (SISI), Imphal, All Manipur Entrepreneurs Association (AMEA), Imphal, Manipur, Institute of Co-operative Management, Imphal, Manipur etc. Out of these, 59.0 per cent belongs to Imphal West District and the remaining 41.0 per cent belongs to Imphal East District. Between the two districts, nearly equal numbers of entrepreneurs had not joined any entrepreneurship development programmes.

The fact that some entrepreneurs undertook entrepreneurship training while the majority of them stays out of it necessitates to analyze whether it has anything to do with their age, religion, etc. Moreover, the usefulness of the training received and the reasons thereof for not attending it are enquired into in the following lines.

Table 4.15
Entrepreneurship Development Programmes and Districts

Undertaking of Entrepreneurship Development Programmes	District		Both
	Imphal West	Imphal East	
Yes			
Count	23	16	39
% within EDP	59	41	100.0
% within District	41.1	32	36.8
% of Total	21.7	15.1	36.8
No			
Count	33	34	67
% within EDP	49.3	50.7	100.0
% within District	58.9	68	63.2
% of Total	31.1	32.1	63.2
Total			
Count	**56**	**50**	**106**
% within EDP	52.8	47.2	100.0
% within District	100.0	100.0	100.0
% of Total	52.8	47.2	100.0

Source : Field Survey

(i) Age

It can be seen from Table 4.16 that the maximum per centage of entrepreneurs who received entrepreneurial training belongs into the age group 21-30 years (43.6 per cent). It was followed by those in the age group 31-40 years (41.0 per cent). It is quite interesting to note that only 0.9 per cent of the total entrepreneurs (1 out of 106) joined EDP in the age group 20 years and below. Further, no entrepreneurs in the age group 51 years and above joined any entrepreneurial training.

Table 4.16
Age of Entrepreneurs Vs Entrepreneurship Development Programmes

Age of Entrepreneurs	Undertaking of Entrepreneurship Development Programmes		
	Yes	No	Total
20 years & below			
Count	1	7	8
% within Age	12.5	87.5	100
% within EDP	2.6	10.4	7.5
% of Total	0.9	6.6	7.5
21 -30			
Count	17	31	48
% within Age	35.4	64.6	100
% within EDP	43.6	46.3	45.3
% of Total	16	29.2	45.3
31-40			
Count	16	15	31
% within Age	51.6	48.4	100
% within EDP	41	22.4	29.2
% of Total	15.1	14.2	29.2
41-50			
Count	5	8	13
% within Age	38.5	61.5	100
% within EDP	12.8	11.9	12.3
% of Total	4.7	7.5	12.3

(contd.)

Age of Entrepreneurs	Undertaking of Entrepreneurship Development Programmes		
	Yes	No	Total
51 years & above			
Count		6	6
% within Age		100	100
% within EDP		9	5.7
% of Total		5.7	5.7
Total			
Count	39	67	106
% within Age	36.8	63.2	100
% within EDP	100	100	100
% of Total	36.8	63.2	100

Source : Field Survey.

(ii) Education

Table 4.17 observes that educational level of entrepreneurs influences the undertaking of EDPs. The highest per centage of entrepreneurs who joined entrepreneurial trainings was graduates (53.8 per cent) while the minimum were under-matriculates (2.6 per cent).

Educational level-wise, 70.0 per cent of the post graduate entrepreneurs received EDP training as against 53.8 per cent of the graduate entrepreneurs. In contrast only 25.0 per cent of the under-graduate entrepreneurs joined EDP training while that was only 17.6 per cent in case of matriculate entrepreneurs.

Hence, it can be concluded that higher the level of education, the greater is the awareness of EDPs among the entrepreneurs covered by the study.

(iii) Religion

Religion of entrepreneurs also influences the undertaking of EDPs. It can be seen from Table 4.18 that all the Christian and Sikh entrepreneurs had not undertaken any entrepreneurship development programmes.

Table 4.17
Educational Qualification of Entrepreneurs Vs Entrepreneurship Development Programmes

Educational Qualification of Entrepreneurs	Undertaking of Entrepreneurship Development Programmes		
	Yes	No	Total
Under Matriculates			
Count	1	11	12
% within Qualification	8.3	91.7	100
% within EDP	2.6	16.4	11.3
% of Total	0.9	10.4	11.3
Matriculates			
Count	3	14	17
% within Qualification	17.6	82.4	100
% within EDP	7.7	20.9	16
% of Total	2.8	13.2	16
Under-graduates			
Count	7	21	28
% within Qualification	25	75	100
% within EDP	17.9	31.3	26.4
% of Total	6.6	19.8	26.4
Graduates			
Count	21	18	39
% within Qualification	53.8	46.2	100
% within EDP	53.8	26.9	36.8
% of Total	19.8	17	36.8
Post-Graduates			
Count	7	3	10
% within Qualification	70	30	100
% within EDP	17.9	4.5	9.4
% of Total	6.6	2.8	9.4
Total			
Count	39	67	106
% within Qualification	36.8	63.2	100
% within EDP	100	100	100
% of Total	36.8	63.2	100

Source : Field Survey

39.6 per cent of the Hindu entrepreneurs had joined EDPs while only 20.0 per cent Muslim entrepreneurs thought right to attend the EDPs

It can thus be concluded that knowledge of EDPs were common among Hindus and Muslims whereas it was not so among the Christian and Sikh entrepreneurs.

Table 4.18
Religion of Entrepreneurs Vs Entrepreneurship Development Programmes

Undertaking of Entrepreneurship Development Programmes	Hindu	Muslim	Christian	Sikh	Total
Yes					
Count	38	1			39
% within EDP	97.4	2.6			100
% within Religion	39.6	20			36.8
%.of Total	35.8	0.9			36.8
No					
Count	58	4	2	3	67
% within EDP	86.6	6	3	4.5	100
% within Religion	60.4	80	100	100	36.8
%.of Total	54.7	3.8	1.9	2.8	36.8
Total					
Count	96	5	2	3	106
% within EDP	90.6	4.7	1.9	2.8	100
% within Religion	100	100	100	100	100
%.of Total	90.6	4.7	1.9	2.8	100

Source : Field Survey

(iv) Feasibility study

An attempt is made here to examine whether the undertaking of feasibility study influences the entrepreneurs to join any entrepreneurial training programmes.

As can be seen from Table 4.19, majority of the entrepreneurs who had undertaken feasibility study either by themselves (30.8 per cent) or through other agencies (51.3 per cent) had joined EDPs. Only 17.9 per cent thought it necessary to attend EDPs after not undertaking feasibility study.

Table 4.19
Feasibility Study Vs Entrepreneurship Development Programmes

Undertaking of Entrepreneurship Development Programme	Undertaking of Feasibility Study			
	Self	Agencies	No Study	Total
Yes				
Count	12	20	7	39
% within EDP	30.8	51.3	17.9	100
% within Feasibility Study	42.9	64.5	14.9	36.8
% of Total	11.3	18.9	6.6	36.8
No				
Count	16	11	40	67
% within EDP	23.9	16.4	59.7	100
% within Feasibility Study	57.1	35.5	85.1	63.2
% of Total	15.1	10.4	37.7	63.2
Total				
Count	28	31	47	106
% within EDP	26.4	29.2	44.3	100
% within Feasibility Study	100.0	100.0	100.0	100.0
% of Total	26.4	29.2	44.3	100

Source : Field Survey

On the other hand, majority of the entrepreneurs who had not undertaken any feasibility study (59.7 per cent) thought unnecessary to attend the EDPs. 23.9 per cent entrepreneurs who conducted feasibility study themselves were confident enough by not attending EDPs, while 16.4 per cent of the entrepreneurs who conducted the feasibility study through other agencies were also self confident to carry on the industrial unit without attending any EDPs.

In short, it can be concluded that those who conducted any feasibility study before starting an unit attends EDPs more than those who had not conducted the study.

(v) Generation of entrepreneurs

In respect of generation, it has been noticed in Table 4.20 that majority of the entrepreneurs who attended EDPs belongs to first generation entrepreneurs (94.9 per cent) followed by second generation entrepreneurs (5.1 per cent).

Table 4.20
Generation of Entrepreneurs Vs Entrepreneurship Development Programmes

Undertaking of Entrepreneurship Development Programmes	Generation of Entrepreneurs			
	First	Second	Third	Total
Yes				
Count	37	2		39
% within EDP	94.9	5.1		100
% within Generation	44	9.5		36.8
% of Total	34.9	1.9		36.8
No				
Count	47	19	1	67
% within EDP	70.1	28.4	1.5	100
% within Generation	56	90.5	100	63.2
% of Total	44.3	17.9	0.9	63.2
Total				
Count	84	21	1	106
% within EDP	79.2	19.8	0.9	100
% within Generation	100	100	100	100
% of Total	79.2	19.8	0.9	100

Source : Field Survey.

Generation-wise, only 44.0 per cent of the first generation entrepreneurs attended EDPs while that was only 9.5 per cent in the case of second generation entrepreneurs. It is interesting to note that third generation entrepreneurs never attends any EDPs.

It can thus be concluded that first generation entrepreneurs are more enthusiastic than the other generations regarding the attendance of EDPs. In other words, the other generations are more experienced with their business skills that they need not attend any EDPs.

(vi) Rural/urban background

Table 4.21 shows that urban background of the entrepreneurs do not give them an advantage to attend EDPs. For example, only 35.7 per cent of the entrepreneurs having urban background attended some sort of entrepreneurial training whereas 64.3 per cent of them had not joined any training programmes.

Table 4.21
Rural/Urban Background of Entrepreneurs Vs Entrepreneurship Development Programmes

Undertaking of Entrepreneurship Development Programmes	Background of Entrepreneurs		
	Urban	Rural	Total
Yes			
Count	15	24	39
% within EDP	38.5	61.5	100
% within Background	35.7	37.5	36.8
% of Total	14.2	22.6	36.8
No			
Count	27	40	67
% within EDP	40.3	59.7	100
% within Background	64.3	52.5	63.2
% of Total	25.5	37.7	63.2
Total			
Count	42	64	106
% within EDP	39.6	60.4	100
% within Background	100	100	100
% of Total	39.6	60.4	100

Source : Field Survey

On the other hand, 37.5 per cent of the entrepreneurs having rural background had undertaken EDPs. It is thus clear that rural background of the entrepreneurs cannot be a disadvantage for attending the entrepreneurship development programmes.

Table 4.22
Usefulness of Attending Entrepreneurship Development Programmes

Undertaking of Entrepreneurship Development Programmes	No response	Very useful	Useful	Not very useful	Not useful	Total
Yes						
Count	1	28	7	1	2	39
% within EDP	2.6	71.8	17.9	2.6	5.1	100
% within Responses	1.5	100	100	100	100	36.8
% of Total	0.9	26.4	6.6	0.9	1.9	36.8
No						
Count	67					67
% within EDP	100					100
% within Responses	98.5					63.2
% of Total	63.2					63.2
Total						
Count	68	28	7	1	2	106
% within EDP	64.2	26.4	6.6	0.9	1.9	100
% within Responses	100	100	100	100	100	100
% of Total	64.2	26.4	6.6	0.9	1.9	100

Source : Field Survey

The usefulness of attending EDPs from 39 entrepreneurs are also enquired. Table 4.22 shows the responses from the entrepreneurs. 71.8 per cent of those entrepreneurs who had taken training programmes (28 out of 39) found that EDPs are very useful to their enterprises while 17.9 per cent rated it as useful. Only 5. 1 per cent rated attending EDPs as not useful. It can thus be concluded that attending some sort of entrepreneurial training can go a long run in the smooth functioning of the industrial units.

Further, it will be very interesting to know as to why 63.2 per cent (67 out of 106) entrepreneurs have not attended any entrepreneurial development programmes. As can be observed from Table 4.23, 34.9 per cent (37 out of 106) entrepreneurs are not aware of any such programmes while 18.9 per cent (20 out of 106) felt inconvenient to attend EDPs even if they are aware of it. It is worthwhile to mention here that 9.4 per cent (10 out of 106) entrepreneurs do not think they are useful.

District-wise, 39.3 per cent (22 out of 56) entrepreneurs of Imphal West District are not aware of EDPs while equal number of entrepreneurs in Imphal East District are at the same time, not aware of EDPs and felt inconvenient to attend such programmes (30.0 per cent each). Moreover, 41.1 per cent (23 out of 56) entrepreneurs of Imphal West District had attended EDPs and thus having no reason for not attending EDPs while only 30.0 per cent (15 out of 50) of Imphal East District had attended EDPs.

REFERENCES

1. Davenport Robert W., Financing the small Manufacturing in Developing Countries, Mc Graw Hill Book Company, New York, 1967, pp. 12-13.
2. D.C. Mc Cleland & D.G. Winter, 'Motivating Economic Achievement', The Free Press, New York, 1969.
3. S.K. Gupta, 'Entrepreneurship Development Training Programme in India', Small Enterprise Development', Vol. 1, No. 4, December 1990.

Table 4.23
Reasons for not Attending Entrepreneurship Development Programmes

Districts	Reasons					
	No Response (Attended EDP)	Not aware	Thought as not useful	Inconve- nient	Others	Total
Imphal West						
Count	23	22	5	5	1	56
% within District	41.1	39.3	8.9	8.9	1.8	100
% within Reason	60.5	59.5	50	25	100	52.8
% of Total	21.7	20.8	4.7	4.7	0.9	52.8
Imphal East						
Count	15	15	5	15		50
% within District	30	30	10	30		100
% within Reason	39.5	40.5	50	75		47.2
% of Total	14.2	14.2	4.7	14.2		47.2
Total						
Count	38	37	10	20	1	106
% within District	35.8	34.9	9.4	18.9	0.9	100
% within Reason	100	100	100	100	100	100
% of Total	35.8	34.9	9.4	18.9	0.9	100

Source : Field Survey

CHAPTER V

PERFORMANCE AND GROWTH OF ENTREPRENEURS

5.1 Introduction

After analysing the entrepreneurial efforts in promoting the industrial units in the previous chapter, it is attempted to examine the entrepreneurial performance and growth of the enterprises in this chapter. Mere numerical strength of enterprises does not mean much achievement in the economic development of the nation. The performance of enterprises must be measured by the contribution they make to the development of the nation. The economists are as much concerned with the growth of the enterprises as they are with the starting of new units. However, there are certain difficulties as regards to evaluation of the performance and growth of an enterprise. Firstly, there are difficulties in defining the term growth. Secondly, growth cannot be measured by an exact criteria as it poses certain problems. Finally, evaluating the growth of the enterprises is not altogether different from evaluating the entrepreneurial performance, implying that enterprise and entrepreneur are not different entities. The third problem makes the first two problems more complicated.

As discussed earlier in Chapter I, Berna[1] dealt with expansion of the firm, with reference to the effective interest in the technological improvement and product diversification. Expansion and growth usually means enhancement of the initial installed capacity of the enterprise and thus expansion may be taken as an index of the growth of industrial units. One of the arguments put forward by Berna in support of the need for expansion of industrial units in underdeveloped countries is that they are generally established on less than optimum scale[2]. As such, growth has no meaning without expansion or product characterization, and the efforts to utilize the existing facilities fully should also be taken into consideration. Limited amount of initial capital at the disposal of entrepreneurs, their caution due to inexperience in business and the restricted markets for their products are some of the reasons attributed by Berna for starting the industrial units on less than optimum scale in underdeveloped countries[3]. More or less, the same can be said about the industrial units under study.

In a situation like this, if the growth is construed as merely the additional capacity created over and above the initial installed capacity, it may not jump to a meaningful measurement of the growth of enterprises. As such, the efforts to utilize the existing production capacity fully should also be taken into consideration for assessing the growth of enterprises.

Another problem is the difficulty in quantification of the growth. Finding out the differences between initial capital employed and the latest capital employed appears to be a simple way of measuring the growth. But, the method presents several problems in case of units rendering services and making heterogeneous products. Even if it is possible to measure the production and utilization capacities, they may not provide a useful basis for comparison in view of the varied nature of the enterprises and their products.

Growth of enterprises may also be measured by its increased investment, employment, sales, production, profits etc. Each of these measures has its own merits and demerits. Irrespective of merits and demerits, it has not been found possible to gather information on some of these variables. Even in cases where information could be gathered, it is not found possible to do so either for all the years or a period of four or five years consecutively. As a result, data was collected from the enterprises under study only with reference to the initial year and the latest year. The initial year refers to the first year of the functioning of the enterprise and the latest year refers to the year of survey i.e., the accounting year ended during 2002 or earlier.

As discussed earlier, the performance of the enterprise cannot be differentiated from that of an entrepreneur. However, whether it is entrepreneurs or enterprises, the evaluation is made on the basis of group performance instead of individual units of entrepreneurs. In this study, the performance is sought to be analysed on the basis of capital employed, size of employment, sales turnover, time devoted by entrepreneurs to the enterprises etc.

5.2 Capital employed

One of the method of judging the performance of an enterprise is to observe the changes in the capital employed over a period of time. In fact, the growth achieved in capital employed stands a good testimony for the effective performance of entrepreneurship. Keeping this point in view, an attempt is made here to examine the growth of capital employed. It has already mentioned that since data was not available for all the years of existence of enterprises under study, the analysis has been made on the basis of the capital employed figures with reference to the initial year and the latest year covered under the study.

It may be seen from Table 5.1 that in the initial year of starting the enterprises, the capital employed was less than Rs. 2 lakhs in as many as 69.8 per cent (74 out of 106) of the enterprises in both the districts. The industrial units with a maximum of Rs. 10 lakhs and above were only 8.5 per cent (9 out of 106). An average capital of Rs. 3.5 lakhs was invested in each of the enterprises or units in the initial year.

District-wise, it may be observed that the units with capital upto Rs. 2 lakhs accounted a greater percentage (69.6) in Imphal West District and followed by capital ranging between Rs. 2 – 4 lakhs (10.7 per cent) In Imphal East District also, capital upto Rs. 2 lakhs constituted a maximum of 70.0 per cent units and followed by capital ranging between Rs. 2 – 4 lakhs (16.0 per cent). Capital of Rs. 4 – 6 lakhs was invested in 8.9 per cent of the units in Imphal West District while the units with the same amout of capital formed 4.0 per cent in Imphal East District. Capital of Rs. 10 lakhs and above was invested almost equally in both the districts (8.0 per cent). On the basis of average capital employed, it can be said that greater investment was made in the units of Imphal West Distict (average Rs. 3.5 lakhs) than in the units of Imphal East Districts (average Rs. 3.2 lakhs).

Coming to the latest year, it is very interesting to note that the capital invested in different enterprises or units in the two districts under study increased considerably. On the one hand, units with capital of upto Rs. 2 lakhs decreased from 69.8 per cent in the initial year to 25.5 per cent in the latest year. On the other hand, those with capital of Rs. 10 lakhs and above registered an increase from 8.5 per cent in the initial year to 32.1 per cent in the latest year. The trend is also the same in case capital ranging between Rs. 6 and 8 lakhs. There was no such units in the initial year but 4.7 per cent (5 out 106) were found in the latest year. It can also be understood from the fact that the average investment in an enterprises was Rs. 3.4 lakhs in the initial year whereas it was Rs. 11.9 lakhs in the latest year.

So far as the district-wise position is concerned it could be seen from the table that there was a trend of declining in the number of units with amount of capital of Rs. 2 lakhs and below and an increase in the units with more amount of capital investment in the latest year. While the average capital employed in each enterprise in Imphal West District increased from Rs. 3.5 lakhs in the initial year to Rs. 11.4 lakhs in the latest year, in Imphal East District, it increased from Rs. 3.2 lakhs to Rs. 12.5 lakhs.

It can thus be concluded from the above analysis that there has been a significant growth in the size of the enterprises measured on the basis of capital employed.

(i) Religion-wise growth of capital

It is now sought to analyse the growth of investment in the enterprises from the initial year to the latest year across the religions of the entrepreneurs. Table 5.2 observes the average capital employed in the initial year and the latest year in the different units classified on the basis of the entrepreneurs' religions and also the percentage change therein. It can be noted that the average capital employed in the initial year was highest in the units started by Sikh entrepreneurs (Rs. 4.0

Table 5.1
Capital Employed

Capital Employed (Rs. in lakhs)	Imphal West District		Imphal East District		Both	
	Initial year	Latest year	Initial year	Latest year	Initial year	Latest year
Upto 2	39 (69.7)	11 (19.6)	35 (70.0)	16 (32.0)	74 (69.8	27 (25.5)
4(Feb	6 (10.7)	8 (14.3)	8 (16.0)	11 (22.0)	14 (13.2	19 (17.9)
6(Apr	5 (8.9)	10 (17.9)	2 (4.0)	5 (10.0)	7 (6.6	15 (14.2)
8(Jun	-	3 (5.4)	-	2 (4.0)	-	5 (4.7)
10(Aug	1 (1.8)	4 (7.1)	1 (2.0)	2 (4.0)	2 (1.9	6 (5.7)
10 & above	5 (8.9)	20 (35.7)	4 (8.0)	14 (28.0)	9 (8.5	34 (32.1)
Total	56 (100.0)	56 (100.0)	50 (100.0)	50 (100.0)	106 (100	106 (100.0)
Average Capital (Rs. in lakhs)	3.5	11.4	3.2	12.5	3.4	11.9

Source : Field Survey
Note : Figures in parentheses indicate percentages to total.

lakhs) followed by those started by Hindus (Rs. 3.5 lakhs) and Muslim entrepreneurs (Rs. 1.5 lakhs).

It was lowest (Rs. 1 lakh) in the units started by Christian entrepreneurs. On the other hand, in the latest year, the average capital employed was highest in the units started and owned by Sikh entrepreneurs (Rs. 13.3 lakhs) followed by those owned by Hindu entrepreneurs (Rs. 12.4 lakhs) and Muslim entrepreneurs (Rs. 4.5 lakhs). The units owned by Christian entrepreneurs had the least capital employed (average Rs. 2.2 lakhs). It is clear from the above analysis that Sikh entrepreneurs were the biggest investors and those of Christian were smallest.

Table 5.2
Capital Employed across Religions of Entrepreneurs

Religion	Average Capital (Rs.in lakhs)		Changes (in %ages)
	Initial year	Latest year	
Hindu	3.5	12.4	257.5
Muslim	1.5	4.5	202.7
Christian	1.0	2.2	120.0
Sikh	4.0	13.3	233.3
Total	**3.4**	**11.9**	**255.2**

Source : Field Survey.

However, it is worthwhile to mentioned that the percentage growth in the capital employed from the initial year to the latest year is very interesting to be observed. The percentage growth was highest (257.5 per cent) in the enterprises owned by Hindu entrepreneurs followed by the enterprises owned by Sikh entrepreneurs (233.3 per cent). The growth rate of Christian entrepreneurs stood at the lowest level (120.0 per cent).

(ii) Industry-wise growth of capital

An attempt is here made to analyse the growth in the capital employed in the enterprises on the basis of the type of industry they belong to. As can be observed from Table 5.3, the average capital employed in each of the enterprises belonging to different industries shows a significant growth from the initial year to the latest year. In the initial year, the average capital employed was highest at R. 6.2 lakhs in plastics and rubber based industries followed by automobile and engineering works (Rs. 5.3 lakhs). It was lowest in entrepreneurs relating to metal based industries (Rs. 0.3 lakhs). In the latest year, units belonging to automobile and engineering works reached the highest average investment of Rs. 24.1 lakhs followed by those belonging to wood based industries (Rs. 12.6 lakhs) and plastics and rubber based industries (Rs. 11.6 lakhs). At the same time, the least average capital employed was found in the metal based units (Rs. 1.6 lakhs).

Table 5.3
Capital Employed and Type of Industry

Type of Industry	Average Capital Employed (Rs. in lakhs)		Change (%age)
	Initial year	Latest year	
Food based	2.9	9.2	178.2
Metal based	0.3	1.6	458.6
Handlooms & Handicrafts	0.4	4.7	1194.4
Plastics & Rubber based	6.2	11.6	86.9
Wood based	4.0	12.6	218.1
Printing & Stationery	2.7	10.1	275.5
Automobile & Engineering	5.3	24.1	350.4
Others	.9	3.1	248.3
Total	3.4	11.9	255.2

Source : Field Survey.

So far as the growth of capital is concerned, units falling under handlooms and handicrafts showed the highest growth rate i.e., more than twelve times. The next highest growth was achieved by those units belonging to metal based industries i.e., more than five times. The growth rate in terms of average capital employed was the least in case of units belonging to plastics and rubber based industries (below two times).

It can thus be concluded that handloom and handicrafts units required lower capital investment in the initial year but reached the maximum capital investment in the latest year as far as the growth rate is concerned. On the other hand, plastics and rubber based industries had the maximum capital investment in the initial year but a least growth rate in the latest year.

(iii) Growth of capital and forms of organisation

Very interestingly, an attempt is made here to examine the growth of capital of enterprises on the basis of the different forms of organisation.

Table 5.4 observes that units organised as private limited companies had the highest average capital employed both in the initial year (Rs. 11.8 lakhs) as well as the latest year (Rs. 24.9 lakhs) followed by partnership firms. However, as far as the growth rate of average capital employed is concerned, it was the sole proprietorship concerns which recorded a growth rate of more than 4 times. On the other hand, it was the least i.e., a little more than two times in case of private limited company.

Table 5.4
Capital Employed and Forms of Organisation

Type of Industry	Average Capital Employed (Rs. in lakhs)		Change (%age)
	Initial year	Latest year	
Private limited company	11.8	24.9	110.6
Partnership	7.7	21.1	175.0
Sole proprietorship	2.4	10.1	320.4
Total	3.4	11.9	255.2

Source : Field Survey

5.3 Size of employment

The growth in the size of employment made by the enterprises is also another measure for assessing the entrepreneurial performance. Hence, an attempt is made here in this section to analyse the size of employment in the enterprises under study.

Table 5.5 observes the number of workers employed in the units for both initial and latest year.

In both the districts, it can be noted that in the initial year, 90.6 per cent of the units had not more than 10 workers each. Those having workers of 25 and above constituted only 3.8 per cent of the units. It is interesting to mention here that 20.8 per cent of the units had no paid workers in the initial year. On the average, there were 8 workers employed in each units in the initial year. District-wise, however, we can find that more number of workers were employed in units of Imphal West District (average 10 workers) compared to those of Imphal East District (average 5 workers).

Coming to the latest year, there had been considerable growth in the size of employment made by the units under study. It can be proved from the fact that the average number of workers employed in each units in both the districts increased from 8 in the initial year to 20 in the latest year. District-wise, in Imphal West District, the increase was from 10 to 20 and in Imphal East District, it was from 5 to 20 workers.

(i) Religion-wise growth of employment

It is now attempted to analyse the growth of employment in the units from the initial year to the latest year across the religions of the entrepreneurs. Table 5.6 reveals the average size of employment in the initial and latest year and also the percentage change in between them.

It can be noted that in the initial year, average size of employment was highest (8.2) in units owned by Hindu entrepreneurs and lowest (2.5) in those owned by Christian entrepreneurs. In the latest year, though the maximum average size of employment was again found in the units of Hindu

Table 5.5
Size of Employment

No. of Workers employed	Imphal West District		Imphal East District		Both	
	Initial year	Latest year	Initial year	Latest year	Initial year	Latest year
No paid workers	8	1	14	2	22	3
	(14.3)	(1.8)	(28.0)	(4.0)	(20.8)	(2.8)
1 – 5	35	13	25	20	60	33
	(62.5)	(23.2)	(50.0)	(40.0)	(56.6)	(31.1)
5 – 10	8	26	6	11	14	37
	(14.3)	(46.4)	(12.0)	(22.0)	(13.2)	(34.9)
10-15	2	3	1	5	3	8
	(3.6)	(5.4)	(2.0)	(10.0)	(2.8)	(7.6)
15 – 20	-	5	1	5	1	10
		(8.9)	(2.0)	([illegible].0)	(0.9)	(9.4)
20 – 25	1	3	1	1	2	4
	(1.8)	(5.4)	(2.0)	(2.0)	(1.9)	(3.8)
25 & above	2	5	2	6	4	11
	(3.6)	(8.9)	(4.0)	(12.0)	(3.8)	(10.4)
Total	56	56	50	50	106	106
	(100.0)	(100.0)	(100.0)	(100.0)	(100.0)	(100.0)
Average number of workers employed	9.9	19.5	5.5	19.9	7.8	19.7

Source : Field Survey
Note : Figures in parentheses indicate percentages to total.

entrepreneurs (20.6), the lowest size of employment (9.0) was found in the units of Muslim entrepreneurs.

Table 5.6
Size of Employment and Religions of Entrepreneurs

Religions	Average Size of Employment		Changes (%age)
	Initial year	Latest year	
Hindu	8.2	20.6	151.6
Muslim	5.4	9.0	66.7
Christian	2.5	10.5	320.0
Sikh	3.3	14.0	320.4
Total	7.8	19.7	151.9

Source : Field Survey.

As far as the growth of employment is concerned, we find that the highest growth (320.4 per cent) was achieved by units owned by Sikh entrepreneurs. On the other hand, units of Muslim entrepreneurs could achieve the least growth in employment (66.7 per cent).

(ii) Industry-wise growth in employment

Table 5.7 reveals the average workforce employed in each of the units classified according to their type of industry and the percentage change in the size of employment from the initial year to the latest year. It can be noticed that the units falling under the category of automobile & engineering works were found to have the highest size of employment (17.9 per cent). On the other hand, in the initial year, it was the lowest in units belonging to 'others' type of industry (1.8). In the latest year, on the other hand, the average size of employment was maximum in the units falling under the category of handlooms & handicrafts industries (56.4) and the lowest was again found in 'others' type of industry (3.5).

With regards to growth in size of employment, we can notice that units falling under the category of handlooms & handicrafts industry had achieved the highest growth (858.8

per cent) from the initial year to the latest year, whereas units falling under the category of printing and stationery works revealed the least growth (53.4 per cent).

Table 5.7
Size of Employment and Type of Industry

Type of Industry	Average Size of Employment		Change (%age)
	Initial year	Latest year	
Food based	4.0	6.6	64.8
Metal based	2.18	12.7	355.6
Handlooms & Handicrafts	5.9	56.4	858.8
Plastics & Rubber based	4.2	8.4	101.9
Wood based	7.3	17.5	138.8
Printing & Stationery	5.9	9.1	53.4
Automobile & Engineering	17.9	35.0	95.8
Others	1.8	3.5	94.4
Total	7.8	19.7	151.9

Source : Field Survey.

It can, thus, be concluded that growth in employment was highest in handloom & handicrafts type of industries followed by metal based and wood based industries.

(iii) Growth of employment Vs forms of organisation

An enquiry has been made into the size and growth of employment in the units classified on the basis of their forms of organisation. Table 5.8 observes that private limited companies had the highest average workforce both in the initial and the latest year.

However, it was the sole proprietorship concerns that had achieved the highest growth of 223.5 per cent from the initial to the latest year. While partnership firms could achieved growth of 103.6 per cent in the size of employment, private limited companies maintained only an increase of 2.3 per cent in the size of employment.

It can be understood from the above analysis that the sole proprietorship concerns were able to employ more number of workforce as compared to other forms of organisation.

Table 5.8
Size of Employment Vs Forms of Organisation

Forms of Organisation	Average Size of Employment		Change (%age)
	Initial year	Latest year	
Food based	4.0	6.6	64.8
Private Limited Company	55.3	56.5	2.3
Partnership	7.3	14.9	103.6
Sole Proprietorship	5.8	18.7	223.5
Total	7.8	19.7	151.9

Source : Field Survey

5.4 Sales turnover

The growth of enterprises can also be measured by changes in sales turnover between the initial and the latest year. Table 5.9 observes the district-wise sales turnover in terms of rupees in lakhs for the initial year and the latest year. In the initial year, 75.5 per cent of the total units in both the districts had sales turnover of less than Rs. 2 lakhs. A maximum turnover of Rs. 10 lakhs and above was made only by 3.8 per cent of the total units. On an average, sales turnover of Rs. 2.1 lakhs was made in each of the enterprises in the initial year.

District-wise, in the initial year, it may be seen that Imphal West District had 83.9 per cent of units having sales turnover of less than Rs. 2 lakhs while that of Imphal East District had only 30.4 per cent. Sales turnover of Rs. 2-4 lakhs was made in only 5.4 per cent of the enterprises in Imphal West District while the enterprises with the same amount of sales turnover formed 20.0 per cent in Imphal East District. On the basis of average sales turnover, it can be observed that greater sales was made in the enterprises of Imphal East District (average Rs. 2.2 lakhs) than in the enterprises of Imphal West District (average Rs. 2.0 lakhs).

Table 5.9
Sales Turnover

Sales Turnover (Rs in lakhs)	Imphal West District		Imphal East District		Both	
	Initial year	Latest year	Initial year	Latest year	Initial year	Latest year
Upto 2	47 (83.9)	17 (30.4)	33 (66.0)	11 (22.0)	80 (75.5)	28 (26.4)
2 – 4	3 (5.4)	11 (19.7)	10 (20.0)	15 (30.0)	13 (12.3)	26 (24.5)
4 – 6	1 (1.8)	8 (14.3)	4 (8.0)	11 (22.0)	5 (4.7)	19 (17.9)
6 – 8	-4 (7.1)	-2 (4.0)	-6 (5.7)			
8 -10	2 (3.6)	2 (3.6)	2 (4.0)	1 (2.0)	4 (3.8)	3 (2.8)
10 & above	3 (5.4)	14 (25.0)	1 (2.0)	10 (20.0)	4 (3.8)	24 (22.6)
Total	56 (100.0)	56 (100.0)	50 (100.0)	50 (100.0)	106 (100.0)	106 (100.0)
Average Turnover (Rs. in lakhs)	2.0	14.8	2.2	7.5	2.1	11.3

Source : Field Survey
Note : Figures in parentheses indicate percentages to total.

So far as the latest year is concerned, it is worthwhile to mention that the sales turnover made by different enterprises in both the districts under study increased considerably. While the enterprises having turnover of less than Rs. 2 lakhs, decreased from 75.5 per cent in the initial year to 26.4 per cent in the latest year, enterprises having turnover of Rs. 10 lakhs and above increased from 3.8 per cent in the initial year to 22.6 per cent in the latest year. This clearly indicates that the sales turnover increased in the enterprises from the initial year to the latest year. It can also be justified from the fact that the average sales turnover in an enterprise was Rs. 2.1 lakhs in the initial year whereas it increased to Rs. 11.3 lakhs in the latest year.

District-wise, it could be seen that there was a decline in the number of unit with sales turnover of less than Rs. 2 lakhs and an increase in the units with more amount of sales turnover exceeding Rs. 2 lakhs in the latest year. On the one hand, in Imphal West District, units with sales turnover of less than Rs. 2 lakhs decreased from 83.9 per cent in the initial year to 30.4 per cent in the latest year. At the same time, units having sales turnover of Rs. 10 lakhs and above increases from 5.4 per cent in the initial year to 25.0 per cent in the latest year. On the other hand, in Imphal East District, units having less than Rs. 2 lakhs sales turnover decreased from 66.0 per cent in the initial year to 22.0 per cent in the latest year. Regarding sales turnover of Rs. 10 lakhs and above, units increased from 2 per cent in the initial year to 20.0 per cent in the latest year. While the average sales turnover made in each enterprises in Imphal West District increased from Rs. 2.0 lakhs in the initial year to Rs. 14.8 lakhs in the latest year, in Imphal East District, it increased from Rs. 2.2 lakhs to Rs. 7.5 lakhs.

From the above analysis, it can be concluded that there has been a significant growth in the performance of the enterprises measured on the basis of sales turnover.

Further, an attempt is made here to examine the average sales turnover made by different units across the various types of industries, religions of entrepreneurs and forms of organisation.

(i) Religion-wise growth in sales

An enquiry has been made into the growth of sales in different enterprises classified on the basis of entrepreneurs' religions. Table 5.10 observes the average sales turnover in the initial and latest year and also the percentage change in between them. It is noted that in the latest year, average sales turnover was highest (Rs. 21.0 lakhs) in units owned by Sikh entrepreneurs and minimum (Rs. 5.1 lakhs) in those owned by Christian entrepreneurs.

Table 5.10
Religion-wise Sales Turnover

Religions	Average Sales Turnover Change (Rs. in Lakhs)		Change (%age)
	Initial year	Latest year	
Hindu	2.1	11.3	433.7
Muslim	1.8	9.4	427.0
Christian	1.0	5.1	405.0
Sikh	2.3	21.0	819.7
Total	2.1	11.3	444.7

Source : Field Survey.

On analyzing the growth of sales from the initial year to latest year, it is found that, the highest growth (819.7 per cent) was made by entrepreneurs owned by Sikh entrepreneurs. On the other hand, enterprises owned by Christian entrepreneurs could achieve the least growth sales (405.0 per cent).

(ii) Sales turnover across types of industries

Table 5.11 shows the average sales turnover of each of the enterprises classified on the basis of the industries they belong to and the growth in turnover measured as a percentage change from initial year to latest year. It may be seen that in the initial year, sales turnover was maximum at Rs. 3.1 lakhs in wood based industries followed by plastic and rubber based industries (Rs. 2.8 lakhs).

It was the lowest in units relating to handlooms and handicrafts industries (Rs. 0.8 lakhs). In the latest year, units belonging to automobile and engineering works recorded the highest average sales turnover of Rs. 20.4 lakhs followed by those belonging to wood based industries (Rs. 13.7 lakhs). It was in 'others' type of industries, the average sales turnover in each enterprise was least (Rs. 1.7 lakhs).

Table 5.11

Sales Turnover and Type of Industry

Type of Industry	Average Sales Turnover (Rs. in lakhs)		Change (%age)
	Initial year	Latest year	
Food based	2.9	9.4	229.0
Metal based	1.0	4.2	340.0
Handlooms & Handicrafts	0.8	4.0	401.3
Plastic & Rubber based	2.8	13.0	271.0
Wood based	3.1	13.7	337.5
Printing & Stationery	1.5	7.1	373.3
Automobile & Engineering	2.1	20.4	882.2
Others	1.0	1.7	65.7
Total	2.1	11.3	444.7

Source : Field Survey

So far as the growth of sales turnover is concerned, units belonging to automobile and engineering works showed the highest growth rate i.e., more than nine and half times. The next highest increase was made by units belonging to handlooms and handicrafts industries i.e., more than five times.

It can be concluded that automobile and engineering works, handlooms and handicrafts industries and plastic and rubber based industries have done well in improving the sales turnover considerably from the initial year to the latest year.

(iii) Sales turnover Vs forms of organisation

After examining the growth of sales on the basis of the forms of organisation of the enterprises, it can be seen in Table 5.12 that partnership firms had the highest average sales turnover in the initial year (Rs. 6.1 lakhs) and private limited companies had the highest average sales turnover in the latest year (Rs. 62.3 lakhs). It is worthwhile to mention that sole proprietorship concerns had the least average sales turnover both in the initial year (Rs. 1.4 lakhs) and the latest year (Rs. 8.2 lakhs).

Table 5.12
Sales Turnover and Forms of Organisation

Forms of Organisation	Average Sales Turnover (Rs. in lakhs)		Change (%age)
	Initial year	Latest year	
Private Limited Company	5.4	62.3	1044.5
Partnership	6.1	18.0	196.2
Sole Proprietorship	1.4	8.2	484.3
Total	2.1	11.3	444.7

Source : Field Survey.

As far as the growth of sales from the initial year to the latest year, the maximum growth in sales turnover was achieved by private limited company (1044.5 per cent).

While, there was 484.3 per cent increase in average sales in sole proprietorship concerns, only 196.2 per cent increase in sales could be achieved by partnership firms from initial year to the latest year.

5.5 Capital turnover

The performance of an enterprise can be measured on the basis of the speed or rate with which capital employed is rotated in the process of doing business. Efficient rotation of capital would lead to higher profitability. Table 5.13 observes information relating to times with which capital employed is converted into sales in the initial year and the latest year in the two districts under study.

In the initial year, 73.6 per cent (78 out of 106) units in both the districts had capital turnover of upto 2 times. A maximum turnover of 10 and above times was achieved by only 7.6 per cent. On an average, capital turnover of 3.4 times was made in each of the enterprises in the initial year.

District-wise, in the initial year, it may be observed that Imphal West District had 76.8 per cent of the units having capital turnover upto 2 times while that of Imphal East District had only 70 per cent. Capital turnover of 2-4 times was made by 8.9 per cent units in Imphal West District while the units with the same times of capital turnover formed only 6 per cent in Imphal East District. However, it was in the capital turnover of 10 and above times that Imphal East District units (10.0 per cent) performed better than its counterparts in Imphal West District (5.4 per cent).

As regards to the latest year, it is worthwhile to mention that capital turnover made by different units in both the districts under study increased with the exception in the capital turnover of 10 and above times. While the units having capital turnover upto 2 times decreased from 73.6 per cent in the initial year to 67.9 per cent in the latest year, units having capital turnover of 2-4 times increased from 7.6 per cent in the initial year to 17.0 per cent in the latest year. However, it was in the capital turnover of 10 and above times that units in the initial year decreased from 7.6 per cent to 1.9 per cent in the latest year. On the average, the capital turnover decreased from 3.4 times in the initial year to 2.5 times in the latest year.

District-wise, it can be noted that there was a decline in the number of units with capital turnover of upto 2 times and an increase in the units with more times of capital turnover in the range 2-4 in the latest year. In Imphal West District, units with capital turnover of upto 2 times decreased from 76.8 per cent in the initial year to 69.6 per cent in the latest year. At the same time, units having capital turnover of 2-4 times increases from 8.9 per cent in the initial year to 17.9 per cent

Table 5.13
Capital Turnover

No. of Times	Imphal West District		Imphal East District		Both	
	Initial year	Latest year	Initial year	Latest year	Initial year	Latest year
Upto 2	43 (76.8)	39 (69.6)	35 (70.0)	33 (66.0)	78 (73.6)	72 (67.9)
2 – 4	5 (8.9)	10 (17.9)	3 (6.0)	8 (16.0)	8 (7.6)	18 (17.0)
4 – 6	4 (7.1)	3 (5.4)	4 (8.0)	4 (8.0)	8 (7.6)	7 (6.6)
6 – 8	1 (1.8)	2 (3.6)	2 (4.0)	2 (4.0)	3 (2.8)	4 (3.8)
8 – 10	—	—	1 (2.0)	3 (6.0)	1 (0.9)	3 (2.8)
10 & above	3 (5.4)	2 (3.6)	5 (10.0)	—	8 (7.6)	2 (1.9)
Total	**56 (100.0)**	**56 (100.0)**	**50 (100.0)**	**50 (100.0)**	**106 (100.0)**	**106 (100.0)**
Average Turnover	**2.2**	**2.8**	**4.7**	**2.2**	**3.4**	**2.5**

Source : Field Survey
Note: Figures in parentheses indicate percentages to total.

in the latest year. On the other hand, units having capital turnover of upto 2 times decreased from 70.0 per cent in the initial year to 66.0 per cent in the latest year in the Imphal East District. As regards to capital turnover of 2-4 times, units increased from 6.0 per cent in the initial year to 16.0 per cent in the latest year. Capital turnover exceeding 4 times are more or less remained unchanged or decreased in both the districts except in Imphal East District wherein units in the capital turnover range of 8-10 increased from 2.0 per cent in the initial year to 6.0 per cent in the latest year. As such, the average capital turnover made by each enterprises in Imphal West District increased from 2.2 times in the initial year to 2.8 times in the latest year whereas it decreased from 4.7 times to 2.2 times in Imphal East District.

Thus, it can be concluded that, there has been a significant growth in the performance of the enterprises in Imphal West District than in Imphal East District measured on the basis of capital turnover.

Further, an enquiry is made here to analyse the average capital turnover made by different units on the basis of various types of industries, religions of entrepreneurs and forms of organisation preferred by the entrepreneurs.

(i) Religion Vs capital turnover

Table 5.14 observes the average capital turnover made by units in the initial and latest year and also the percentage change in between them on the basis of entrepreneurs' religions. It is found that the average capital turnover was maximum (6.3 times) in unit owned by Muslim entrepreneurs and minimum (0.5 times) in those owned by Sikh entrepreneurs in the initial year. In the latest year also, the same trend in the average capital turnover happened. It was maximum in units owned by Muslim entrepreneurs (4.6 times). However, on analysing the growth in capital turnover from the initial year to the latest year, it's found that the highest growth (220.0 per cent) was made by units owned by Sikh entrepreneurs. On the other hand, units owned by Hindu and Muslim entrepreneurs had failed even to maintain the existing capital turnover. Consequently, they have achieved only a negative growth.

Table 5.14
Religion-wise Capital Turnover

Religion	Average Capital Turnover (No. of times)		Change (%age)
	Initial year	Latest year	
Hindu	3.3	2.5	- 24.2
Muslim	6.3	4.6	- 27.0
Christian	1.3	2.0	53.8
Sikh	0.5	1.6	220.0
Total	3.4	2.5	- 26.5

Source : Field Survey.

(ii) Capital turnover across types of industries

An attempt has been made into the growth of capital turnover in different enterprises classified on the basis of type of industries started by the entrepreneurs. It can be seen from Table 5.15 that printing and stationery works had the maximum average capital turnover (6.8 times) in the initial year followed by metal based industries (6.0 times). It was lowest in plastic and rubber based industries (0.8 times).

In the latest year, however, the minimum average capital turnover was achieved by printing and stationery works (0.8 times). It was maximum in the unit belonging to handlooms and handicrafts industries (4.2 times) followed by food and metal based industries (4.0 times each).

Regarding the growth of capital turnover, units belonging to food based industries showed the highest growth rate (90.5 per cent) followed by plastic and rubber based industries (75.0 per cent) and 'others' type of industries (23.3 per cent). However, printing and stationery works, wood based and metal based industries failed to achieve a growth rate as far as capital turnover is concerned.

Table 5.15
Capital Turnover and Type of Industry

Type of Industry	Average Capital Turnover (No. of times)		Change (%age)
	Initial year	Latest year	
Food based	2.1	4.0	90.5
Metal based	6.0	4.0	-33.3
Handlooms & Handicrafts	4.2	4.2	Nil
Plastics & Rubber based	0.8	1.4	75.0
Wood based	5.8	2.7	-53.4
Printing & Stationery	6.8	0.8	- 88.2
Automobile & Engineering	1.0	1.1	10.0
Others	3.0	3.7	23.3
Total	3.4	2.5	-26.5

Source : Field Survey.

(iii) Capital turnover Vs forms of organisation

For ascertaining the growth of capital turnover on the basis of the forms of organisation, Table 5.16 observes that in the initial year, partnership firms had the maximum capital turnover (7.6 times) followed by sole proprietorship (2.9 times). In the latest year, sole proprietorship had the maximum capital turnover (2.6 times) followed by partnership firms (2.2 times). It is worthwhile to mention that private limited companies had the least average capital turnover in the latest year (1.5 times).

As regards to the growth of capital turnover from the initial year to the latest year, the growth was achieved by private limited companies (114.3 per cent). For other forms of organisation i.e., partnership firms and sole proprietorship had negative growth rate.

5.6 Institutional borrowings of enterprises

After discussing the capital turnover of the enterprises, it is now the turn of institutional borrowings made by the units so as to analyse the entrepreneurial performance. Not only the entrepreneurs' own capital but also borrowings from outside agencies are needed for starting and running the industrial unit. Dependence on these borrowings may be increased or decreased from the initial year to the latest year. But more dependence on it means that the concerned units are having the burden of paying interest. As such, an attempt is made to judge the growth of enterprises on the basis of degree of dependence on borrowings.

Table 5.16
Capital Turnover and Forms of Organisation

Type of Industry	Average Capital Turnover (No. of times)		Change (%age)
	Initial year	Latest year	
Private Limited Company	0.7	1.5	114.3
Partnership	7.6	2.2	-71.1
Sole proprietorship	2.9	2.6	-10.3
Total	3.4	2.5	-26.5

Source : Field Survey.

Table 5.17 analyses the district-wise dependence on institutional borrowings in terms of rupees in lakhs for the initial year and the latest year. In the initial year, 24.5 per cent of the total units had to depend on borrowings amounting to less than Rs. 2 lakhs. A maximum borrowings of more than Rs. 10 lakhs were taken by only 11.3 per cent of the total units. It is worthwhile to mention that 50.9 per cent units had not depended on any borrowings for its activities. On an average, borrowings of Rs. 8 lakhs were taken in each of the enterprises in the initial year.

District-wise, in the initial year, it can be noted that Imphal West District had 30.4 per cent units who depended on borrowings of less than Rs. 2 lakhs while that of Imphal East District had only 18.0 per cent. Borrowings in the range of Rs. 2-4 lakhs were taken by 3.6 per cent units in the Imphal West District while it was 8.0 per cent in the Imphal East District.

Table 5.17
Borrowings of Enterprises

Amount of Borrowings (Rs. in lakhs)	Imphal West District		Imphal East District		Both	
	Initial year	Latest year	Initial year	Latest year	Initial year	Latest year
Less than 2	17 (30.4)	6 (10.7)	9 (18.0)	5 (10.0)	26 (24.5)	11 (10.4)
2 – 4	2 (3.6)	3 (5.4)	4 (8.0)	1 (2.0)	6 (5.7)	4 (3.8)
4 – 6	5 (8.9)	1 (1.8)	3 (6.0)	1 (2.0)	8 (7.6)	2 (1.9)
6 – 8	—	2 (3.6)	—	1 (2.0)	—	3 (2.8)
8 – 10	—	—	—	2(4.0)	—	2 (1.9)
10 & above	8 (14.3)	3 (5.4)	4 (8.0)	2 (4.0)	12 (11.3)	5 (4.7)
No. of entrepreneurs having no borrowings	24 (42.9)	41 (73.2)	30 (60.0)	38 (76.0)	54 (50.9)	79 (74.5)
Total	56 (100.0)	56 (100.0)	50 (100.0)	50 (100.0)	106 (100.0)	106 (100.0)
Average Borrowings (Rs. in lakhs)	8.2	1.5	7.6	1.5	8.0	1.5

Source : Field Survey
Note : Figures in parentheses indicate percentages to total.

Regarding the number of entrepreneurs having no borrowings, it was 42.9 per cent units in Imphal West District while that of Imphal East District was 60.0 per cent. On the basis of average borrowings, it is found that greater dependence on borrowings was made by units in Imphal West District (average Rs. 8.2 lakhs) than in the units of Imphal East District (average Rs. 7.6 lakhs).

Coming to the latest year, it is interesting to observe that the dependence on borrowings by the different units in both the districts under study decreased significantly. Borrowings of less than Rs. 2 lakhs were decreased from 24.5 per cent in the initial year to 10.4 per cent in the latest year. At the same time, units borrowings of Rs. 4-6 lakhs also decreased from 7.6 per cent in the initial year to 1.9 per cent in the latest year. It was just an exception that borrowings in the range of Rs. 8-10 lakhs were taken by 1.9 per cent units in the latest year. It can be verified from the fact that the number of entrepreneurs having no borrowings have increased from 50.9 per cent in the initial year to 74.5 per cent in the latest year. On the average also, borrowings decreased from Rs. 8.0 lakhs in the initial year to Rs. 1.5 lakhs in the latest year.

District-wise, it can be noticed that dependence on borrowings by the different units have decreased from the initial year to the latest year. In Imphal West District, units borrowing amount less than Rs. 2 lakhs decreased from 30.4 per cent in the initial year to 10.7 per cent in the latest year. In Imphal East District also, in the same range of borrowings, it decreased from 18.0 per cent to 10.0 per cent. Regarding the amount of borrowings of Rs. 10 lakhs and above, units decreased from 14.3 per cent in the initial year to 5.4 per cent in the latest year in the Imphal West District while it was from 8.0 per cent to 4.0 per cent in the Imphal East District. Number of units having no borrowings have also increased from 42.9 per cent in the initial year to 73.2 per cent in the latest year in the Imphal West District while that of Imphal East District was from 60.0 per cent to 76.0 per cent. On the one hand, in Imphal West District, the average borrowings taken by unit decreased from Rs. 8.2 lakhs in the initial year to Rs. 1.5 lakhs in the latest year. On the other hand, in Imphal East District, the average borrowings decreased from Rs. 7.6 lakhs in the initial year to Rs. 1.5 lakhs in the latest year.

It can be concluded from the above analysis that there has been a significant growth in the performance of the enterprises measured on the basis of degree of dependence on borrowings. In addition, a further attempt is made here to determine the average amount of borrowings, sources of borrowings, amount of repayment of borrowings etc.

1. Average amount of institutional borrowings

After discussing the district-wise institutional borrowings, an attempt is made here to inter-linked the average amount of borrowings taken by the various units across the various types of industries, religions of entrepreneurs and forms of organisation.

(i) Entrepreneurs' religions Vs average amount of borrowings

Table 5.18 analyses the average amount of institutional borrowings taken by the different units in the initial and latest year and also the percentage change in between them on the basis of entrepreneurs' religions. It is found that maximum amount of average institutional borrowings in the initial year were taken by Hindu entrepreneurs (Rs. 8.6 lakhs) followed by Sikh entrepreneurs (Rs. 5.8 lakhs).

Table 5.18
Religion-wise Institutional Borrowings

Religion	Average Capital Turnover (Rs. in lakhs)		Change (%age)
	Initial year	Latest year	
Hindu	8.6	1.6	-81.4
Muslim	1.0	0.04	-96.0
Christian	-	-	Nil
Sikh	5.8	3.3	-43.1
Total	8.0	1.5	-81.3

Source : Field Survey

On the other hand, in the latest year, the average institutional borrowings was highest in the units started and owned by Sikh entrepreneurs (Rs. 3.3 lakhs) followed by those owned by Hindu entrepreneurs (Rs.1.6 lakhs) and Muslim entrepreneurs (Rs.0.04 lakhs). It is worthwhile to mention here that Christian entrepreneurs had not taken any institutional borrowings both in the initial as well as in the latest year. Thus it is clear from the above analysis that Sikh and Hindu entrepreneurs depended more on institutional borrowings as compared to Muslim and Christian entrepreneurs.

Regarding the percentage change from the initial year to the latest year, dependence on borrowings by Muslim entrepreneurs decreased by 96.0 per cent followed by Hindu entrepreneurs (81.4 per cent) and Sikh entrepreneurs (43.1 per cent).

Table 5.19
Institutional Borrowings and Type of Industry

Type of Industry	Average Capital Turnover (Rs. in lakhs)		Change (%age)
	Initial year	Latest year	
Food based	9.2	0.7	-92.4
Metal based	0.5	0.06	-88.0
Handlooms & Handicrafts	0.5	0.9	80.0
Plastics & Rubber based	7.0	3.8	-45.7
Wood based	10.0	1.5	-85.0
Printing & Stationery	3.7	0.4	-89.2
Automobile & Engineering	12.8	2.9	-77.3
Others	4	-	-100.0
Total	8.0	1.5	- 81.3

Source : Field Survey

(ii) Types of industries Vs average amount of borrowings

An attempt is made here to ascertain the growth of enterprises on the basis of decrease of dependence on institutional borrowings across the various types of industries they belong to. Table 5.19 shows that the average institutional borrowings taken by each of the enterprises belonging to different industries decreases significantly from the initial to the latest year. In the initial year, the highest average borrowings were taken by automobile and engineering works (Rs. 12.8 lakhs) followed by wood based (Rs. 10.0 lakhs) and food based (Rs. 9.2 lakhs) industries. It was the lowest in the enterprises relating to metal based and handlooms and handicrafts industries (Rs. 0.5 lakhs each).

In the latest year, units belonging to plastic and rubber based industries had taken the maximum average institutional borrowings (Rs. 3.8 lakhs) followed by those belongings to automobile and engineering works (Rs. 2.9 lakhs) and wood based industries (Rs. 1.5 lakhs). At the same time, the least average borrowings were taken by metal based industries (Rs. 0.06 lakhs).

So far as the decrease of dependence on borrowings is concerned, 'others' type of industries stopped taking institutional borrowings in the latest years. At the same time, units belonging to food based industries decreased their dependence on institutional borrowings by 92.4 per cent from the initial year to the latest year followed by printing and stationery works (89.2 per cent), metal based industries (88.0 per cent), wood based industries (85 per cent) etc. However, it is very interesting to note that handlooms and handicrafts increased their dependence on institutional borrowings by 80.0 per cent.

From the above analysis, it can be concluded that while handlooms and handicrafts industries increased their dependence on institutional borrowings for carrying out their performance, all other types of industries decreased their dependence on institutional borrowings for their performance.

(iii) Forms of organisation Vs average amount of borrowings

Interlinking the various forms of organisation and average amount of borrowings, Table 5.20 observes that private limited companies had taken the maximum average institutional borrowings in the initial year (Rs. 30.5 lakhs)

Table 5.20
Institutional Borrowings and Forms of Organisation

Forms of Organisation	Average Capital Turnover (Rs. in lakhs)		Change (%age)
	Initial year	Latest year	
Private Limited Company	30.5	0.03	-99.9
Partnership	14.5	0.8	-94.5
Sole proprietorship	4.8	1.7	-64.6
Total	8.0	1.5	-81.3

Source : Field Survey.

followed by partnership firms (Rs. 14.5 lakhs). However, in the latest year, it was the sole proprietorship that had taken the maximum average borrowings (Rs. 1.7 lakhs). Regarding the change in the dependence on borrowings from the initial year to the latest year, it can be found that private limited companies had almost stopped depending on institutional borrowings (99.9 per cent) for their performance.

It can be concluded that dependence on institutional borrowings by the units under study were significantly decreased from the initial year to the latest year.

2. Sources of institutional borrowings

After going through the linkages of average institutional borrowings taken by the various units across the various types of industries, religions of entrepreneurs and forms of organisation, it will be incomplete to analyse the institutional borrowings of enterprises without knowing its sources from which the concerned enterprises had availed such borrowings. As such, an attempt is made here to ascertain the various sources of institutional borrowings both in the initial year and in the latest year.

Table 5.21 shows the district-wise sources of institutional borrowings in the initial year as well as in the latest year. In the initial year, 18.9 per cent of the total units had been given financial assistance by the commercial banks. Next to commercial banks, it was Manipur Industrial Development Corporation Ltd. (MANIDCO) (14.2 per cent), NEDFI (6.6 per cent), others (5.7 per cent) and NSIC (3.8 per cent) that had proved as importance sources of institutional borrowings in the initial year.

District-wise, in the initial year, the main source of institutional borrowings in Imphal West District was commercial banks (23.2 per cent) while that of Imphal East District was MANIDCO (16.0 per cent). The least role was played by NSIC and 'others' in giving financial assistance to units located in Imphal West District while it was NEDFI and NSIC in Imphal East District.

Regarding the latest year also, commercial banks still played the main role of providing financial assistance to 15.1 per cent of the total units under study. It was followed by other sources (6.6 per cent), NSIC (2.8 per cent) and MANIDCO (0.9 per cent).

District-wise, it can be seen that majority of the units in Imphal West District (14.3 per cent) and in Imphal East District (16.0 per cent) depended on commercial banks for financial requirements in latest year. It is noteworthy to mention here that MANIDCO and NEDFI had stopped giving financial assistance to the units located in Imphal West District in the latest year. It was the same in case of NEDFI in Imphal East District.

It can be concluded that commercial banks proved themselves as the main sources of institutional borrowings both in the initial and latest year under study.

3. Repayment of borrowings

Taking of financial assistance is as much important as repayment of it. Otherwise, indebtedness of the industrial units

Table 5.21
Sources of Institutional Borrowings

Sources of Institutional Borrowings	Imphal West District		Imphal East District		Both	
	Initial year	Latest year	Initial year	Latest year	Initial year	Latest year
Commercial Banks	13 (23.2)	8 (14.3)	7 (14.0)	8 (16.0)	20 (18.9)	16 (15.1)
MANIDCO	7 (12.5)	—	8 (16.0)	1 (2.0)	15 (14.2)	1 (0.9)
NEDFI	6 (10.7)	—	1 (2.0)	—	7 (6.6)	—
NSIC	3 (5.4)	2 (3.6)	1 (2.0)	1 (2.0)	4 (3.8)	3 (2.8)
Others*	3 (5.4)	2 (3.6)	3 (6.0)	2 (4.0)	6 (5.7)	7 (6.6)
No. of Entrepreneurs having no borrowings	24 (42.9)	41 (73.1)	30 (60.0)	38 (76.0)	54 (50.9)	79 (74.5)
Total	56 (100.0)	56 (100.0)	50 (100.0)	50 (100.0)	106 (100.0)	106 (100.0)

Source : Field Survey
***Other** includes Industries Department, Assam Financial Corporation. Co-operative Banks etc.
Note : Figures in parentheses indicate percentages to total.

will become a great hindrance for the smooth running of the units. Not only the interest burden will rise but also the credit worthiness of the unit will decrease in the financial market if the unit has not repaid the institutional borrowings in time. Keeping this view in mind, an enquiry is made to analyse the amount of borrowings repaid in the initial year and the latest year.

Table 5.22 observes the district-wise repayment of borrowings in percentages in relation to amount of institutional borrowings. In the initial year, 23.6 per cent of the total units were able to repay 75 to 100 per cent of their borrowings. It is worthwhile to mention that out of 18 units (17.0 per cent) who repaid upto 25 per cent of their borrowings, the repayment record of 10 units is nil. On an average, borrowings of Rs. 4 lakhs were repaid.

District-wise, in the initial year, 5 units each from Imphal East and Imphal West Distircts had not repaid their initial borrowings till date. On one hand, while 26.8 per cent units of Imphal West District had repaid 75 to 100 per cent of their initial borrowings, only 20.0 per cent units of Imphal East District could do so. On the other hand, 2 units from each districts were able to repay 50 to 75 per cent of the initial borrowings in both the districts under study. On the average, borrowings repaid by units located in Imphal West District (Rs. 5.0 lakhs) were more than those of units located in Imphal East District (Rs. 2.4 lakhs). In the latest year, 12.3 per cent of the total units were able to repay their latest 75 to 100 per cent borrowings as against 3.8 per cent who had already repaid upto 50 per cent of their latest borrowings. Including 4 units whose repayment record was nil, 8 units were able to repay only upto 50 per cent of their latest borrowings. On the average, repayment of borrowings in the latest year (Rs. 0.6 lakhs) were less than those of the initial year (Rs. 4.0 lakhs).

District-wise, 14.3 per cent units located in Imphal West District and 10.0 per cent units located in Imphal East District repaid 75 to 100 per cent of their latest borrowings. On the average, Rs. 0.8 lakhs latest borrowings were repaid in Imphal West District while it was only Rs. 0.5 lakhs in Imphal East District.

Table 5.22
Amount of Borrowings Repaid

Borrowings Repaid (in %age)	Imphal West District		Imphal East District		Both	
	Initial year	Latest year	Initial year	Latest year	Initial year	Latest year
Upto 25	12 (21.4)	2 (3.6)	6 (12.0)	2 (4.0)	18 (17.0)	4 (3.8)
25 – 50	3 (5.4)	1 (1.8)	2 (4.0)	3 (6.0)	5 (4.7)	4 (3.8)
50 – 75	2 (3.6)	4 (7.1)	2 (4.0)	2 (4.0)	4 (3.8)	6 (5.7)
75 – 100	15 (26.8)	8 (14.3)	10 (20.0)	5 (10.0)	25 (23.6)	13 (12.3)
No. of entrepreneurs having no borrowings	24 (42.9)	41 (73.2)	30 (60.0)	38 (76.0)	54 (50.9)	79 (74.5)
Total	56 (100.0)	56 (100.0)	50 (100.0)	50 (100.0)	106 (100.0)	106 (100.0)
Average Borrowings Repaid (Rs. In lakhs)	5.0	0.8	2.4	0.5	4.0	0.6

Source : Field Survey
Note : Figures in parentheses indicate percentages to total.

From the above asnaysis, it can be understood that the ability of the units under study to make repayment of institutional borrowings was significant. Nearly half of the units who had taken institutional borrowings have already repaid full or more than 75 per cent of their borrowings. It was only 19.2 per cent units in the latest year (10 out of 52) and 14.8 per cent units in the initial year (4 out of 27) that had failed to make repayment of institutional borrowings. Further, an attempt is made here to inter-linkéd the ability of enterprises to repay institutional borrowings with religions of entrepreneurs, types of industries and forms of organsation.

(i) Religions of entrepreneurs Vs repayment of borrowings

Table 5.23 finds the ability of the enterprises to repay institutional borrowings in the initial year and latest year in percentage and also on the basis of entrepreneurs' religions. It can be noted that Sikh entrepreneurs had already repaid their initial borrowings (100.0 per cent) followed by Muslim entrepreneurs (88.0 per cent) and Hindu entrepreneurs (49.7 per cent).

Table 5.23
Religion-wise Repayment of Borrowings

Religion	Average Capital Turnover (In %age)		Change (%age)
	Initial year	Latest year	
Hindu	49.7	43.3	-12.9
Muslim	88.0	100.0	13.6
Christian	-	-	Nil
Sikh	100.0	35.0	-65.0
Total	50.7	42.9	-15.4

Source : Field Survey

In the latest year Muslim entrepreneurs had the maximum ability to repay borrowings (100.0 per cent) followed by Hindu

(43.3 per cent) and Sikh (35.0 per cent) entrepreneurs. Thus, it is clear from the above analysis that Muslim entrepreneurs performed well as far as repayment of institutional borrowings is concerned.

Regarding the percentage change from the initial year to the latest year, it is found that Muslim entrepreneurs had increased their performance by 13.6 per cent measured on the basis of ability of repay borrowings. On the other hand, Hindu and Sikh entrepreneurs could not maintained their repayment percentages by 12.9 per cent and 65 per cent respectively.

(ii) Types of industries Vs repayment of borrowings

Table 5.24 observes the growth of enterprises on the basis of ability to repay institutional borrowings by the various types of industries they belong to.

Table 5.24
Types of Industries and Repayment of Borrowings

Types of Industries	Average Capital Turnover (In %age)		Change (%age)
	Initial year	Latest year	
Food based	44.6	Nil	-100
Metal based	53.6	100	86.6
Handlooms & Handicrafts	98.1	63.2	-35.6
Plastics & Rubber based	33.0	31.3	-5.2
Wood based	10.0	86.0	760.0
Printing & Stationery	62.4	0.1	-99.8
Automobile and Engineering	68.8	43.0	-37.5
Others	32.7	-	-
Total	50.7	42.9	-15.4

Source : Field Survey.

The performance of handlooms and handicrafts industries in the initial year was significant as compared to other types of industries. It has repaid 89.1 per cent of initial institutional borrowings followed by automobile and engineering works (68.8 per cent), printing and stationery works (62.4 per cent), metal based industries (53.6 per cent) etc. The ability to repay borrowings was the least in wood based industries (10.0 per cent).

In the latest year, units belonging to metal based industries had already repaid all of their borrowings (100.0 per cent). It was followed by wood based industries who are able to repay 86.0 per cent of their borrowings. It is worthwhile to mention here that food based industries have not yet started repayment of institutional borrowings. At the same time, it has been found that 'others' type of industries had not taken any borrowings in the latest year.

Regarding the change from the initial year to the latest year in percentages, it can be noted that wood based industries had made the maximum effort in repayment of borrowings. While it increases its ability to repay borrowings by 760.0 per cent, metal based industries also did a significant job by increasing its repayment record by 86.6 per cent. The performance of food based industries and printing and stationery works were very poor as far as repayment of borrowings was concerned.

From the above analysis, it can be concluded that except food based industries and printing and stationery works, there has been a significant growth in the performance of enterprises measured on the basis of ability to repay institutional borrowings.

(ii) Forms of organisation Vs repayment of borrowings

Borrowings taken by the different forms of organisation were to be repaid. And as such, Table 5.25 finds out the average repayment of borrowings in percentages both in the initial and the latest year.

In the initial year, private limited companies had performed better as far as repayment of borrowings was concerned. While they were able to repay 79.4 per cent of their initial borrowings, sole proprietorship concerns and partnership firm could managed only 53.5 per cent and 25.5 per cent respectively.

Table 5.25
Forms of Organisation and Repayment of Borrowings.

Forms of Organisation	Average Capital Turnover (In %age)		Change (%age)
	Initial year	Latest year	
Private Limited Co.	79.4	100.0	25.9
Partnership	25.5	35.1	37.6
Sole Proprietorship	53.5	43.4	-18.9
Total	50.7	42.9	-15.4

Source : Field Survey.

In the latest year, the same trend happens in the repayment of borrowings. Private limited companies had already completed repayment of latest borrowings while sole proprietorship concerns has repaid 43.4 per cent of their latest borrowings. For partnership firms, they could managed only 35.1 per cent as far as repayment of latest borrowings is concerned.

Regarding the change in percentage from the initial year to the latest year, the performance of partnership firms and private limited companies was significant as compared to sole proprietorship concerns. While the ability to repay institutional borrowings for the former two forms of organisation increases, that of the later one decreases from initial to latest year.

5.7 Entrepreneurial effort

In addition to the measures of entrepreneurial performance and growth discussed above, the time devoted by the entrepreneurs to their units can also be analysed as an important means of assessing the performance of enterprises. It is assumed that the time devoted by the entrepreneurs to their respective enterprises determines the degree of entrepreneurial success. In view of this, an attempt has been made to analyse the time devoted by the entrepreneurs. For convenience and simplicity, the time devoted is not measured in clock hours. Instead, entrepreneurial time is taken as the full time attention of an entrepreneur on an unit. The measurement of the time is not with reference to a particular point of time and the assessment is on average and it is on the basis of the self assessment of the entrepreneur himself. In the study, the entrepreneurs are requested to denote the percentage of time devoted by them on the basis of full attention which can be given to an unit.

Distribution of the average time devoted by the entrepreneurs on their units in percentages is shown in Table 5.26. In both the two districts, as much as 67.0 per cent of the entrepreneurs were found to be devoting 75 to 100 per cent of their full time to their units. Those entrepreneurs devoting 50 to 75 per cent of their full time constituted 19.8 per cent.

On an average, the time devoted by the entrepreneurs was 87.2 per cent in both the districts. District-wise, it was in Imphal East District that the average time devoted was more (91.6 per cent) than in Imphal West District (83.3 per cent).

Table 5.26
Time Devoted by Entrepreneurs

Entrepreneurial Time in %age	Imphal West District	Imphal East District	Both
0 – 25	-	1 (2.0)	1 (0.9)
25 – 50	10 (17.9)	3 (6.0)	13 (12.3)
50 – 75	14 (25.0)	7 (14.0)	21 (19.8)
75 – 100	32 (57.1)	39 (78.0)	71 (67.0)
Total	56 (100.0)	50 (100.0)	106 (100.0)
Average Entre-preneurial Time	83.3	91.6	87.2

Source: Field Survey
Note : Figures in parentheses indicate percentages to total.

District-wise, 78.0 per cent of the Imphal East District entrepreneurs devoted 75 to 100 per cent of their full time while it was only 57.1 per cent entrepreneurs in Imphal West District. It is worth mentioning here that except one entrepreneur in Imphal East District, there was no one who devoted less than 25 per cent of their full time.

It can thus be concluded that entrepreneurs whose units are located in Imphal East District devoted more entrepreneurial time on an average as compared to those from Imphal West District. This prompted us to further analyse the time devoted by entrepreneurs with regards to religions of entrepreneurs.

Table 5.27 observes the average time devoted by entrepreneurs classified on the basis of their respective religions.

Table 5.27
Entrepreneurs' Religion and their Devoted Time

Religions	Average Time Devoted (in percentage)
Hindu	87.2
Muslim	80.0
Christian	100.0
Sikh	91.7
Total	87.2

Source : Field Survey.

The highest attention of the entrepreneurs is received by the units owned and started by Christian entrepreneurs (100.0 per cent) followed by Sikh (91.7 per cent), Hindu (87.2 per cent) and Muslim (80.0 per cent) entrepreneurs.

In addition, Table 5.28 finds the time devoted by the entrepreneurs on the basis of different forms of organisations. It can be noted that it was in sole proprietorship concerns that the entrepreneurs were devoting the highest time (89.7 per cent) followed by partnership firms (78.8 per cent) and private limited companies (67.5 per cent). It may be due to the fact that in sole proprietorship concerns the risk involved is entirely to be borne by the sole entrepreneur himself which prompts him to be more attentive and committed towards shaping the enterprise more successful by devoting greater part of his full time.

Table 5.28
Time Devoted and Forms of Organisation

Form of Organisation	Average Time Devoted (in percentage)
Private Limited Company	57.5
Partnership	78.8
Sole Proprietorship	89.7
Total	87.2

Source : Field Survey

REFERENCES

1. James J. Berna, op. cit., pp. 11-13
2. Ibid., p. 11.
3. Ibid.

CHAPTER VI

PROBLEMS ENCONUNTERED BY ENTERPRISES

6.1 Introduction

Having analyzed the performance and growth of the enterprises in the preceding chapter, the attention can be drawn on the major problems encountered by the enterprises under study. It is a fact that the variations in growth of enterprises may be due to several problems faced by the enterprises from time to time. These problems may also differ from place to place, from one type of industry to another and like that. Even within a specified category of enterprises or entrepreneurs, again the problems may differ from enterprise to enterprise or entrepreneur to entrepreneur. The problems may be relating to raw materials, marketing, power, labour, finance, technical and managerial assistance etc. The overall performance of an enterprise may be adversely affected by these problems. The entrepreneurs are enquired to list out the problems by major heads like underutilization of capacity, marketing, finance, raw-materials, labour, power etc.

6.2 Underutilization of installed capacity

It is assumed that utilization capacity of enterprises gives a true and fair view of their performance. In other words, unutilized capacity of an enterprise is an index of its problems and all the problems faced by an enterprise leads to underutilization of installed capacity. Hence, it is attempted to use the standard of unutilized capacity to measure the magnitude of the aggregate of all the problems encountered by the enterprises.

Table 6.1 observes the annual average unutilized capacity (in percentages) over the years since starting for the units under study. Only one unit from Imphal West District and 4 units from Imphal East District reported 100 % capacity utilization. Including these 5 units, 46.2 per cent (49 out of 106) had unutilized capacity to the extent of less than 25 per cent. On the other hand, only 0.9 per cent units (1 out of 106) had unutilized capacity of 75 per cent and above. The unutilized capacity of 37.7 per cent units(40 out of 106) is ranging between 25 to 50 per cent and that of 15.1 per cent (16 out of 106) units is ranging between 50 to 75 per cent. Average unutilized capacity of all the 106 units is 29.3 per cent.

Table 6.1
Distribution of Average Unutilised Capacity

Annual Average Unutilised Capacity (%)	Imphal West District	Imphal East District	Both
0 – 25	24 (42.9)	25 (50.0)	49 (46.2)
25 – 50	20 (35.7)	20 (40.0)	40 (37.7)
50 – 75	12 (21.4)	4 (8.0)	16 (15.1)
75 – 100	—	1 (2.0)	1 (0.9)
Total	56 (100.0)	50 (100.0)	106 (100.0)
Average unutilised capacity (per cent)	33.4	24.8	29.3

Source : Field Survey
Note: Figures in parentheses indicate percentages to total.

District-wise, equal number of units under study in both the two districts had unutilized capacity ranging from 25-50 per cent. While 21.4 per cent of the units (12 out of 56) of Imphal West District had unutilized capacity ranging between 50-75 per cent, that of Imphal East District is only 8.0 per cent (4 out of 50). It is also interesting to note that the only one unit which had unutilized capacity ranging between 75 per cent and above is located in Imphal East District. Regarding average unutilized capacity, Imphal West District had 33.4 per cent and that of Imphal East District had 24.8 per cent.

Thus, it can be concluded that the units located in Imphal West District had more unutilized capacity as compared to that of Imphal East District.

(i) Religion Vs unutilized capacity

It is now attempted to analyze the religion-wise average unutilized capacity. As shown in Table 6.2, the average unutilized capacity was highest in enterprises owned by Hindu entrepreneurs (30.1 per cent) followed by those owned by Sikh entrepreneurs (21.7 per cent) and Muslim entrepreneurs (19.0 per cent).

It was lowest (17.5 per cent) in the entrepreneurs started by Christian entrepreneurs.

Table 6.2
Religion-wise Average Unutilised Capacity

Religions	Average age of the units (in years)	Average unutilised capacity (%age)	Total units
Hindu	13.6	30.1	96
Muslim	10.6	19.0	5
Christian	15.0	17.5	2
Sikh	25.3	21.7	3
Total	13.8	29.3	106

Source : Field Survey

Moreover, the average unutilized capacity of Muslim, Christian and Sikh entrepreneurs is less than the average for all the units under study. Again, it is apparent from the table that units started by Sikh entrepreneurs (25.3 years) are the oldest followed by Christian entrepreneurs (15 years). The units owned by Muslim entrepreneurs are the youngest of all (10.6 years) but the average unutilized capacity of those units is less than the average of all the units.

(ii) Type of industry Vs unutilised capacity

Table 6.3 observes the average unutilized capacity with reference to different types of industries. The average unutilized capacity is highest in plastic and rubber based industries (40.4 per cent) followed by food based and 'others' type of industries (35 per cent each). It was the lowest in handlooms and handicrafts industries (18.1 per cent). With regards to the average age of the units, the younger of industries have the higher average unutilized capacities. For example, plastic and rubber based industries which have the highest average unutilized capacity are the second youngest by average age of the units (12.3 year). Likewise, the youngest of all the units i.e. food based industries (11.2 years) have the second highest unutilized capacity along with 'others' type of industry (35 per cent each).

Table 6.3
Industry-wise Average Unutilised Capacity

Tpye of Industry	Average age of the units (in years)	Average unutilised capacity (%age)	Total units
Food based	11.2	35	17
Metal based	18.4	24.6	14
Handloom & Handicrafts	17.1	18.1	8
Plastic & rubber based	12.3	40.4	12
Wood based	15.6	29.7	15
Printing and Stationery	12.6	24.5	10
Automobile and Engineering	12.3	27	25
Others	12.6	35	5
Total	13.8	29.3	106

Source : Field Survey

It can thus be concluded that handlooms and handicrafts industries and printing and stationery industries have the least average unutilized capacities while plastic and rubber based industries have the highest average unutilized capacities.

(iii) Forms of organization Vs unutilized capacity

An attempt is made here to analyze the different forms of organisation and their average unutilized capacity. Table 6.4

shows that sole proprietorship concerns have the highest average unutilized capacity (30.4 per cent). By establishing a relationship with the average age of the units it can be seen that private limited companies which are the youngest (7.8 years) units have the least average unutilized while the sole proprietorship concerns which are the oldest units (14.1 years) have the highest average unutilized capacity. On the other hand, partnership firms which are a little younger than sole proprietorship concerns (13.6 years) have a lesser average unutilized capacity (23.8 per cent).

Table 6.4
Forms of Organization and Average Unutilized Capacity

Forms of Organization	Average age of the units (in years)	Average unutilised capacity (%age)	Total units
Private limited Company	7.8	21.3	4
Partnership	13.6	23.8	12
Sole Proprietorship	14.1	30.4	90
Total	13.8	29.3	106

Source : Field Survey

(iv) Causes of underutilization

The problems faced by the enterprises are all reflected in the underutilization of its capacity and as such these problems can be solved if the reasons for underutilization are traced. So, an attempt is made here to analyze the entrepreneurs' self evaluation of the reasons for underutilization.

Table 6.5 observes the reasons given by entrepreneurs for underutilization, their weighted score, rating and ranking etc. Power scarcity was ranked as number one reason for underutilization of capacity by 19.4 per cent of the entrepreneurs followed as reason number two by lack of finances and slackness of demand (16.3 per cent). The third important reason for underutilization of capacity was lack of raw-materials faced by 12.2 per cent of the entrepreneurs while this is the overall situation in both the districts, some different aspects can be seen in the individual districts. Power scarcity was the reason number one for underutilization of capacity in Imphal West District (22.4 per cent) whereas that of Imphal East District was lack of finances (18.9 per cent). As regards to reason number two, it was slackness of demand in Imphal West District (19.5 per cent) while that of Imphal East District was power scarcity (16.0 per cent).

The other important reasons cited by all the entrepreneurs are 'competition' (11.3 per cent), 'others' (7.6 per cent), 'want of skilled labour' (7.8 per cent) etc.

6.3 Marketing

After analyzing the reasons for underutilization of capacity, an enquiry is made here to know the magnitude and the intensity of the marketing problems faced by the enterprises currently. As again in the case of reasons for underutilization of capacity, a self-assessment of entrepreneurs regarding the marketing problems they faced is sought. Table 6.6 shows the number one and number two problems faced by the enterprises related with marketing. 88 enterprises (83.0 per cent) specified number one problem and 39 of them (36.8 per cent) mentioned the second problem also. 52 of the total 106 (49.1 per cent) enterprises faced competition from small units as problem number one. In addition, 24 units (22.6 per cent) had to compete with large firms. Some other important number one problems are problems of transport and 'other' like seasonal demand, lack of goodown facilities etc. Out of the 39 units mentioning a second important problem, 14 of them complained of competition from small firms again and slackness in demand is number two problem for 12 units.

In the district-wise situation, it can be noted that competition from small as well as large firms is the number one problem for the majority of the units (43 out of 56) in Imphal West District. The number two problem in this district is slackness in demand for ten units. The same case occurred in Imphal East District. Competition from small and large firms happens to be the problem number one and two for majority of the units in this district.

Table 6.5
Reasons for Unutilised Capacity

Reasoms	Imphal West District					Rank	Imphal East District					Both			Rank
	Entrepreneurs' Ranking			Weigh-ted score	Rat-ing (%)		Entrepreneurs' Ranking			Weigh-ted	Rat-ing (%)	Rank	Weight-ted score	Rat-ing (%)	
	One	Two	Three				One	Two	Three						
Slackness of demand	16	1	4	54	19.5	2	5	7	1	30	12.6	3	84	16.3	2
Lack of raw – materials	7	7	1	36	13	4	5	6	-	27	11.3	4	63	12.2	3
Competition	4	7	5	31	11.2	5	3	6	6	27	11.3	4	58	11.3	4
Lack of whole time interest in the enterprise	1	2	1	8	2.9	9	1	1	-	5	2.1	7	13	2.5	8
Mechanical breakdowns	2	3	1	13	4.7	8	4	3	3	21	8.8	6	34	6.6	7
Strained industrial relations	-	-	-	-			-	-	-	-	-	-	-	-	-
Power scarcity	11	12	5	62	22.4	1	8	5	4	38	16	2	100	19.4	1

(contd.)

Table 6.5 *(contd.)*

Reasoms	Imphal West District					Rank	Imphal East District					Both				Rank
	Entrepreneurs' Ranking One	Two	Three	Weighted score	Rating (%)		Entrepreneurs' Ranking One	Two	Three	Weighted	Rating (%)	Rank	Weighted score	Rating (%)		
Want of skilled labour	3	5	-	19	6.9	6	4	4	1	21	8.8	6	40	7.8		6
Lack of finances	7	5	8	39	14.1	3	9	6	6	45	18.9	1	84	16.3		2
Others*	4	1	1	15	5.4	7	7	1	1	24	10.1	5	39	7.6		5
No. of entrepreneurs not responding	1	13	30	0	-	-	4	11	28	0	-	-	0	-		-
Total	56	56	56	277	100		50	50	50	238	100		515	100		

Table 6.6
Problems of Marketing Encountered at present

Problems	Imphal West District		Imphal East District		Both	
	Problem Number		Problem Number		Problem Number	
	One	Two	One	Two	One	Two
Competition from Small Units	28 (50.0)	4 (7.1)	24 (48.0)	10 (20.0)	52 (49.1)	14 (13.2)
Competition from Large firms	15 (26.8)	2 (3.6)	9 (18.0)	2 (4.0)	24 (22.6)	4 (3.8)
Slackness in demand	2 (3.6)	10 (17.9)	-	2 (4.0)	2 (1.9)	12 (11.3)
Price Control	-	1 (1.8)	2 (4.0)	-	2 (1.9)	1 (0.9)
Distribution Control	-	1 (1.8)	-	1 (2.0)	-	2 (4.7)
Problems of transport	2 (3.6)	3 (5.4)	2 (4.0)	2 (4.0)	4 (3.8)	5 (4.7)
Others*	2 (3.6)	1 (5.4)	2 (4.0)	-	4 (3.8)	1 (0.9)
No. of entrepreneurs having no problem	7 (12.5)	34 (60.7)	11 (22.0)	33 (66.0)	18 1(7.0)	67 (63.2)
Total Units	56 (100.0)	56 (100.0)	50 (100.0)	50 (100.0)	106 (100.0)	106 (100.0)

Source : Field Survey
Note: Figures in parentheses indicate percentages to total.
* **Others** includes seasonal demand, lack of goodown facilities etc.

The number one marketing problem faced by different types of industry is given in Table 6.7. It can be seen that no type of industry is free from marketing problem. Only 18 units out of 106 (17.0 per cent) had no problems of marketing. They are five from automobile and engineering works, four from food based units, three each from handlooms and handicrafts, two from metal based units and one from plastic and rubber based units. As compared to other types of industry, handlooms and handicrafts (37.5 per cent) and food based (23.5 per cent) industries are in an advantageous position as regards to having no marketing problem. More or less the marketing problems are same for all types of industry.

Competition from large scale units is insignificant for metal based and wood based units. But it is significant for plastic and rubber based, handlooms and handicrafts and printing and stationery units. But the main problem is competition from small units which is faced by all types of industries. Slackness in demand is suffered by metal based and printing and stationery units. Other problems like seasonal demand, lack of godown facilities etc are mostly encountered by automobile and engineering and food based units.

6.4 Raw materials

It is attempted here to examine the raw-material problems faced by the enterprises currently. The problems might be scarcity of raw-materials or its high prices or low quality. Sometimes it might be transport or other problems. As can be seen from Table 6.8, 77 units (72.6 per cent) mentioned number one problem and 56 (52.8 per cent) of them specified the number two problem of raw-materials also. 25 out of the total 106 (23.6 per cent) units under study complained scarcity as number one problem. Moreover, 24 units had to suffer from high prices as against 21 units (19.8 per cent) whose number one problem is the problem of transport. Out of the units mentioning number two problem relating to raw-materials, 26 suffered from high prices (24.5 per cent), 14 from problems of transport (13.2 per cent), 10 from scarcity (9.4 per cent), 5 from low quality (4.7 per cent) and 1 from other problems (0.9 per cent) such as price fluctuation, seasonal availability of raw-materials etc. While this is the overall situation, in the district-wise

Table 6.7
Number One Marketing Problem Faced by Different Industries

Type of Industry	Number One Problem				Total units having problem	Total units having no problem	Total Units
	Competition from small units	Competition from large units	Slackness in demand	Others			
Food based	7 (13.5)	3 (12.5)	-	3 (30.0)	13 (14.8)	4 (22.2)	17 (16.0)
Metal based	9 (17.3)	1 (4.2)	1 (50.0)	1 (10.0)	12 (13.6)	2 (11.1)	14 (13.4)
Handlooms & Handicrafts	3 (5.8)	2 (8.3)	-	-	5 (5.7)	3 (16.7)	8 (7.6)
Plastic & Rubber based	3 (5.8)	7 (29.2)	-	1 (10.0)	1 (12.5)	1 (5.6)	12 (11.3)
Wood based	10 (19.2)	1 (4.2)	-	1 (10.0)	12 (13.6)	3 (16.7)	15 (14.2)
Printing and stationery	5 (9.6)	3 (12.5)	1 (50.0)	1 (10.0)	10 (11.4)	-	10 (9.4)

(contd.)

Table 6.7 *(contd.)*

Type of Industry	Number One Problem				Total units having problem	Total units having no problem	Total Units
	Competition from small units	Competition from large units	Slackness in demand	Others			
Automobile and Engineering	13	4	-	3	20	5	25
	(25)	(16.7)		(30.0)	(22.7)	(27.8)	(23.6)
Others	2	3	-	-	5	-	5
	(3.9)	(12.5)			(5.7)		(4.7)
Total	52	24	2	10	88	18	106
	(100.0)	(100.0)	(100.0)	(100.0)	(100.0)	(100.0)	(100.0)

Source : Field Survey
Note: Figures in parentheses indicate percentages to total.

classification of some units, different aspects can also be seen. Problems of transport and high prices was the number one problem for majority of the enterprises in Imphal West District (26.8 per cent each) whereas that of Imphal East District was scarcity of raw-materials (32.0 per cent). Regarding the problem number two, Imphal West District enterprises suffered mainly from high prices and scarcity (37.5 per cent) of raw-materials whereas Imphal East District enterprises complained mainly for high prices and problems of transport (42.0 per cent).

Further, table 6.9 shows the distribution of the number one problems of raw-materials by different types of industries. Altogether 26 units complained about scarcity of raw-materials as problem number one. Most of them are wood based units (26.9 per cent), food based and automobile and engineering units (19.2 per cent each). Next to scarcity, high prices of raw-materials proves as a serious problem for 24 units. Among them, 9 are metal based units (37.5 per cent) followed by food based (16.7 per cent), plastic and rubber based (12.5 per cent) etc. Moreover, out of the units facing problems of transport, automobile and engineering units are the maximum (38.1 per cent). It can thus be concluded that out of the total 106 units under study, 28 units (26.4 per cent) have no problems relating to raw-materials. Among them, automobile and engineering and handlooms and handicrafts units are in an advantageous position as compared to other types of industries.

6.5 Power

After the problems relating to raw-materials have been analyzed, now the attention is drawn towards the problems of power faced by the enterprises. Table 6.10 observes the distribution of number one and number two power problems of the enterprises. 90 enterprises (84.9 per cent) mentioned number one problem and 78 of them (73.6 per cent) specified the second problem also. 67 of the units (63.2 per cent) suffered from uncertainty of power supply as number one problem followed by 19 units (17.9 per cent) whose main complaints was scarcity of power supply. Out of the units who specified a second main problem, 54 units (50.9 per cent) were affected by scarcity of power followed by 18 units (26.9 per cent) who specified uncertainty of power supply. District-wise also, the problems relating to power is also quite the same.

Table 6.8
Problems of Raw-Materials Encountered at present

Problems	Imphal West District		Imphal East District		Both	
	Problem Number		Problem Number		Problem Number	
	One	Two	One	Two	One	Two
Scarcity	9 (16.1)	8 (14.3)	16 (32.0)	2 (4.0)	25 (23.6)	10 (9.4)
High Prices	15 (26.8)	13 (23.2)	9 (18.0)	13 (26.0)	24 (22.6)	26 (24.5)
Low Quality	2 (3.6)	3 (5.4)	1 (2.0)	2 (4.0)	3 (2.8)	5 (4.7)
Problem of transport	15 (26.8)	6 (10.7)	6 (12.0)	8 (16.0)	21 (19.8)	14 (13.2)
Others *	2 (3.6)	1 (1.8)	2 (4.0)	—	4 (3.8)	1 (0.9)
No. of entrepreneurs having no problem	13 (23.2)	25 (44.6)	16 (32.0)	25 (50.0)	29 (27.4)	50 (47.2)
Total Units	56 (100.0)	56 (100.0)	50 (100.0)	50 (100.0)	106 (100.0)	106 (100.0)

Source : Field Survey
Note: Figures in parentheses indicate percentages to total.
* **Others** includes price fluctuation, seasonal availability of raw-materials etc.

Table 6.9
Number One Raw-Materials Problems Faced by Different Industries

Type of Industry	No. One Problem					Total units having problem	Total units having no problem	Total units
	Scarcity	High Prices	Low quality	Transport	Others			
Food based	5	4	-	3	-	12	5	17
	(19.2)	(16.7)		(14.3)		(15.4)	(17.9)	(16.0)
Metal based	4	9	-	-	-	13	1	14
	(15.4)	(37.5)				(16.7)	(3.6)	(13.2)
Handlooms &	1	2	2	-	-	5	3	8
Handicrafts	(3.9)	(8.3)	(66.7)			(6.4)	(10.7)	(7.6)
Plastic & Rubber	2	3	-	4	-	9	3	12
based	(7.7)	(12.5)	-	(19.1)	-	(11.5)	(10.7)	(11.3)
Wood based	7	2	-	1	-	10	5	15
	(26.9)	(8.3)		(4.8)		(12.8)	(17.9)	(14.2)
Printing and	1	2	1	4	2	10	-	10
stationery	(3.9)	(8.3)	(33.3)	(19.1)	(50.0)	(12.8)	-	(9.4)

(contd.)

Table 6.9 - (*contd.*)

Type of Industry	No. One Problem					Total units having problem	Total units having no problem	Total units
	Scarcity	High Prices	Low quality	Transport	Others			
Automobile and Engineering	5 (19.2)	2 (8.3)	-	8 (38.1)	-	15 (19.2)	10 (35.7)	25 (23.6)
Others	1 (3.9)	-	-	1 (4.8)	2 (50.0)	4 (5.1)	1 (3.6)	5 (4.7)
Total	26 (100.0)	24 (100.0)	3 (100.0)	21 (100.0)	4 (100.0)	78 (100.0)	28 (100.0)	106 (100.0)

Source : Field Survey
Note : Figures in parentheses indicate percentages to total

Table 6.10
Problems of Power Encountered at Present

Problems	Imphal West District		Imphal East District		Both	
	Problem Number		Problem Number		Problem Number	
	One	Two	One	Two	One	Two
Scarcity	12	27	7	27	19	54
	(21.4)	(48.20	(14.0)	(54.0)	(17.9)	(50.9)
Uncertainty	34	11	33	7	67	18
	(60.70	(19.60	(66.0)	(14.0)	(63.2)	(17.0)
High Cost	1	5	1	1	2	6
	(1.80	(8.90	(2.0)	(2.0)	(1.9)	(5.7)
Other	2	-	-	-	2	-
	(3.60)				(1.9)	
No. of Entrepreneur having	7	13	9	15	16	28
no problem	(12.50	(23.20	(18	(30.0)	(15.1)	(26.4)
Total Units	56	56	50	50	106	106
	(100.0)	(100.0)	(100.0)	(100.0)	(100.0)	(100.0)

Source : Field Survey
Note: Figures in parentheses indicate percentages to total.

Table 6.11
Number One Power Problem Faced by Different Industries

Type of Industry	No. One Problem				Total units having problem	Total units having no problem	Total units
	Scarcity	Un-certainty	High Prices	Others			
Food based	5	10	1	-	16	1	17
	(26.3)	(14.9)	(50.0)		(17.8)	(6.3)	(16)
Metal based	2	8	1	-	11	3	14
	(10.5)	(11.9)	(50.0)		(12.2)	(18.8)	(13.2)
Handlooms &	1	5	-	-	6	2	8
Handicrafts	(5.3)	(7.5)			(6.7)	(12.5)	(7.5)
Plastic & Rubber	4	8	-	-	12	-	12
based	(21.1)	(11.9)			(13.3)		(11.3)
Wood based	3	9	-	-	12	3	15
	(15.8)	(13.4)			(13.3)	(18.8)	(14.2)
Printing and stationery	1	7	-	2	10	-	10
	(5.3)	(10.4)		((100.0)	(11.1)		(9.4)

Automobile and	3	18	-	-	21	4	25
Engineering	(15.8)	(26.9)			(23.3	(25.0)	(23.6)
Others	-	2	-	-	2	3	5
		(3.0)			(2.2)	(18.8)	(4.7)
Total	19 (100.0)	67 (100.0)	2 (100.0)	2 (100.0)	90 (100.0)	16 (100.0)	106 (100.0)

Source : Field Survey
Note: Figures in parentheses indicate percentages to total.

Regarding the industry-wise problem related with power, it can be seen from Table 6.11 that scarcity of power was felt mainly by food based industries (26.3 per cent) followed by plastic and rubber based industries (21.1 per cent).

However, the main problem of power i.e., uncertainty of power supply was suffered maximum by automobile and engineering units (26.9 per cent) followed by food based (14.9 per cent), wood based (13.4 per cent) units etc. The problem of high cost appeared to be genuine as most of the units installed generators for running the units without any power breakdowns or power-offs. It can also be noted that power cut-off or roaster systems have become a regular phenomenon of the Indian power system and Manipur is not an exception.

6.6 Labour

In the overall situation, 45 out of 106 units (42.5 per cent) complained of number one problem of labour as is shown in Table 6.12. Among them, 33 units (31.1 per cent) suffered from the problem of absenteeism, problem of training was reported by 7 units (6.6 per cent) and in the case of 4 units (3.8 per cent) the problem was 'others' which includes non-availability of skilled workers, high wage rate etc. In addition, 12 units also mentioned a second problem. Out of them, training was reported by 6 units and for another 3 units, their second problem was absenteeism.

As regards the industry-wise problem number one of labour, Table 6.13 observes that training of labour was a problem for all types of industries except metal based, wood based and other types of industries. However, the problem of absenteeism of labour was mainly suffered by automobile and engineering (36.4 per cent) followed by wood based units (21.2 per cent), food based (12.1 per cent) units etc. Labour turnover in plastic & rubber based units was on account of other local concerns offering high wages and absenteeism had been due to lack of social discipline. On the whole, employer-employee relations were satisfactory.

6.7 Finance

It has been found that the important problem faced by the enterprises from their commencement was finance. As can be

Table 6.12
Problems of Labour Encountered at Present

Problems	Imphal West District Problem Number		Imphal East District Problem Number		Both Problem Number	
	One	Two	One	Two	One	Two
Training	4 (7.1)	3 (5.4)	3 (6)	3 (6)	7 (6.6)	6 (5.7)
Turnover	-	2 (3.6)	1 (1	-	1 (0.9	2 (1.9)
Absenteeism	17 (30.4)	2 (3.6)	16) (32	1 (2)	33 (31.1)	3 (2.8)
Others*	3 (5.4)	1 (1.8)	1 (2)		4 (3.8)	1 (0.9)
No. of Entrepreneurs having no problem	32 (57.1)	48 (85.7)	29 (58)	46 (92)	61 (57.5)	94 (88.7)
Total Units	56 (100.0)	56 (100.0)	50 (100.0)	50 (100.0)	106 (100.0)	106 (100.0)

Source : Field Survey
Note: Figures in parentheses indicate the percentages to total.
* **Others** includes non-availability of skilled workers, high wage rate etc.

Table 6.13
Number One Labour Problem Faced by Different Industries

Type of Industry	No. One Problem				Total units having problem	Total units having no problem	Total units
	Training	Turn-over	Absente-eism	Others			
Food based	1	-	4	1	6	11	17
	(14.3)		(12.1)	(25.0)	(13.3)	(18	(16
Metal based	-	-	1	1	2	12	14
			(3.0)	(25.0)	(4.4)	(19.7)	(13.2)
Handlooms & Handicrafts	1	-	2	-	3	5	8
	(14.3)		(6.1)		(6.7)	(8.2)	(7.5)
Plastic & Rubber based	2	1	1	-	4	8	12
	(28.6)	(100.0)	(3)		(8.9)	(13.1	(11.3)
Wood based	-	-	7	-	7	8	15
			(21.1)		(15.6)	(13.1)	(14.2)
Printing and stationery	1	-	5	2	8	2	10
	(14.3)		(15.2)	(50)	(17.8)	(3.3)	(9.4)

Automobile & Engineering	2	-	12	-	14	11	25
	(28.6)		(36.4)		(31.1)	(18.0)	(23.6)
Others	-	-	1	-	1	4	5
			(3.0)		(2.2)	(6.6)	(4.7)
Total	7	1	33	4	45	61	106
	(100.0)	(100.0)	(100.0)	(100.0)	(100.0)	(100.0)	(100.0)

Source : Field Survey
Note: Figures in parentheses indicate percentages to total.

Table 6.14
Problems of Finance Encountered at Present

Problems	Imphal West District Problem Number		Imphal East District Problem Number		Both Problem Number	
	One	Two	One	Two	One	Two
Shortage of Working Capital	31 (55.4)	12 (21.4)	17 (34.0)	14 (28.0)	48 (45.3)	26 (24.5)
Shortage of fixed capital	11 (19.6)	16 (28.6)	23 (46)	13 (26)	34 (32.1)	29 (27.4)
High rates of interest	-	3 (5.4)	1 (2)	2 (4.0)	1 (0.9)	5 (4.7)
Red(tape in Government a gencies	2 (3.6)	1 (1.8)	1 (2.0)	1 (2.0)	3 (2.8)	2 (1.9)
Meagre assistance from Government agencies	2 (3.6)	4 (7.1)	-	2 (4.0)	2 (1.9)	6 (5.7)
Others*	1 (1.8)	-	-	-	1 (0.9)	-

No. of entrepreneurs having no problem	9 (16.1)	20 (35.7)	8 (16.0)	18 (36.0)	17 (16.0)	38 (35.8)
Total Units	56 (100.0)	56 (100.0)	50 (100.0)	50 (100.0)	106 (100.0)	106 (100.0)

Source : Field Survey
Note: Figures in parentheses indicate percentages to total.
* **Others** includes delayed payment of accounts, credit sales, inadequate banking facilities etc.

Table 6.15
Number One Finance Problem Faced by Different Industries

Type of Industry	No. One Problem				Total units having problem	Total units having no problem	Total units
	Shortage of working capital	Shortage of fixed capital	High rates of interest	Others			
Food based	9	5	-	-	14	3	17
	(18.8)	(14.7)			(15.7)	(17.6)	(16)
Metal based	7	6	-	1	14	-	14
	(14.6)	(17.6)		(16.7)	(15.7)		(13.2)
Handlooms & Handicrafts	3	3	-	-	6	2	8
	(6.3)	(8.8)			(6.7)	(11.8)	(7.5)
Plastic & Rubber based	6	3	1	1	11	1	12
	(12.5)	(8.8)	(100.0)	(16.7)	(12.4)	(5.9)	(11.3)
Wood based	5	5	-	2	12	3	15
	(10.4)	(14.7)		(33.3)	(13.5)	(17.6)	(14.2)
Printing and stationery	6	2	-	-	8	2	10
	(12.5)	(5.9)			(9.0)	(11.8)	(9.4)

Automobile & Engineering	10	9	-	1	20	5	25
	(20.8)	(26.5)		(16.7)	(22.5)	(29.4)	(23.6)
Others	2	1	-	1	4	1	5
	(4.2)	(2.9)		(16.7)	(4.5)	(5.9)	(4.7)
Total	48	34	1	6	89	17	106
	(100.0)	(100.0)	(100.0)	(100.0)	(100.0)	(100.0)	(100.0)

Source : Field Survey
Note: Figures in parentheses indicate the percentages to total.

observed form Table 6.14, only 17 units (16.0 per cent) and 38 units (35.8 per cent) reported as having no number one and two finance problems respectively. In the overall situation, majority of the units faced shortage of working capital (45.3 per cent) as number one financial problem. However, it was shortage of fixed capital for another 32.4 per cent of the units.

High rates of interest, red-tape in government agencies, meagre assistance from government agencies etc. are some of the other financial problems faced by comparatively less number of units.

As regards to number two problem of finance, 29 units (27.4 per cent) complained about shortage of fixed capital as against 26 units (24.5 per cent) who were suffering from shortage of working capital. Meagre assistance from government agencies and high rates of interest were faced by 6 and 5 units respectively.

No particular type of financial problem is peculiar to any particular type of industry as could be seen from Table 6.15. The problem of shortage of working capital is almost universal as it is faced by each and every industry. Comparatively, handlooms and handicrafts, wood based and automobile and engineering units are in advantageous position as less percentage of these units are facing the problem of shortage of working capital. For example, 3 out of 8 (handlooms and handicrafts), 5 out of 15 (wood based) and 10 out of 25 (automobile and engineering) units are facing the problem of shortage of working capital. As to the shortage of fixed capital also, almost all types of industries are not free from this problem. Metal based, handlooms and handicrafts, wood based and automobile and engineering units are facing acute shortage of fixed capital (23 units).

6.8 Technical and managerial assistance

Coming to the problem of technical and managerial assistance, altogether 44 units reported a number one problem. Of them, 16 units also mentioned a number two problem of it. 22 units (20.8 per cent) complained about ineffective consultancy service provided by government agencies (Table 6.16) followed by 13 units (12.3 per cent) who suffered from lack of skilled

Table 6.16
Problems of Technical and Managerial Assistance Encountered of Present

Problems	Imphal West District		Imphal East District		Both	
	Problem Number		Problem Number		Problem Number	
	One	Two	One	Two	One	Two
Ineffective consultancy services provided by Govt. agencies	10 (17.9)	-	12 (24.0)	-	22 (20.8)	-
Expensive consultancy services provided by private agencies	3 (5.4)	2 (3.6)	3 (6.0)	7 (14.0)	6 (5.7)	9 (8.5)
Lack of skilled workforce	6 (10.7)	1 (1.8)	7 (14.0)	3 (6.0)	13 (12.3)	4 (3.8)
Lack of proficient manager	1 (1.8)	2 (3.6)	1 (2.00)	1 (2.0)	2 (1.9)	3 (2.8)
Others*	-	-	1 (2.0)		1 (0.9)	-

(contd.)

Table 6.16 - *(contd.)*

Problems	Imphal West District		Imphal East District		Both	
	Problem Number		Problem Number		Problem Number	
	One	Two	One	Two	One	Two
No.of entrepreneurs having no problem	36 (64.3)	51 (91.1)	26 (52.0)	39 (78.0)	62 (58.5)	90 (84.9)
Total Units	56 (100.0)	55 (100.0)	50 (100.0)	50 (100.0)	106 (100.0)	106 (100.0)

Source : Field Survey
Note: Figures in parentheses indicate the percentages to total.
* **Others** includes lack of organized technical services, irresponsible attitude of suppliers of plant and machinery etc.

consultancy service provided by government agencies (Table 6.16) followed by 13 units (12.3 per cent) who suffered from lack of skilled workmen as number one technical and managerial assistance problem. Among the problem number two, expensive consultancy services provided by private agencies were suffered by 9 units (8.5 per cent) followed by 4 units (3.8 per cent) who reported lack of skilled workforce. Lack of proficient manager was also felt by 3 units (2.8 per cent) as an important number two technical and managerial assistance problem.

Distribution of the number one problem of technical and managerial assistance faced by different types of industries is shown in Table 6.17. Altogether 22 units are facing the problem of ineffective consultancy services provided by government agencies. Most of these units are automobile and engineering (5), food based and wood based (4 each) and plastic and rubber based (3) units.

Other than the problems of ineffective consultancy services provided by government agencies, other important problems of technical and managerial assistance are lack of skilled workmen and expensive consultancy services provided by private agencies. Lack of skilled workmen are also common to all types of industries whereas expensive consultancy services are felt by food based, automobile and engineering (2 each) and metal based and printing and stationery works (1 each). Lack of proficient manager was reported by 1 unit each of wood based and automobile and engineering unit.

Table 6.17
Number One Technical and Managerial Problem Faced by Different Industries

Type of Industry	No. One Problem				Total units having problem	Total units having no problem	Total units
	Ineffective consultancy service provided by Govt. agiencies	Expensive consultancy service provided by Pvt. agiencies	Lack of skilled workmen	Others			
Food based	4	2	2	-	8	9	17
	(18.2)	(33.3)	(15.4)		(18.2)	(14.5)	(16.0)
Metal based	3	1	2	-	6	8	14
	(13.6)	(16.7)	(15.4)		(13.6)	(12.9)	(13.2)
Handlooms & Handicrafts	-	-	2	-	2	6	8
			(15.4)		(4.6)	(9.7)	(7.5)
Plastic & Rubber based	3	-	1	1	5	7	12
	(13.6)		(7.7)	(33.3)	(11.4)	(11.3)	(11.3)

Wood based	4	-	2	1	7	3	15
	(18.2)		(15.4)	(33.3)	(15.9)	(12.9)	(14.2)
Printing and stationery	1	1	2	-	4	6	10
	(4.5)	(16.7)	(15.4)		(9.1)	(9.7)	(9.4)
Automobile & Engineering	5	2	2	1	10	15	25
	(22.7)	(33.3)	(15.4)	(33.3)	(22.7)	(24.2)	(23.6)
Others	2	-	-	-	2	3	5
	(9.1)				(4.6)	(4.8)	(4.7)
Total	22	6	13	3	44	62	106
	(100.0)	(100.0)	(100.0)	(100.0)	(100.0)	(100.0)	(100.0)

Source : Field Survey

Note: Figures in parentheses indicate percentages to total.

CHAPTER VII

FINDINGS OF THE STUDY AND SUGGESTIONS

In this chapter, the findings and suggestions of the whole study are presented.

Findings of the study

The findings of the study are discussed as hereunder:

7.1 Generation of entrepreneurs

It has been found that 79.2 per cent of entrepreneurs were first generation entrepreneurs, followed by 19.8 per cent second generation and 0.9 per cent third generation entrepreneurs. District-wise, majority of the first generation entrepreneurs are from Imphal East District while majority of the second generation and third generation are from Imphal West District.

i) Age

Majority of the first and second generation entrepreneurs belongs to the age group 21-30 years (46.4 and 42.9 per cent respectively). The third generation belongs to 31-40 years age group.

ii) Type of industry started

Handlooms and handicrafts and 'others' types of industries are preferred only by the first generation entrepreneurs.

The lone third generation entrepreneur was interested in the metal based industry.

iii) Forms of organisation preferred

Seventy-five per cent of the private limited companies were established by first generation entrepreneurs as against 25.0

per cent by the second generation. In case of partnership firms also, the trend is also the same. The only third generation entrepreneur started his unit as a partnership firm.

7.2 Religion of entrepreneurs

Entrepreneurs in the two districts under study are mostly Hindus, followed by Muslims, Sikhs and Christians respectively. Hindus are the single largest group (90.6 per cent), whereas Christians stood as the smallest group (1.9 per cent).

(i) Entry into entrepreneurship

a) Time of entry

It is very interesting to note that 90.5 per cent of all the entrepreneurs who commenced their industrial units before 1980 were Hindus and 4.8 per cent each were Christians and Sikhs. Muslim entrepreneurs started entering into entrepreneurship during the period 1990-1995. District-wise, the industrial units in Imphal West District had greater length of existence than those in Imphal East District.

b) Age of entry Vs religion

The highest percentage of the entrepreneurs (45.3 per cent) entered into entrepreneurship at the age of 21-30 years (average age 25.5 years). Christian entrepreneurs started their units at the earlier age (average age 21.5 years) while the Muslim entrepreneurs started their units at a later stage (average age 36.8 years).

(ii) Type of industry chosen

23.6 per cent of the entrepreneurs started their industrial units in automobile and engineering works and 16.0 per cent of the entrepreneurs preferred food based industries. It is very interesting to note here that 100.0 per cent of the handlooms and handicrafts industries and 'others' group of industries were undertaken by the Hindu entrepreneurs only.

(iii) Forms of organisation preferred

Sole proprietorship is the most popular of all the forms of organisation. It gained popularity among all the religions except Sikh. It is worth mentioning that all the Muslim and Christian entrepreneurs run their units as the sole trading concerns.

Private limited companies were started only by the Hindu entrepreneurs.

7.3 Occupational background

More people from students, professional and business background were attracted towards industrial entrepreneurship than those from the government service and agriculture.

(i) Occupational background and age of entering into entrepreneurship

21-30 years age group is mostly preferred by the entrepreneurs with student background followed by government service background and agricultural background. 51 years and above age group is preferred by the majority of the entrepreneurs having agricultural background.

(ii) Occupational background and type of industry chosen

Entrepreneurs hailing from professional background started industries falling under the category of automobile and engineering works. Those whose occupational background was agriculture were found uniformly in food based, metal based and printing and stationery industries.

(iii) Occupational background and forms of organisation

Private limited companies were started by the highest percentage of the entrepreneurs who were having professional background. Majority of the entrepreneurs started units as sole proprietorship concerns. It is very interesting to note that entrepreneurs having agricultural and government service background preferred only the sole proprietorship concerns.

7.4 Educational Background

It is interesting to note that majority of the entrepreneurs under study were graduates and post-graduates (49 out of 106). Only 11.3 per cent of the total entrepreneurs were under-matriculates. In other words, a low level of education has not deterred the under-matriculates to be ahead of others in industrial entrepreneurship.

(i) Educational qualification of entrepreneurs and their age at the time of entry

Graduate entrepreneurs formed the highest percentage (41.7 per cent) who entered industry at the age group of 21-30 years. On the other hand, 50.0 per cent of the entrepreneurs who started their units in the age group of 51 & above years were only educated upto under-matric. On the basis of these observations, it is felt that education plays a pivotal role to the cause of the furtherance of entrepreneurship. It can thus be concluded that people with higher educational levels are finding their entry into industry earlier.

(ii) Entrepreneurs' education and their generation

About seventy-seven per cent graduate entrepreneurs were first generation while the rest are second generation. It is very interesting to note that all the post-graduate entrepreneurs are first generation entrepreneurs. On the other hand, the only third generation entrepreneur is educated upto twelve standard. Thus, it can be concluded that higher the level of education the greater is the chance to start industry as a first generation entrepreneur.

(iii) Entrepreneurs' education and their religion

The spread of schooling has cut across the business of religion. It may be noticed that majority of the graduates and all of the post-graduates were Hindus. It seems none of the entrepreneurial religions are placed in a disadvantageous position, by comparison.

(iv) Entrepreneurs' educational qualification and type of industry chosen

Entrepreneurs with high educational level preferred automobile and engineering industries whereas that of with low educational level opted for metal based industries.

(v) Entrepreneurs' educational qualification and forms of organisation preferred

Private limited company and partnership as a form of organisation is not yet popular in Manipur. Sole proprietorship concern is the most popular in all the levels of entrepreneurs' education.

7.5 Parental occupation of entrepreneurs

Government service was the parental occupation of the highest percentage of the entrepreneurs (31.1 per cent) followed by agriculture (26.4 per cent). District-wise, agriculture was the pre-dominant parental occupation in Imphal East District (32.0 per cent), while government service was the dominant occupation in the Imphal West District (37.5 per cent).

(i) Parental occupation of entrepreneurs and age at the time of entry

Majority of the entrepreneurs whose parental occupation were agriculture, government service and profession entered the industry at the age of 21-30 years. On the other hand, a good number of entrepreneurs whose parental occupation was business entered into the entrepreneurial activity either at the age of 21-30 years or 31-40 years.

(ii) Parental occupation of entrepreneurs and type of industry preferred

Most of the entrepreneurs, irrespective of their parental occupation, started their units related to automobile and engineering industries. Among them, entrepreneurs whose parental occupation was agriculture, government service and profession formed the highest (28.0 per cent each). Next to it, most of the units related to food based industries were started mainly by the entrepreneurs whose parental occupation was business and government service (35.3 per cent each).

7.6 Parental education of entrepreneurs

It is interesting to note that majority of the entrepreneurs' parents were under-matriculates (38.7 per cent). While graduates constituted 12.3 per cent, post-graduates accounted for only 1.9 per cent.

(i) Parental education and entrepreneurs' age at the time of entry

About fifty-four per cent (53.8%) of the entrepreneurs having a parental education of graduate preferred the age group of 21-30 years. For the parental education of post-graduate also, 21-30 yeas is the chosen age group to start an industry. Further, it is observed that those who started industry at the later stage of 41-50 years, illiterates formed the highest (61.5 per cent). It indicates that higher level of parental education induces entrepreneurs to make an early entry into industrial entrepreneurship.

(ii) Parental education and entrepreneurs' education

Almost all the entrepreneurs under study are not only first generation entrepreneurs but also they are first among the generation that are educated. But it does not mean that the low level of parental education proves hindrance to entrepreneurship as majority of the entrepreneurs were having parental education upto matriculation only.

(iii) Parental education and religion

Hindu entrepreneurs are more educated than other as regards their parental education. The parental education of under-graduation, graduation and post-graduation were found only for them. For the Muslim entrepreneurs, their parents were educated upto matriculation whereas it was only upto under-matriculates for the Christian and Sikh entrepreneurs.

(iv) Parental education and type of industry opted

Automobile and engineering units are opted by majority of the entrepreneurs having different parental education except those having upto under-graduation, followed by food based and wood based industry.

(v) Parental education and forms of organisation preferred

Sole proprietorship concerns are started by those entrepreneurs having parental education only upto under-matriculation. On the other hand, private limited companies are equally started by those entrepreneurs having parents who were illiterates and educated upto post-graduation. It can thus be concluded that less parental education has not deterred the entrepreneurs to start units either on company form or partnership from rather than the ordinary sole proprietorship concerns.

(vi) Parental education and generation of entrepreneurs

Parental education upto graduation (92.3 per cent) and post-graduation induced their wards to start industry as first generation entrepreneurs. On the other hand, majority of the second generation entrepreneurs and the only third generation entrepreneur were having parental education upto under-matriculation. Thus, it can be concluded that higher the parental education, the greater is the chance to become entrepreneurs as first generation.

7.7 Economic status of entrepreneurs

The average monthly income of entrepreneurs of Imphal West District is Rs. 2951.79 while that of Imphal East District is Rs. 2394.70. It is worthwhile to mention here that 41.5 per cent of the entrepreneurs were unemployed or students whose particulars are not available. Religion-wise, the average monthly income of Hindu entrepreneurs were found to be the highest followed by Muslim, Sikh and Christian entrepreneurs.

7.8 Rural/urban background of entrepreneurs

It is observed that urban experience is not a precondition of industrial entrepreneurship. Majority of the entrepreneurs under study had rural background (60.4 per cent).

(i) Rural/urban background and type of industries preferred

The highest percentage of the entrepreneurs with rural background started automobile and engineering units (29.7 per cent) followed by metal based units (15.6 per cent) and food based units (14.1 per cent). Those with urban background, who started food based units constituted the highest (10.0 per cent).

(ii) Rural/urban background and forms of organisation

Private limited company and partnership form of organisation was preferred by the entrepreneurs hailing from rural and urban background in the ratio 1:3. As regards the sole proprietorship concern, 42.2 per cent had come from urban background whereas 57.8 per cent had rural background. Partnership form of organisation is also mainly preferred by those entrepreneurs hailing from rural background.

(iii) Rural/urban background and generation of entrepreneurs

76.2 per cent of the entrepreneurs hailing from urban background are first generation entrepreneurs, followed by 21.4

per cent second generation and 2.4 per cent third generation entrepreneurs. On the other hand, entrepreneurs having rural background are constituted by 81.3 per cent first and 18.8 per cent second generation entrepreneurs. It is interesting to note that the only third generation entrepreneur hails from urban background.

7.9 Pattern of Families

84 of the total entrepreneurs (79.2 per cent) were in joint families at the time of starting their units and 22 (20.8 per cent) were in nuclear families. Religion-wise, all the Christian and Sikh entrepreneurs were in joint families. Among the Hindu entrepreneurs, 79.2 per cent were from joint families as against 20.8 per cent from nuclear family. The ratio of joint family and nuclear family in respect of Muslim entrepreneurs is 3:2.

7.10 Entrepreneurs' Ambitions

Ambitions motivate men. It activise men, broaden their vision and make the life more meaningful. As regards the entrepreneurs' ambitions, the ambition of gaining independent living or self-employment was ranked first in Imphal West District as well as in Imphal East District. In both the districts put together, 'to make money' received second rank.

7.11 Reasons Compelling Entrepreneurs to Enter Industry

Sometimes the compulsion rather than the ambition leads the man to success. But it is not an easy task to differentiate between one's ambition and compulsion. The main compulsion that has compelled the entrepreneurs in both the districts was the diversification of economic interest. It may be interesting to note that 6 entrepreneurs had no compelling reason to start industry. Thus, what is an ambition for one entrepreneur may be a compulsion for another.

It is the entrepreneurs' attitude that ultimately makes the difference.

7.12 Factors Facilitating Entrepreneurship

It has been observed that there are at least two important factors facilitating entrepreneurship apart from a few others.

They are previous experience in manufacturing and encouragement of family members/relatives/friends.

7.13 Expectations of entrepreneurs

It is quite natural that many of the entrepreneurs expect a lot from the state government and other non-government agencies. Whether these expectations get fulfilled or not, they initiate a useful function in stimulating the desire of the entrepreneur to start an industry. For example, many of the entrepreneurs (73 out of the total 106) expected financial assistance from State Government, Manipur Industrial Development Corporation (MANIDCO) and other state and national agencies.

7.14 Entrepreneurs' expectations and its fulfilment

Only 25 out of the total 106 entrepreneurs could fulfilled their expectations. This explains the realistic attitude of the entrepreneurs in general. The expectancy gap is broader perhaps because many of them have the expectations of getting financial assistance from government or other sources.

7.15 Choice of type of industries

Previous employment in the industry influenced the entrepreneurs much in their preference of type of industries. Selecting an industry type on reason likes easy to set up or easy availability of machinery or raw-materials is weakness of entrepreneurs. Banking on initial easiness is not enterprising. They may face problems in the future if they hesitate to take more pains in the beginning. But it does not mean that choosing industries on such ground will err the entrepreneurs in all the cases.

7.16 Reasons influencing entrepreneurs to locate their unit in the district

It has been observed that the entrepreneurs are very much reluctant to move away from their hometowns or native places. Overall idealness of the place for the industry was rated as number one rank by Imphal West District entrepreneurs while it was nearness to markets in the case of Imphal East District.

7.17 Discouraging factors in the process of setting up/commencement of the unit

The main factor responsible for slow commencement of the industrial unit was shortage of working capital. This automatically points to the inadequate banking facilities in the state or poor banking habits of the entrepreneurs. But it is interesting to note that 22 out of 56 entrepreneurs of Imphal West District and 19 out of 50 entrepreneurs of Imphal East District started their units without having any discouraging headache at the beginning.

7.18 Friend, philosopher and guide of the entrepreneurs

51.9 per cent of the entrepreneurs (55 out of 106) gave the names of either their family members or relatives as friend, philosopher and guide. Only 10.4 per cent of the entrepreneurs were not motivated by any outside individual but they received the motivation from within.

7.19 Satisfaction with location of unit

After the study, it is found that majority of the entrepreneurs under study are satisfied with the location of their units. It will go hand-in-hand with the development of entrepreneurship in small scale industries. Satisfaction with location of unit includes satisfaction with common facilities like banks, post-office, water, electricity, raw-materials servicing ventures, testing laboratories for raw-materials and products etc.

But, it is interesting to note the reasons for dissatisfaction from 21 entrepreneurs who are not satisfied with the location of their unit. Inadequate common facilities were rated highest as reason number one by majority of the entrepreneurs of both Imphal West and Imphal East Districts. To be more precise, lack of water supply, erratic power condition and more specially, lack of testing laboratory for raw-materials and products are some of the inadequate common facilities availed by the entrepreneurs.

7.20 Feasibility study of the enterprise

More than half of the entrepreneurs under study undertook feasibility study of their respective projects. While some carried out the study themselves (26.4 per cent), other took the help of outside agencies (29.2 per cent). It is very interesting to note that 44.3 per cent of the total entrepreneurs didn't find any reason to conduct the study.

(i) Age of entrepreneurs

It has been noticed that with the increase in the age of entrepreneurs starting from 21-30 years group, less number of entrepreneurs depends upon outside agencies for conducting their feasibility study. More interestingly, all the entrepreneurs in the 51 & above year's group didn't conduct any feasibility study. It is, perhaps, due to the difference in the maturity level of entrepreneurs.

(ii) Educational level of entrepreneurs

It is interesting to conclude that the number of entrepreneurs who never conducted any feasibility study decreases with the increase in the educational level of the entrepreneurs. For example 11 out of 12 under-matriculate entrepreneurs didn't conduct any feasibility study whereas only 10 out of 39 graduate entrepreneurs didn't find any reason to conduct the study. Hence, educational background has a direct relation with the undertaking of feasibility study of the project.

(iii) Religion of entrepreneurs

It was in the case of Sikh entrepreneurs that two-thirds conducted the study either by themselves or through other agencies. In case of Muslim entrepreneurs, only 20 per cent (1 out of 4) conducted the study themselves.

(iv) Rural/urban background of entrepreneurs

In the present study, it has been found that rural background cannot be a disadvantage to the entrepreneurs in carrying out the feasibility study. For example, out of the 64 entrepreneurs with rural background, 39 entrepreneurs conducted the study by themselves (17 entrepreneurs) or through other agencies (22 entrepreneurs). On the other hand, out of 42 entrepreneurs with urban background, 11 entrepreneurs conducted the study themselves and 9 entrepreneurs depended on outside agencies for conducting the study.

(v) Type of industry

Entrepreneurs who started plastic & rubber based industries had not undertaken any feasibility study by themselves. The highest percentage of entrepreneurs who conducted the study themselves were found in the automobile and engineering works (7.5 per cent) whereas that of entrepreneurs who depended on outside agencies were found in plastic & rubber based industries (8.6 per cent).

(vi) Generation of entrepreneurs

The first generation entrepreneurs depended mostly on outside agencies. The source is just the opposite in case of second generation entrepreneurs. Most of them have faith in themselves for conducting the study. The third generation entrepreneur conducted the study only by himself.

(vii) Forms of organisation

All the entrepreneurs who started their units as private limited companies conducted the study either by themselves or through other agencies. In case of those entrepreneurs who formed partnership firms, half of them conducted the study through outside agencies.

7.21 Time lag between commencement of production and other stages of production.

In Imphal West District, 32.14 per cent entrepreneurs reported a time lag of less than one year, 25.0 per cent a time lag of 1-2 years, 16.1 per cent 2-3 years, 8.9 per cent 3-4 years and 14.3 per cent 4 and above years between commencement of production and conception of idea to start unit. On the other hand, in Imphal East District, between conception of idea to start unit and commencement of production, a time lag of less than one year was reported by 46.0 per cent of the entrepreneurs, while 1-2 years was reported by another 26.0 per cent, 2-3 years delay was reported by 16.0 per cent and 3-4 years delay was reported by 4.0 per cent, 6.0 per cent reported a delay of 4 years & above.

7.22 Financing the enterprises

In the promotion of an enterprise, the availability of enough finance is the most important factor, without it, the idea to start business or industry will always remain a simple wish. Even if the necessary finance is available, there are many obstacles in financing the small scale industries. These obstacles are always rated as high risks.

(i) Initial capital invested

In both the districts, highest percentage of enterprises (69.8 per cent) invested an amount upto Rs. 2 lakhs. District-wise, greater amount of capital was invested in units in Imphal West District (average capital Rs. 3.5 lakhs) than in the units of Imphal East District (average capital Rs. 3.2 lakhs)

(ii) Entrepreneurs own capital

It has been found that the highest percentage (51.9 per cent) of entrepreneurs invested their own capital to extent ranging from 75-100 per cent followed by those (21.7 per cent) who invested own capital ranging upto 25.0 per cent. Further, it is interesting to note that more entrepreneurs in Imphal East District invested own capital even beyond 75 per cent of the total initial capital.

(iii) Sources of initial capital

On enquiry, it reveals that the respondents depended more on family income as a source of initial capital. Next after family income, government agencies and commercial banks proves as another important source of initial capital.

7.23 Skills of business – Entrepreneurship Development Programmes (EDPs)

Running a business, whether large or small, requires the managerial skill. Since a small entrepreneur cannot employ management experts to manage his/her business, he/she needs to be imparted basic and essential managerial skills in the financial areas like finance, production and marketing.

Keeping the importance of EDPs in the development of entrepreneurship, attempt was made to evaluate the entrepreneurial quality or skill of the sample respondents. 36.8 per cent of the entrepreneurs undertook training under EDPs conducted by various agencies like District Industry Centre (DIC) of the government, Small Industry Services Institute (SISI), All Manipur Entrepreneurs Association (AMEA), Imphal, Institute of Co-operative Management, Imphal, etc.

(i) Age

Maximum percentage of entrepreneurs who received entrepreneurial training belongs into the age group 21-30 years. It is quite interesting to note that only one out of the total 106 entrepreneurs joined EDP in the age group of 20 years and below. Further, no entrepreneurs in the age group 51 years and above joined any entrepreneurial training.

(ii) Education

The highest percentage of entrepreneurs who joined entrepreneurial trainings was graduates (53.8 per cent) while the minimum were under-matriculates (2.6 per cent). Hence, it can be concluded that higher the education, the greater is the awareness of EDPs among the entrepreneurs covered by the study.

(iii) Religion

Religion of entrepreneurs also influences the undertaking of EDPs. All the Christian and Sikh entrepreneurs had not undertaken any EDPs.

(iv) Feasibility study

Majority of the entrepreneurs who had undertaken feasibility study either by themselves (30.8 per cent) or through other agencies (52.3 per cent) had joined EDPs. Only 17.9 per cent thought it necessary to attend EDPs after not undertaking feasibility study. Thus, it can be concluded that those who conducted any feasibility study before starting an unit attends EDPs more than those who had not conducted the study.

(v) Generation of entrepreneurs

It has been found that majority of the entrepreneurs who attended EDPs belongs to first generation entrepreneurs (94.9 per cent) followed by second generation entrepreneurs (5.1 per cent). It is worthwhile to mention that the lone third generation entrepreneur never attends any EDPs. It can thus be concluded that first generation entrepreneurs are more enthusiastic than the other generations regarding the attendance of EDPs. In other words, the other generations are more experienced with their business skills that they need not attend any EDPs.

(vi) Rural/urban background

After study, it has been found that urban background of the entrepreneurs do not give them an advantage to attend EDPs. For example, only 35.7 per cent of the entrepreneurs having urban background attended some sort of entrepreneurial training whereas 37.5 per cent of the entrepreneurs having rural background had undertaken EDPs.

Further, it has been observed that 71.8 per cent of those entrepreneurs who had undertaken training programmes found that EDPs are very useful to their enterprises. No doubt, it will be very interesting to know as to why 67 out of 106 entrepreneurs have not attended any EDPs. 37 out of 106 entrepreneurs are not aware of any such programmes while 20 felt inconvenient to attend EDPs even if they are aware of it. It is worthwhile to mention here that 9.4 per cent (10 out of 106) entrepreneurs do not think they are useful.

7.24 Capital employed

There has been a significant growth in the size of the enterprises measured on the basis of capital employed. On the one hand, units with capital of upto Rs. 2 lakhs decreased from 69.8 per cent in the initial year to 25.5 per cent in the latest year. On the other hand, those with capital of Rs. 10 lakhs and above registered an increase from 8.5 per cent in the initial year to 32.1 per cent in the latest-year.

(i) Religion-wise growth of capital

It is clear from the study that Sikh entrepreneurs were the biggest investors and those of Christian were smallest. However, the percentage growth in the capital employed from the initial year to the latest year is very interesting to be observed. The percentage growth was highest (257.5 per cent) in the enterprises owned by Hindu entrepreneurs followed by the enterprises owned by Sikh entrepreneurs (233.3 per cent). The growth rate of Christian entrepreneurs stood at the lowest level (120.0 per cent).

(ii) Industry-wise growth of Capital

So far as the growth of capital is concerned, units falling under handlooms and handlooms showed the highest growth rate i.e., more than twelve times. The next highest growth was achieved by those units belonging to metal based industries i.e., more than five times. The growth rate in terms of average capital employed was the least in case of units belonging to plastics and rubber based industries (below two times).

(iii) Growth of capital and forms of organisation

It has been observed that units organised as private limited companies had the highest average capital employed both in the initial year (Rs. 11.8 lakhs) as well as in the latest year (Rs. 24.9 lakhs) followed by partnership firms. However, as far as the growth rate of average capital employed is concerned, it was th sole proprietorship concerns which recorded a growth rate of more than 4 times.

7.25 Size of employment

There had been a considerable growth in the size of employment made by the units under the study. It can be proved from the fact that the average number of workers employed in each unit in both the districts increased from 8 in the initial year to 20 in the latest year.

(ii) Religion-wise growth in employment

The average size of employment was highest (8.2) in units owned by Hindu entrepreneurs and lowest in those owned by Christian entrepreneurs. As far as the growth of employment is concerned, we found that the highest growth (320.4 per cent) was achieved by units owned by Sikh entrepreneurs. On the other hand, that of Muslim entrepreneurs was the least (66.7 per cent).

(ii) Industry-wise growth in employment

Growth in employment was highest in handlooms and handicrafts type of industries followed by metal based and wood based industries. It was the least for the units falling under the category of printing and stationery works.

(iii) Growth of employment Vs forms of organisation

Private limited companies had the highest average workforce both in the initial and the latest year. However, it was the sole proprietorship concerns that had achieved the highest growth of 223.5 per cent from the initial to the latest year.

7.26 Sales turnover

After the study, it can be concluded that there has been a significant growth in the performance of the enterprises measured on the basis of sales turnover. While the enterprises having turnover of less than Rs. 2 lakhs decreased from 75.5 per cent in the initial year to 26.4 per cent in the latest year, enterprises having turnover of Rs. 10 lakhs and above increased from 3.8 per cent in the initial year to 22.6 per cent in the latest year. It can also be justified from the fact that the average sales turnover in an enterprise was Rs. 2.1 lakhs in the initial year whereas it increased to Rs. 11.3 lakhs in the latest year.

(i) Religion-wise growth in sales

The average sales turnover was highest in the units owned by Sikh entrepreneurs (Rs. 21.0 lakhs) and minimum (Rs. 5.1 lakhs) in those units owned by Christian entrepreneurs in the latest year.

(ii) Sales turnover across types of industries

As far as the growth of sales turnover is concerned, units belonging to automobile and engineering works showed the highest rate (882.2 per cent) followed by units belonging handlooms and handicrafts industries (401.3 per cent).

(iii) Sales turnover Vs forms of organisation

The maximum growth in sales turnover was achieved by private limited company (1044.5 per cent) from the initial year to latest year. It is worthwhile to mention that sole proprietorship concerns had the least average sales turnover both in the initial year (Rs. 1.4 lakhs) and the latest year (Rs. 8.2 lakhs).

7.27 Capital turnover

The performance of the enterprises was also measured on the basis of the speed or rate with which capital employed is rotated in the process of doing business. After the study, it was observed that there has been a significant growth in the performance of the enterprises in Imphal West District than in Imphal East District measured on the basis of capital turnover.

(i) Religion Vs capital turnover

The average capital turnover was maximum, (6.3 times) in units owned by Muslim entrepreneurs and minimum (0.5 time) in those owned by Sikh entrepreneurs in the initial year. In the latest year also, the same trend in the average capital turnover happened. However, as far as growth from the initial year to the latest year is concerned, the highest growth (220.0 per cent) was made by units owned by Sikh entrepreneurs. On the other hand, units owned by Hindu and Muslim entrepreneurs had failed even to maintain the existing capital turnover.

(ii) Capital turnover across types of industries

Regarding the growth of capital turnover, units belonging to food based industries showed the highest growth rate (90.5 per cent) followed by plastic and rubber based industries (75.0 per cent) and 'others' type of industries (23.3 per cent).

(iii) Capital turnover Vs forms of organisation

As regards to the growth of capital turnover, it was achieved only by private limited companies (114.3 per cent). For other forms of organisation i.e., partnership firms and sole proprietorship had negative growth rate.

7.28 Institutional borrowings of enterprises

Measured on the basis of degree of dependence on borrowings, it can be concluded that there has been a significant growth in the performance of the enterprises. Borrowings of less than Rs. 2 lakhs were decreased from 24.5 per cent in the initial year to 10.4 per cent in the latest year. At the same time, units borrowings Rs. 4-6 lakhs also decreased from 7.6 per cent in the initial year to 1.9 per cent in the latest year. On the average borrowings decreased from Rs. 8.0 lakhs in the initial year to Rs. 1.5 lakhs in the latest year.

1. Average amount of borrowings

To find out the average amount of institutional borrowings an attempt was made to inter-linked the average amount of borrowings taken by the various units across the various types of industries, religion of entrepreneurs and forms of organisation.

(i) Entrepreneurs' religions Vs average amount of borrowings

Maximum amount of average institutional borrowings were taken by Hindu entrepreneurs (Rs. 8.6 lakhs) in the initial year. On the other hand, in the latest year, it was highest in the units started and owned by Sikh entrepreneurs (Rs. 3.3 lakhs). Regarding the percentage change from initial year to latest year, dependence on borrowings by Muslim entrepreneurs decreased by 96.0 per cent followed by Hindu entrepreneurs (81.4 per cent) and Sikh entrepreneurs (43.1 per cent).

(ii) Types of industries Vs average amount of borrowings

After the study, it can be concluded that while handlooms and handicrafts industries increased their dependence on institutional borrowings (80.0 per cent) for carrying out their performance, all other types of industries decreased their dependence on institutional borrowings for their performance.

(iii) Forms of organisation Vs average amount of borrowings

In the initial year, private limited companies had taken the maximum average institutional borrowings (Rs. 30.5 lakhs). However, in the latest year, it was the sole proprietorship concerns that had taken the maximum (Rs. 1.7 lakhs). As far as the change in the dependence on borrowings is concerned, almost all the units under study decreased from the initial year to the latest year.

2. Sources of institutional borrowings

Commercial banks proved themselves as the main sources of institutional borrowings both in the initial and latest year under study. In the initial year, 18.9 per cent of the total units had been given financial assistance by it. In the latest year also, 15.1 per cent of the total units under study were given financial assistance by the commercial banks. Other important sources of institutional borrowings are MANIDCO, NEDFI and NSIC. However, it is note worthy to mention here that MANIDCO and NEDFI had stopped giving financial assistance to the units located in Imphal West District in the latest year. It was the same in case of NEDFI in Imphal East District.

3. *Repayment of borrowings*

From the study, it can be concluded that the ability of the units under study to make repayment of borrowings was significant. Nearly half of the units who had taken institutional borrowings have already repaid full or more than 75.0 per cent of the borrowings. It was only 19.2 per cent units in the latest year (10 out of 52) and 14.8 per cent units in the initial year (4 out of 27) that had fail to make repayment of institutional borrowings.

(i) Religions of entrepreneurs Vs repayment of borrowings

In the initial year, Sikh entrepreneurs had repaid all of their institutional borrowings. In the latest year, Muslim entrepreneurs had the maximum ability to repay borrowings (100.0 per cent) followed by Hindu (43.3. per cent). Regarding the percentage change from the initial year to the latest year, we found that Muslim entrepreneurs had increased their performance by 13,.6 per cent, measured on the basis of ability to repay borrowings. On the other hand, Hindu and Sikh entrepreneurs could not maintain their repayment by 12.9 per cent and 65.0 per cent repayment respectively.

(ii) Types of industries Vs repayment of borrowings

The performances of handlooms and handicrafts industries in the initial year were significant as compared to other types of industries. In the latest year, units belonging to metal based industries had already repaid all of their borrowings (100.0 per cent). Regarding the change from the initial year to the latest year in percentage, it was found that wood based industries had made the maximum effort in repayment of borrowings. However, the performance of food based industries and printing and stationery works were very poor as far as repayment of borrowings was concerned.

(iii) Forms of organisation Vs repayment of borrowings

In the initial as well as latest year, private limited companies had performed better as far as repayment of borrowings was concerned. Regarding the change in percentage from the initial year to the latest year, the performance of partnership firms and private limited companies was significant as compared to sole proprietorship concerns.

7.29 Entrepreneurial effort

It is assumed that the time devoted by the entrepreneurs to their respective enterprises determines the degree of entrepreneurial success. On an average, the time devoted by the entrepreneurs was 87. 2 per cent in both the districts. District-wise, it was in Imphal East District that the average time devoted was more (91.6 per cent) than in Imphal West District (83.3 per cent).

Religion-wise, the highest attention of the entrepreneurs is received by the units owned and started by Christian entrepreneurs (100.0 per cent) followed by Sikh (91.7 per cent), Hindu (87.2 per cent) and Muslim (80.0 per cent) entrepreneurs.

Further, it can be noted that it was in sole proprietorship concerns that the entrepreneurs devoted the highest time (89.7 per cent) followed by partnership firms (78.8 per cent) and private limited companies (57.5 per cent).

7.30 Underutilisation of installed capacity

Unutilised capacity of an enterprise is an index of its problems and all the problems faced by an enterprise leads to underutilisation of installed capacity. It is worthwhile to mention that only one unit from Imphal West District and 4 units from Imphal East District reported 100 per cent capacity utilisation. Regarding average unutilised capacity, Imphal West District had 33.4 per cent and that of Imphal East District had 24.8 per cent.

(i) Religion Vs unutilised capacity

The average unutilised capacity was highest in enterprises owned by Hindu entrepreneurs (30.1 per cent) and the least was found in those owned by Christian entrepreneurs. It is interesting to note that units owned by Muslim entrepreneurs are the youngest of all (10.6 years) but their average unutilised capacity is less than that of all other units.

(ii) Type of industry Vs unutilised capacity

The average unutilised capacity is highest in plastic and rubber based industries. It was the least in handlooms and handicrafts industries.

(iii) Forms of organisation Vs unutilised capacity

By establishing a relationship with the average age of the units, it was found that private limited companies which are the youngest (7.8 years) units have the least average unutilised capacity while sole proprietorship concerns which are the oldest units (14.1 years) have the highest average unutilised capacity.

(iv) Causes of underutilisation

Power scarcity was ranked as number one reason for underutilisation of capacity followed by lack of finances and slackness of demand as reason number two. The other important reasons cited by all the entrepreneurs are 'competition', 'want of skilled labour' etc.

7.31 Marketing

Regarding the marketing problems faced by the entrepreneurs, competition from small units was cited as the problem number one by 52 of the total 106 enterprises. In addition, 24 units had to complete with large firms. In district-wise situation, it can be noted that competition from small as well as large firms was the number one problem for the majority of the units in both the districts under study. But as compared to other types of industry, handlooms and handicrafts (37.5 per cent) and food based (23.5 per cent) industries are in an advantageous position as regard to having no marketing problem.

7.32 Raw-materials

Twenty-five out of the total 106 (23.6 per cent) units under study complained scarcity as number one problem of raw-materials. Moreover, 24 units had to suffer from high prices as against 21 units (19.8 per cent) whose number one problem was the problem of transport. District-wise, problem of transport and high prices was the number one problem for majority of the enterprises in Imphal West District (26.8 per cent each) whereas that of Imphal East District was scarcity of raw-materials (32.0 per cent). Regarding the industry-wise problem, out of the total 106 units under study, 28 units (26.4 per cent) have no problems relating to raw-materials. Among them, automobile and engineering and handlooms and handicrafts units are in an advantageous position as compared to other type of industries.

7.33 Power

The main problem of power i.e., uncertainty of power was suffered maximum by automobile and engineering units (26.9 per cent) followed by food based (14.9 per cent), wood based (13.4 per cent) units etc. The problem of high cost appeared to be genuine as most of the units installed generators for running the units without any power break downs or power-offs. It can also be noted that power cut-off or roaster systems have become a regular phenomenon of the Indian power system and Manipur is not an exception.

7.34 Labour

Regarding the labour problems, 33 units (31.1 per cent) suffered from the problem of absenteeism, problem of training was reported by 7 units (6.6 per cent) and in case of 4 units (3.8 per cent), the problem was 'others' which includes non-availability of skilled workers, high wage rate etc. Industry-wise, problems related to training of labour was a problem for all types of industries. However, the problem of absenteeism of labour was mainly suffered by wood based units (21.2 per cent), food based (12.1 per cent) units etc. On the whole, employer-employee relations were satisfactory.

7.35 Finance

It has been found that the most important problem faced by the enterprises from their commencement was finance. In the overall situation, majority of the units faced shortage of working capital (45.3 per cent).

No particular type of financial problem is peculiar to any particular type of industries. The problem of shortage of working capital is almost universal as it is faced by each and every industry. Comparatively, handlooms and handicrafts , wood based and automobile and engineering units are in advantageous position as less percentage of these units are facing the problem of shortage of working capital.

7.36 Technical and managerial assistance

Out of the total 106 units, 22 units (20.8 per cent) complained about inefficient consultancy service provided by government agencies, followed by 13 units (12.3 per cent) who suffered from lack of skilled workmen as number one technical and managerial assistance problem. Lack of skilled workmen are common to all types of industries whereas expensive consultancy services are felt by food based, automobile and engineering (2 units each) and metal based and printing and stationery works (1 unit each). Lack of proficient manager was reported by 1 unit each of wood based and automobile and engineering unit.

SUGGESTIONS

The following suggestions are made to resolve the various issues relating to entrepreneurship in small scale industries. The suggestions are given categorically to the government, to the banks and other financial institutions and to the entrepreneurs.

7.37 Suggestions to the Government

i) In order to run industrial enterprise on efficient lines, proper training, motivation and wide expose become extremely important. It is universally accepted that "entrepreneurs can be taught and made." In India in general and in Manipur in particular, illiteracy has been the main stumbling block for entrepreneurship development. Therefore, the first step to adopt is to provide suitable education and training to the people. The encouragement and development of entrepreneurship culture should become the core part of the our education system, so that the young men and women can become "job givers" and not "job seekers".

ii) Unutilised capacity of an industry is an index of its problems and all the problems faced by industry leads to underutilisation of installed capacity. Power scarcity is the main reason for underutilisation of capacity. In fact, power cut-off or roaster system becomes a regular phenomenon in Manipur. Every possible steps should be taken to improve the power condition of the state on priority basis.

iii) Severe penalties may be levied on entrepreneurs found misusing the funds or otherwise seeking financial assistance by under-hand means. Preventive measures should be taken to provide a check on the malpractices of small units.

iv) The government must provide efficient and effective consultancy services to the entrepreneurs.

v) Unhealthy competition among the small units as well as large units should be discouraged as far as marketing problems are concerned. The state government needs to be active in this regard. As a sign of encouragement to local entrepreneurs, government departments should procure products produced by these entrepreneurs.

vi) Raw-material banks needs to be opened up in Manipur as this state is infamous for long bandhs, strikes and economic blockades. Scarcity of raw-materials and its high prices as a result of it, are the main problem of raw-materials.

vii) Both the central and state government should give wide publicity so as to reach the information to all the entrepreneurs about policies, incentives, schemes, programmes, etc., relating to small scale industries.

viii) As far as possible, in order to reduce the competition from the sectors, the small scale industrial units should operate in the areas reserved for them. Similarly, more number of items should be reserved for the exclusive production of the small scale sector.

ix) Law and Order problems needs to be tackled properly by the Government so that there is a conducive atmosphere for the entrepreneurs to run their businesses without any hindrances.

7.38 Suggestions to banks and other financial institutions

i) It is a common understanding that all who want bank loans are not necessarily genuine entrepreneurs or businessmen. There are some who want to get loan merely to divert it for non-productive purposes. It may not be difficult for banks to identify such persons. But while doing so, banks should not discourage genuine entrepreneurs.

ii) The financial agencies must treat loan seekers as customers and not beggars.

iii) The level of confidence of both entrepreneurs and bankers can be improved by constant follow-up and monitoring. It will help in developing a feeling of partnership among bankers and entrepreneurs in the growth of small enterprises.

iv) The commercial banks and financial agencies may establish more small scale industrial specialised branches at least one in every district head quarters to cater the financial needs of small entrepreneurs.

v) Make application procedures and approval criteria simple and quick loan approvals should be done at the branch level.

vi) Design appropriate saving schemes suitable for the poor; these are valued, and they are an important source of mobilising funds at rural levels.

vii) Timely and adequate finance depending upto the operational cycle of the activity must be available to the entrepreneurs.

viii) Banking services should be available near to the entrepreneurs/enterprise; if necessary, the banker should go to the borrower, rather than other way round.

ix) Banks needs to re-think about their loan giving policies to the entrepreneurs. Shortage of working capital is the main factor responsible for slow commencement of an industrial unit. So, proper handling of this problem is very important.

7.39 Suggestions to the entrepreneurs

i) The entrepreneurs should develop a proper industrial plan before starting a unit. Undertaking of feasibility study either by himself or through outside agencies can be very helpful in this regard.

ii) The entrepreneurs should take proper training through the government and non-governmental agencies before starting a unit, this enables the entrepreneurs to protect their units from sickness.

iii) The entrepreneurs should employ latest techniques of production, skilled labour so as to improve the quality of the products and marketing.

iv) As the competition is found to be a major problem in many units, the entrepreneurs should try to divert to less competitive areas and before they venture, they should analyse the demand.

v) Low level of education should not deterred one to start an industrial venture. Though, it is a fact that people with higher educational levels are finding their entry into industry earlier. Moreover, higher the level of education, the greater is the chance to start industry as a first generation entrepreneur.

vi) The spread of schooling has cut across the business of religion. None of the entrepreneurial religions are placed in a disadvantageous position, by comparison.

vii) Sole proprietorship concern is the most popular form of organisation in Manipur.

viii) Low level of parental education does not proves hindrance to entrepreneurship.

ix) Urban background is not a pre-condition of industrial entrepreneurship.

x) What is an ambition for one entrepreneur may be a compulsion for another. It is the entrepreneurs' attitudes that ultimately make the difference.

xi) Previous experience in manufacturing and encouragement of family members / relatives / friends facilitates entrepreneurship.

xii) Ambitions motivates men. It actives men, broaden their vision and make the life more meaningful.

xiii) Many of the entrepreneurs expect a lot from the state government and other non-government agencies. But never expect its exact fulfilment.

xiv) Previous experience or employment in the industry should form a basis for selecting the right type of industries.

xv) For starting an industry, the availability of enough finance is the most important factor. Without it, the idea to start business or industry will always remain a simple wish.

xvi) One should have some basic and essential managerial skills in the functional areas like finance, production and marketing for entering into industrial entrepreneurship.

xvii) 21-30 years' age group is the right time for starting an industry.

xviii) Attending EDPs can help the entrepreneurs in running enterprises smoothly and profitably.

xix) Labour should be given full opportunity of being trained. The problem of absenteeism of labour needs to looked into with a humane approach. There should be employer-employee friendly relationship inside the industrial unit.

xx) Entrepreneurs need to re-think about their banking habits. Banks are here to help the entrepreneurs but it does not mean that these helps from the banks are taken for granted. Timely repayment of bank loans is the need of the hour.

xxi) The small scale industrial units should maintain proper books of accounts. Statutory obligation should be imposed on the units to maintain and prepare their books of accounts by professional accountant.

xxii) Everyone cannot be a successful entrepreneur. An individual must have certain values and traits to be a successful entrepreneur. The traits and values are need for achievement, need for power, positive work value; moderate job anxiety, risk taking propensity, internal control orientation, high level of aspiration and preference for participative and nuturant-task styles of leadership.

SELECT BIBLIOGRAPHY

A. BOOKS AND RESEARCH WORKS

Agarwal, A.N., 1994: *Growth and Industrial Origin, Indian Economy – Problems, Development and Planning*, New Delhi, Vishwa Prakash.

Agarwal, V.K., 1975: *Initiative Enterprise and Economic Choices in India*, New Delhi, Munshiram Manoharlal Publisher Pvt. Ltd.

Ahmed, Nissar, 1987: *Small Scale and Cottage Industries*, New Delhi, Deep and Deep Publication.

Akhouri, M.M.P. and S.V.S., 1978: *Small Entrepreneurship Development in North Eastern India*, Hyderabad, SIET.

Balkrishnan, G., 1961: *Financing of Small Scale Industries in India: 1950-52*, Bombay, Asia Publishing House.

Batra, G.S. and Daugal, R.C., 2000: *Entrepreneurship and Small Scale Industries*, New Delhi Deep & Deep Publication Pvt. Ltd.

Berna, J.J., 1960: *Industrial Entrepreneurship in Madras State*, Bombay, Asia Publishing House.

Bhagwari Jugolish, 1966: *The Economics of Underdeveloped Countries*, London, World University Library.

Bhatia, B.S. and Batra, G.S. , 2000: *Entrepreneurship and Small Business Management*, New Delhi, Deep & Deep Publications Pvt. Ltd.

Bhattacharya, S.N., 1986: *Development of Small Scale and Cottage Industries*, New Delhi, Metropolitan Book Co.

Cantillon, Richard, 1971: *Entrepreneurship and Economic Development*, New York, The Free Press.

Cashin, P. & R. Sahay, 1996: *Regional Economic Growth and Convergence in India*, Finance and Development, IMF, March.

Desai, Vasant, 2000: *Small Scale Industries and Entrepreneuship*, Mumbai, Himalaya Publishing House.

Desai, Vasant, 2002: *Dynamics of Entrpreneurial Development and Management*, Mumbai, Himalaya Publishing House.

Deshpande, M.U. , 1979: *Small Scale Industrial Entrepreneurship in a Developing Region*, Maharashtra, Marathwada University.

Dutta, Amlan, 1961: *Essays on Economic Development*, Calcutta, Book Land Pvt. Ltd.

Entrepreneurship Development Institute of India, 1987: *Developing New Entrepreneurs*, Ahmedabad, EDII.

Galbraith, J.R., 1969: *The New Industrial Estates*, Calcutta, Oxford and IBM Publishing Company.

Gangadhara Rao, N. 1973: *Entrepreneurship and Growth of Enterprise in Industrial Estates*, New Delhi, Deep & Deep Publications.

Geoffrey G. Meredith, 1994, Robert E. Nelson, Philip A. Neck: *The Practice of Entrepreneurship*, New Delhi, Sultan Chand & Sons.

Gupta, C.B. and Khanka, S.S., 1996: *Entrepreneurship and Small Business Management*, New Delhi, Sultan Chand & Sons.

Gupta, C.B. and Srinivasan, N.P., 2001: *Entrepreneurial Development*, New Delhi, Sultan Chand & Sons.

Joshi, Arun, Lala Shriram, 1975: *A study in Entrepreneurship and Industrial Management*, New Delhi, Orient Longman.

Killy, Peter (Ed.), 1971: *Entrepreneurship and Economic Development*, New York, The Free Press.

Khanka, S.S., 2002: *Entrepreneurial Development*, New Delhi, S. Chand & Company Ltd.

Khanka, S.S., 1990: *Entrepreneurship in Small Scale Industries*, Mumbai, Himalaya Publishing House.

Kumar, S. Ashok, 1990: *Entrepreneurship in Small Industry*, New Delhi, Discovery Publishing House.

Mali, D.D. and Bundopadhyay, R., 1993: *Small Industry Development in North East India: Status and Strategy*, New Delhi, Omsons Publications.

Mali, D.D. and Deka, P., 1987: *Industrial Development in North East India*, New Delhi, Omsons Publications.

Manohar U. Despande, 1982: *Entrepreneurship of Small Scale Industries*, New Delhi, Deep and Deep Publications.

Pieris, Ralph, 1969: *Studies in Sociology of Development*, Rotterdam University Press.

Prasain, G.P., 2003: *Entrepreneurship Development*, New Delhi, Sunmarg Publishers and Distributories.

Prasain, G.P., 2006: *Entrepreneurship and Small Scale Industries*, New Delhi, Akansha Publishing House.

Rao, N. Gangadhara, 1986: *Entrepreneurship and Growth of Enterprise in Indsustrial Estates*, New Delhi, Deep and Deep Publications.

Rao, Subha P., 2001: *Entrepreneurship and Small Business Management*, New Delhi, Discovery Publishing House.

Ricardo, David, 1962: *The Principles of Political Economy and Taxation*, London, J.M. Dent & Sons Ltd.

Say, J.B., 1827: *Production, Distribution and Consumption of Wealth*, Philadelphia, John Grigg No. 9, North Forth Street.

Schumpeter, J.A., 1949: *The Theory of Economic Development*, Cambridge, Havard University Press, Massachussetts.

Sen, S.K., 1964: *Studies in Industrial Policy and Development of India*, Calcutta, Progressive Publishers.

Sharma, K.L., 1967: *Entrepreneurial Performance in Role Perspective*, New Delhi, Abhinav Publications.

Sharma, R.K., 1990: *Industrial Entrepreneurhip*, Ludhiana, Kalyani Publishers.

Vepa Ram, K., 1980: *Modern Small Scale Industries – Problems and Prospects*, New Delhi, Sage Publications.

B. ARTICLES

Bhargava, R.K., 1972: "Importance of Small Scale Industries", *Commerce* (Supplement) 124 (3190), 24 June.

Bhat, A.R., 1972: "Development of Small Industries in Free India", *Commerce*, 125 (3196), 19 August.

Bhat, R.S., 1974: "Growth of Entrepreneurship in Small and Medium Sectors", *Indian Journals of Public Administration*, Vol. XX. No. 3, July- September.

Chandra, Poojary M., 1996: "Small Scale Sector: Myth and Reality", *Economic and Political Weekly*, Vol. XXXI, No. 21, May, 25.

Choudhury, R.P., 1973: "Changing Pattern of Small Business Finance in India", *Indian Journal of Commerce*, Sept.

Deolamkar, Viveks, 1987: "Financial Practices of Small Business in a Backward Region – Analytical Approach", *Indian Journal of Commerce*, Vol. XLI., Part 3, No. 152, July – Sept.

Gaikwad, V.R., and Tripathi, R.N., 1970: "Socio-Psychological Factors Influencing Industrial Entrepreneurship in Rural Areas", National Institute of Community Development, Hyderabad, May.

George Herbertan Evens Jr., 1949: "The Entrepreneur and Economic Theory", *American Economic Review*.

Hazarika, Jatin, 1998: "National Seminar on Entrepreneurship Development – Keynote Address", IIE Guwahati, 10th December.

Himachalam, D., 2001: "Entrepreneurship Development Programme: Need for Revival", *Banking and Finance*, January.

Hussain, Abid, 1998: "Small Enterprises Protection", *Laghu Udyog*, Vol. XXII & XXIII, No. 6 to 7, Jan.- Sept.

Indu, K.S., 1997: "Infrastructure Development for the Small Scale and Tiny Units", *Laghu Udyog*, Vol. XXI & XXII, No. 6 to 8, Jan.-Dec.

Joshi, Navinchandra, 1995: "Rejuvenating Small Industrial Sector", *Yojana*, Vol. 9 No. 13.

Kaushik, K.C., 1997: "50 years of Small Scale Industries in India – Policies and Programmes", *Laghu Udyog*, Vol. XXI & XXXII. No. 6 to 8, January – Dec.

Kaveri, V.S., 2000: "Financing of Small Scale Industries: Issues and Suggestions", National Seminar on Entrepreneurship Development, IIE, Guwahati.

Khan, Nawab Ali, 1984: "Development of Small Scale Sector in India", *Yojana*, Oct. 15.

Khanka, S.S., 2000a: "Development of Small Scale Industries in Assam", *Journal of the North Eastern Council*, Shillong.

Khanka, S.S., 2000b: "Making the Entrepreneurial Society- With reference to North East India", National Seminar on Entrepreneurship Development, IIE, Guwahati.

Lal, Sudarshan, 1974: "What Do We Mean By Small Industries?", *Yojana*, Vol. No. XVII Nos. 23 and 24, January.

Lingaraj, B.P. and Girikumar, T., 1982: "Problems of Small Industries in a Developing Country", *Decision*. Vol. IX, No. 4, October.

Mali, D.D., 2005: "Developing Entrepreneurship in North East – Experiences and Strategies", Keynote Address, ICSSR Sponsored National Seminar on "Entrepreneurship Development in Manipur", Department of *Commerce*, Manipur University.

Mali,D.D., 1998: "Area Approach on Entrepreneurship Development", National Seminar on Entrepreneurship Development, IIE, Guwahati. Dec.

Manalel, James, 1997: "How Beautiful is Small", *SEDME*, Vol. XXIV (4), No. 4 Dec.

Maran, K., 2001:"Role of SSIs in Growing Economy", Industrial Herald, July.

Mathem, P.M., 1997: "Union Budget and Small Enterprises", *Economic and Political Weekly*, Vol. XXXII, No. 14, April 5.

Nagayya, D, 1998a: "Data Base in Researchable Areas in the Small Enterprise Sector", National Seminar on Entrepreneurship Development, IIE, Guwahati, Dec.

Nagayya, D. 1998b: "Entrepreneurship Development: The North Eastern Region – Retrospect and Prospect", National Seminar on Entrepreneurship Development, IE, Guwahati, Dec.

Nagayya, D. and Appa Rao, P.B., 1998: "Perspective of Entrepreneurship Education and Training", National Seminar on Entrepreneurship Development, IIE, Guwahati, Dec.

Nagayya, D. and Rao, K.V., 2000: "Small Scale Industries: Challenges and Strategies in the Liberalised Period", *SBI Monthly Review*, July.

Nixon Singh E., Bijoykumar Singh E., 2002: "Enrepreneurship in Manipur: Problems & Prospects" Paper presented in the Vth Annual Conference of North Eastern Economic Association, Assam, Dec.

Papanek, G.F., 1962: "The Development of Entrepreneurship", *America Economic Review*, Vo. LLI May.

Prasain, G.P., Devi Sancharita R.K., 1997: "Women Traders in Manipur – A Case Study", *Indian Journal of Commerce*, Vol. L. NO. 193, Part IV, Dec.

Reddy, B., Dasaradharami, 2000: "Financing of SSI Sector by Commercial Bank", *Banking and Finance*, Vol. XIII, No. 12, Dec.

Saikia, S.K., 1992: "Problems of Small Units in North Eastern Region", *Yojana*. Vol. 36, No. 13-23, Nov. 30

Singh, Biren, P., 2000: "Role of DIC Thoubal in Rapid Industrialisation" *Manipur Today* Vol. XX, No. 2 April, 23.

Singh, D.P., 1995: "Marking Challenges in Small Scale Industries", *Management Researcher*, Vol. 11, No. 12, July – Dec.

Singh, M.P., 1998: "Growth and Development of SSI, *Laghu Udyog*, Vol. XXII to XXIII, No. 6 to 7 Jan. – Sept.

Srivastava, S.P., 1987: "Institutional Finance for Small Industries", *Indian Journal of Commerce*, Vol, XLI, Part 3, No. 152, July – Sept.

Vepa, Ram K., 1997: "Small Can Be Beautiful – Recommendations on Small Enterprises", *Economic and Political Weekly* Vol. XXXII, NO. 27, July 5.

C. REPORTS AND SURVEYS

All Manipur Entrepreneurs' Association (AMEA), Economic Development Towards 2001 AD

Govt. of Manipur, Director of *Commerce* & Industries, Industrial Policy of Manipur, 2002.

Govt. of Manipur, Directorate of Economic & Statistic, Statistical Abstract of Manipur, 1998.

India, Ministry of Industry, Report of the Expert Committee on Small Enterprises, (Chairman: Abid Hussain), New Delhi, 1997.

Reserve Bank of India (RBI), "Compendium of Circulars on Small Scale Industries" (July 1978 – December 1999) Mumbai, March, 2000.

D. JOURNALS AND PERIODICALS

Banking and Finance, Kolkata

Business Horizons, Bloomington

Business India, Kolkata

Business Week, New York

Business World, New Delhi

Chartered Accountant, New Delhi

Chartered Secretary, New Delhi

Decision, Kolkata

Economic and Political Weekly, New Delhi

IBA Bulletin, Mumbai

Indian Journal of Commerce, New Delhi

Indian Journal of Entrepreneurship, Ahmedabad

Indian Journal of Marketing, New Delhi

Indian Manger, New Delhi

Industrial Herald, Chennai

Journal of Accounting and Finance, Jaipur

Journal of Industry and Trade, Kolkata,
Kangleipak Business Review, Imphal.
Kurushetra, New Delhi
Laghu Udyog, Delhi
Mainstream, Kolkata
Manipur Today, Imphal
Margin, New Delhi
Prajnan, Pune
Productivity, New Delhi
The Strategist, Kolkata
Vikalpa, Ahmedabad
Yojana, New Delhi

Index

T